WONDERS
OF PRAGUE

WONDERS OF PRAGUE

PETR DAVID
VLADIMÍR SOUKUP
ZDENĚK THOMA

KNIŽNÍ KLUB

From left to right: Prague Castle (Pražský hrad), Royal Summer Palace (Královský letohrádek), the River Vltava at the Old Town weir, Wallenstein Garden (Valdštejnská zahrada), Prague city emblem on the Old Town Hall (Staroměstská radnice), Lake (Jezírko) in Prokop Valley (Prokopské údolí), St. Martin's Rotunda, Philosophical Hall (Filozofický sál) in the Library of Strahov Monastery (Strahovský klášter)

Text © Petr David, Vladimír Soukup, 2010
Photographs © Zdeněk Thoma, 2010
Photographs of the crown jewels © Správa Pražského hradu, foto: Jan Gloc
ISBN 978-80-242-2870-9

In the very heart of Europe lies the capital of the Czech Republic, deservedly considered by its charmed visitors to be one of the most beautiful cities in the world. Prague is the capital of a tiny country, which sometimes gets lost on the map of a huge and slightly confused world, frankly, not every inhabitant of planet Earth can tell where the Czech Republic actually lies. Then visitors get a surprise when they see it for the first time – and they love to return.

Prague has a lot to offer. Above all it is an outstanding collection of sights of historical interest, an amazing textbook of architecture, a display of all architectural styles. After all, Prague has always attracted the most prominent artists of their time. Thus we can walk through the city and admire Romanesque buildings as well as wonder at modern creations such as the Dancing House (Tančící dům). We find such treasures as Cubist houses, which actually represent a style reserved primarily for fine art. We can find monuments, both religious and secular, and remarkable sights of technical character. Prague nature deserves admiration as well. The city is divided by the River Vltava, which has inspired many artists, and which waters the greenery of game preserves and parks. Within the boundaries of the city we can also find retreats; wild, rocky valleys and deep ravines, quite unexpected in busy urban areas.

It is a little difficult to choose from the plentiful and varied offer, especially if we are limited by time. Therefore we have attempted to choose the most valuable of Prague's gems, sights and interesting natural areas; in short the best features of all, and introduce them by means of both words and photographs. We would not like to overwhelm you with too much information, but to inspire you and perhaps to guide a little. Therefore the individual objects are arranged so that they follow one after the other as if we were walking through Prague together, gradually from the city centre to the periphery. If you set out with us, you will get to know the most significant sights, and can decide for yourself to what extent are true the words about one of the most beautiful cities in the world.

MORE VALUABLE THAN
THE WHOLE CATHEDRAL

THE CZECH CROWN JEWELS

*Above: czech royal crown –
so-called the crown
of St. Wenceslas*
Opposite page below: *czech
royal sceptre (detail)*
Opposite page above: *czech
royal orb*

A door with seven locks protects the entrance to the coronation chamber in St. Vitus's Cathedral, which holds a relic more valuable than any other, one of the symbols of the Czech nation – the crown jewels. There are seven keys that fit the seven locks. These are in the care of seven different persons and institutions. There is good reason for cautiousness – after all, the set of jewels is priceless; according to some experts its value is greater than the amount needed to build the whole St. Vitus's Cathedral!

For his coronation as Czech king, Charles IV ordered the central item of the crown jewels – the St. Wenceslas's crown – to be made. It is one of the four royal crowns in Europe that have been preserved from the Gothic era. It differs from the other ones in its shape: it resembles the semi-circular caps that indicated the rank of the Přemyslide princes. The motif of four lilies provides evidence of a French influence. The crown weighs 2.368 kg, is made of 21 to 22 carat gold, and is adorned with 96 precious stones and 20 pearls. Later, perhaps sometime during the 16th century, the Habsburgs had an orb and a sceptre created.

They were added to the Czech crown jewels in the 17th and 18th centuries. These objects are made of solid gold, too: the orb with wrought relief that depicts scenes from the Old Testament weighs 780 grams. The 67 cm long sceptre weighs 1.013 kg. The set is completed by a silk coronation cloak edged with ermine, a belt and a stole from the first half of the 17th century.

The Czech crown jewels have been moved several times over the centuries. During the Hussite Wars (1420–1436) Emperor Sikmund held them in Hungary, and after they were returned to Bohemia the Czech estates resolved that they should be kept at the Karlštejn Castle. They survived the turbulent times of the Thirty-Years War in different hiding places. From 1646 the Habsburgs had them in Vienna. In 1791 they were returned to Prague, to be used when Leopold II was crowned Czech king, and there they have remained ever since. From February 1944 until May 1945 they were hidden in a bricked-up kiln in an old Romanesque palace at Prague Castle for fear of air raids. During that time these gems of medieval art were "under the guardianship" of the Third Reich and the hiding place had been secretly established by members of the German occupation forces.

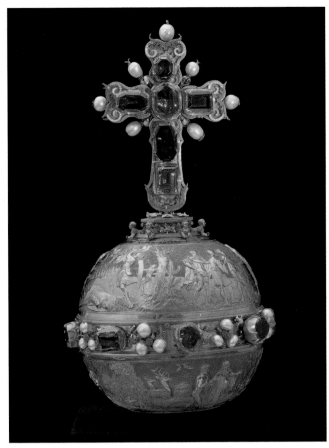

None of the accountable Czech officials knew about the hideaway and the jewels were considered missing. And it is quite possible that they would have remained missing: but then Karl Hermann Frank revealed the hiding place when he was brought to the Prague court in August 1945. The jewels were then ceremonially collected and displayed in St. Vitus's Cathedral. Today they are again in the safety of the coronation chamber. They are presented to the public only on special occasions.

It is said that St. Wenceslas's crown has the power to punish by death any unauthorized person who puts the crown on his or her head. The Reich protector Reinhard Heidrich was supposed to have done so out of haughtiness while viewing the jewels on 13th November 1941. Less than seven months later he was assassinated. It does not pay to laugh at old traditions…

THE BEAUTIFUL COLOUR OF STONES

St. Wenceslas's crown is decorated, in addition to 20 pearls, with 96 precious stones – sapphires, spinelles, emeralds and also one tourmaline-rubellite. The stones were left in their natural shapes and sizes, they were not cut, only polished. Some of them are truly unique; of the nine largest sapphires in the world six are on the Czech crown. During extensive modifications and improvements (1347–1387), some of the stones, mostly green emeralds, were replaced by ones of larger sizes and better quality. A thorn, which allegedly comes from Christ's crown of thorns, is inserted in the sapphire cross at the top of the crown. The royal orb and sceptre are also beautifully decorated with sapphires, spinelles and pearls.

A SYMBOL OF THE CZECH NATION

PRAGUE CASTLE

A BAROQUE GATE

In the middle of the front wing, which separates the first and the second courtyard, there is the Mathias entrance Gate (Matyášova brána), dated from 1614. It faces the Hradčany Square. It is named after the Austrian emperor and Czech king Mathias, who ordered the gate to be built. This monumental piece of architecture, decorated with bossage and crowned with a triangle-shaped gable, is the work of the Italian artist Giovanni Maria Filippi, who worked at Prague castle for Rodolph II, Mathias's predecessor. It is the oldest secular Baroque monument in Bohemia. That is why it is said, with a little exaggeration, that Baroque came into Bohemia under its arches.

In the beginning there was Bořivoj, the first historically recorded Czech prince, who sometime during the year 870 decided to move the central residence of the princely Přemyslide family from the Left Castle (Levý Hradec), above the left bank of the River Vltava, several kilometres further upstream. Here on a rocky bluff above the mouth of the Brusnice stream, a new vast fort was built, called Praha (Prague). The reason was probably the advantageous position of the place. Here the sides of the the Vltava valley, otherwise falling steeply to the river, descend to create a small basin, which was crossed by busy trading routes and which also offered the necessary space for the establishment of settlements. The fort formerly consisted only of wooden structures and was walled by a massive bulwark. During the 10th century it was given a new stone wall with three gates, several stone churches and the princely palace, at first made predominantly of wood, near the southern bulwark. After 1067 Prague Castle

conceded the position of the central princely seat to Vyšehrad. It was Prince Soběslav I, who in late 12th century splendidly rebuilt and newly fortified the whole grounds. In the 13th century the appearance of the Castle did not change significantly, but in 1304 it burned down. Only a reconstruction during the reign of Charles IV, who had it expensively rebuilt in high Gothic style as a representative residence worthy of the imperial court, gave it a new splendour. The work continued during the reign of his son Wenceslas IV until the Hussite Wars and then again in the second half of the 15th century, when the court architect court Benedict Rejt adapted and fortified anew the court grounds for King Vladislav Jagello. It is to his credit that the Renaissance knocked on the gates of Prague castle for the first time; but it was not until the reign of the first Habsburgs after 1526 that this new style entered briskly. The fire in 1541 was a real catastrophe for the ancient seat of Czech rulers. It spread to the Castle from the Less-

Opposite page above: Prague castle from the Petřín Gardens (Petřínské zahrady)

THE ECCENTRIC EMPEROR

Rodolph II (1552–1612), one of the last sovereigns to have resided at Prague Castle, is perhaps the most popular Habsburg in Bohemia. He was an eccentric with boisterous and often inscrutable behaviour, whose life was more and more markedly influenced by mental illness as he got on in years. He surrounded himself with first-class painters and sculptors, as well as politicians, diplomats, scientists and a number of alchemists, mostly charlatans and impostors, who misused the emperor's generoity and gullibility. Rodolph never saw the promised elixir of youth, philosophers' stone or artificially made gold, even though he often visited the alchemists' workshops himself, peeked "under the lids" and tried to hasten the mysterious chemical processes with promises and later even threats.

er Town and severely damaged the Old Royal Palace, the spire of St. Vitus's Cathedral and other buildings. During the reign of Rodolph II at the turn of the 16th and 17th centuries a new, late Renaissance wing was added on the northern side of the second courtyard, with two large halls – the Spanish Hall *(photo left)* and the Gallery, which was adjacent to the famous "kunstchamber" renowned for the art collection of the eccentric emperor. During the rebellion of the Czech estates and the following Thirty-Years War the castle buildings were looted and all the valuables stolen. The largest theft, amounting to dozens of wagons, was taken away from the castle – and from other parts of Prague – by the Swedes in 1648. The most prestigious period in the history of the Prague Castle was de facto over: the Habsburgs moved to Vienna for good and Prague became only one of their provincial residences.

Buildings from different periods of construction, which suffered some damage during the wars for Austrian inheritance in the 18th century, were unified into one style and provided with new façades during the so-called Theresian Reconstruction (1753–1775). Thus they acquired a contemporary, fairly simple Classicist character. The present appearance of the first courtyard also originates from this period.

THE PRIDE OF
CZECH GOTHIC

PRAGUE CASTLE

WHAT IS HIDDEN UNDERGROUND

A visit to the St. Vitus's Cathedral with its exceptionally valuable ornamentation by first-class Czech and world artists is an interesting experience, as is an excursion to its underground. We find the uncovered foundations of two older churches, and also the tomb of Czech kings – Charles IV and his four wives, Wenceslas IV, Ladislav Posthumous, George of Poděbrady and Rodolph II. There are also the remains of Archduchess Marie Amálie of Parma, daughter of empress Marie Therése. Other sovereigns spend their eternal sleep in the royal mausoleum, situated directly above this tomb in the main room of the cathedral. The marble structure dating from 1571–1573 and 1587–1589 was created by the Dutch sculptor Alexander Collin and contains the graves of Ferdinand I, his wife Anna Jagello and their son Maxmilian II. The remains of princes and kings of the Přemyslide family lie in the stone tombs in the gallery chapels, the work of the Parler sculpture workshop. The tomb of Přemysl Ottocar II was made by Peter Parler himself, being not only an exceptional architect but also a sculptor.

St. Vitus's Cathedral, the predominant feature of the Prague castle, is the most significant religious monument in the Czech Republic. Its visual aspect was formed by high Gothic style of the 14th century and Neo-Gothic style of the late 19th century and early 20th century. Its foundation was initiated by King Jan of Luxembourg (Jan Lucemburský), along with the prince royal, Charles IV, who eventually became Czech king and Roman emperor. Its predecessors were two churches of the same dedication – a Pre-Romanesque rotunda, built from 926–930 by Prince Václav, and Prince Spytihněv's Romanesque basilica dating from 1060–1096. On the occasion of celebrating the Prague bishopric being promoted to archbishopric the construction of a monumental Gothic cathedral commenced in their place according to a design by Mathias of Arras. After his death in 1352 Peter Parler, a young architect from Schwabian Gmünd, continued the work. He

decided not to follow Mathias's design in the style of Post-Classic French cathedrals, as it was at that time already somewhat outdated. He impressed his own personal architectural style on the cathedral, characterised by new progressive elements, some of which were being used for the first time in Europe. His art continually developed as the construction proceeded, and every section surprises the viewer with creative ideas, radiating with an effort to design everything unconventionally, individualistically, not according to custom. The reticulated vaulting above the cathedral chancel is very impressive. This had been unknown in Czech architecture. It broke the stereotypical rhythm of the vault spans and conceived the space as a continuous unit *(photo above)*. The dynamic vaulting with three arch ribs in the Southern Narthes is also striking. The arch ribs practically lose their original structural function and become primarily an aesthetic element; Parler's con-

cept being at least one hundred years ahead of its time for European architecture.

By the time of his death in 1399 Peter Parler had managed to finish the eastern part of the cathedral, including a garland of chapels and the lower floors of the Great Southern Spire. His sons then continued the work. The Hussite Wars interrupted the construction, and afterwards the western side of the cathedral was temporarily closed. During the following centuries there were several unsuccessful attempts to complete the cathedral. Only after 1865 was the original Gothic section renovated by Josef Kranner, 1873 marking the laying of the foundation stone of the actual triple nave, built according to the design of architect Josef Mocker. After 1899 architect Kamil Hilbert supervised the construction. He also finally completed the cathedral in 1929.

The gallery of St. Vitus's Cathedral's Great Spire, almost 100 metres high, offers a beautiful sight of Prague literally from bird's-eye view. Peter Parler started its construction in 1396, then his sons continued the work until 1406. In 1541 the Spire was damaged by fire, during which the bells broke off and fell through the lower floors and damaged the structure of the whole building. The repairs were carried out by the head of the construction works at the court, Bonifac Wohlmut, who also finished the upper floor with gallery and the Renaissance casque. The largest bell in Bohemia, called Sikmund, is hung here. It was cast by bell founder Petr Jaroš in 1549. The St. Wenceslas Chapel (kaple sv. Václava – *photo above left*), which is considered to be the heart of the whole cathedral, is adjacent to the ground floor of the Spire. It is located directly above the grave of St. Václav, its walls are decorated with 1345 pieces of polished amethyst and jasper and Gothic wall paintings from the 14th–16th centuries. The entrance to the area below the Spire is from the third courtyard through the Southern Narthes, opened by three arcades with raised lancet arches, above which there is an exceptionally extensive mosaic (95 m^2) depicting the Last Judgment. It is called the Golden Gate, and it is a creation of Venetian masters from 1370–1371.

Left: colourful stained-glass windows

THE RESIDENCE OF
PRINCES AND KINGS

THE PRAGUE CASTLE

**THE KNIGHT
AND THE DRAGON**

The statue of St. George in the third courtyard by the southern frontage of the St. Vitus's Cathedral is one of the most beautiful and valuable pieces of Gothic sculpture in Bohemia, as well as the whole Europe. In 1373 it was cast in bronze by brothers Martin and Jan of Kluž, according to a model created probably by a sculptor from Parler's sculpture workshop. The composition is truly masterful, we can admire the realistically conceived motion of the horse which is rearing and turning, and the dynamic conception of the body of the rider, thrusting his spear into the body of the dragon writhing underneath the horse's hooves. During its existence the sculpture has been damaged several times – e.g. in the fire of 1541, when it was hit by falling charred beams that knocked off St. George's arm with the spear, or at the coronation of Maxmilian II. At that time the sculpture actually broke apart and had to be recast.

The actual residence of Czech princes and kings was the Old Royal Palace, located in the corner of the third courtyard by the former southern wall. Around 1135 Prince Soběslav had the oldest, probably wooden building replaced by a Romanesque palatial building, spectacular at that time. Some sections of it have been preserved to this day: two floors with a 50m long hall and princely apartments, part of the accoupled windows and the bottom section of the so-called Southern Tower by a gate that was lost lat-er. Soběslav's palace was significantly re-constructed by Charles IV, although hardly anything has survived from this construction activity – most of the Gothic buildings were lost during the subsequent late Gothic and Renaissance reconstructions. Vladislav Hall (Vladislavský sál) built between 1492 and 1502 is the largest secular space of the medieval Prague and the most beautiful late Gothic hall in central Europe. It is 62 m long, 16 m wide and 13 m high, topped with a stellar ribbed vault with intertwined curved

ribs, which stretches across the whole second floor of the palace. The 5m high rectangular windows, dating from 1493, mark the first appearance of Renaissance style in Bohemia. Since mid-16th century the hall has been used for various ceremonial meetings, even tournaments were held there. As their participants had to get there in full armour and mounted, access was provided by means of the so-called equestrian staircase with unusually long and low steps.

Among other exceptional sections of the palace there is the original courtroom from the 14th century called the Green Chamber (Zelená světnice), late Gothic rooms of the State Boards Archive (Archiv zemských desek), Vladislav's bedrooms dating from around 1486, the so-called Louis's Wing (Ludvíkovo křídlo), built by Benedikt Ried completely in Renaissance style between 1520 and 1530, a Renaissance hall of the Czech Chancellery (Česká kancelář) with an ornamental portal, which was the scene of the famous defenestration in 1618, and Imperial Court Council Hall (síň říšské dvorské rady), where on 19 June 1621 the 27 leaders of the rebellion of the estates received their death sentence. The Old Assembly (Stará sněmovna – *photo above*) was built during the reign of king Wenc-

eslas IV after 1385 and rebuilt in late Gothic style and then again in Renaissance style after the fire in 1541, when it was given a reticulated vault with intertwined curved ribs. The New State Boards Chancellery (kancelář Nových zemských desek) has decoration of aristocratic coat-of-arms *(photo below)*.

THE OLDEST RESIDENCE OF BISHOPS

The original building of the Prague bishopric, founded in 973, used to be situated at the Prague Castle. There used to reside, side by side, the highest-ranking officials both religious and secular, which was indisputably a thing unique in Europe of that time. It soon became clear, though, that it was not a good arrangement as there were numerous disputes between the princes and bishops. This was also the main reason why after 1067 prince Vratislav moved his seat to Vyšehrad. The brickwork of the oldest Prague bishopric has been preserved in the building of the Old Provostry (Staré probošství) near the south-western corner of the St. Vitus's Cathedral. The stone building was built in the 1st half of the 11th century and rebuilt after 1142. At the eastern side of the building we can see the original Romanesque accoupled window and a section of the greige brickwork going up all the way to the second floor.

ANTIQUITY AND BIZARRENESS

THE PRAGUE CASTLE

PUNISHMENT FOR MURDER

While viewing the St. George Basilica we should not miss an interesting statue called Brigida, located beside the altar. It is a realistic stone statue of a dead girl in an advanced stage of decomposition, including details of the decaying insides, where there are snakes, lizards and frogs crawling. Legend has it that in the times of Rodolph II, and Italian artist Bernardo Spinetti killed his mistress Brigida out of jealousy and threw the body into the Deer Moat (Jelení příkop). The body was found after quite some time, but the murderer still got caught and was convicted. He was sentenced to death, but he requested reprieve, so that he could – as an expression of repentance – chisel out the sculpture of his lover in the condition she had been found in. He worked incessantly day and night, without food and drink, until he completed the sculpture. Only then was he handed over to the executioner.

In the eastern section of the Castle we can find an extraordinarily quaint building complex, which was used mostly by the church and aristocracy in the past. The most dominant are the two towers of the St. George Basilica *(photo above and below right)*, which are among the oldest surviving monuments of Prague. Prince Vratislav founded the original church after 920. Later it became a part of the Benedictine monastery and was reconstructed and enlarged; it got its present-day appearance during the reconstruction following a fire in 1142. In the times of Charles IV some parts were modified in Gothic style, at the beginning of the 16th century the southern columned entrance portal was formed and decorated with a beautiful relief of the fight between St. George and the dragon. Around 1670 an early Baroque façade was added. It faces the George Square (Jiřské náměstí). Several rulers of the Přemysl family were buried in the church. Remains of Romanesque wall paintings have survived here and there in the interior, as well as tombs of the buried princ-

es and a Romanesque crypt, among other things. Beside the chancel there is a late Romanesque two-storied Chapel of St. Ludmila, built between 1200 and 1228 in the times of abbess Agnes, later a Czech saint. Ludmila's plaener tombstone was made at Parler's workshop around 1380. Her daughter-in-law had Ludmila murdered in 921 at Tetín.

Since 973 there was a Benedictine convent by the church, the oldest in Bohemia. Mlada, the sister of prince Boleslav II, was its founder and first abbess. It had an exceptional position among similar religious institutions – only women of the royal family could become abbesses, who moreover had the right (along with the Prague archbishop) to crown Czech queens. During its existence of more than a thousand years the George Convent (Jiřský klášter) went through many reconstructions, its present-day appearance is mostly in early Baroque style from the 2nd half of the 17th century. The remains of brickwork underneath the present-day paradise garden survived from the original pre-Ro-

manesque and Romanesque building. Nowadays the Convent is used by the National Gallery for its exhibitions of its collection from the period of Rodolphine mannerism and Baroque.

The wall of the northern fortification of the Prague Castle is adjacent to the Golden Lane, the smallest lane in Prague, with "dwarfish" houses, which the folk tradition incorrectly associates with alchemists. The 24 original miniature buildings were constructed at the order of emperor Rodolph II after 1597 as homes for the castle riflemen and their families. One by one, the ten houses on the southern side of the lane were pulled down, only the fourteen on the northern side by the wall remained. After the riflemen brigades were abolished towards the end of the 18th century, the houses were sold to various owners, they were occupied by artists and eccentrics, but also by the poor and the rogues' gallery. No 22 was for some time in 1917 occupied by the writer Franz Kafka. Today there is a number of period little shops and galleries.

In Jiřská Street there are Renaissance palaces reconstructed in Baroque style, which

beloved to of prominent Czech aristocracy – Rožmberk and Lobkowitz (originally Pernštejn) families. Today the latter is used by the National Museum, which chose it for its historical exposition The Relics of a National Past. Opposite the Lobkowitz palace there is the former burgavery of the Prague Castle with graffito-decorated façade, today a Museum of Toys, and nearby is the Black Tower, a part of the original Romanesque fortification from the 12th century.

DALIBOR AND HIS VIOLIN

There are three towers that are part of the northern fortification of the Prague Castle, built at the end of the 15th century by Benedikt Ried – Prašná, Bílá and Daliborka (Gunpowder, White and Dalibor Tower, respectively). The latter two served as a prison for the aristocracy. Daliborka was named after its first prisoner Dalibor of Kozojedy, a knight sentenced to death for accepting into serfdom rebel serfs from the neighbouring land. Composer Bedřich Smetana made the idealized story of Dalibor into an opera of the same name. According to the story Dalibor learned to play the violin before his execution, and many admirers came to hear his music, listening secretly by the foot of the tower.

WHERE TULIPS CAME TO EUROPE FROM

THE PRAGUE CASTLE GARDENS

THE EMPEROR
AND HIS LION

In the south-western corner of the Royal Gardens there is the building of the Lion Court, sometimes called Bear Court, today adapted as a period restaurant. The eccentric Emperor Rodolph II had this Renaissance building constructed between 1581 and 1583. He bred various beasts here, mainly lions – as the name suggests. He was particularly fond of one of them. A certain astrologist allegedly read in the stars that the lives of the emperor and the beast were interconnected and that the lion would pass away three days before the emperor's death. When the beast perished in January of 1612, the sovereign commenced to get ready for death, which came exactly as in the prophecy – three days after the lion had died.

Above: spring in the Royal Gardens
Below: the decoration of the "Great mičovna"

The continually developing heavy fire-arms that even the strongest fortifications could not resist hastened the end of the epoch of the castle as an enclosed impregnable fort and opened the door for the Renaissance, which prefers pleasant comfortable living, open space and beauty. Czech king Ferdinand I understood this trend very well, when, at the beginning of the 1530's, he decided to extend the area of the Prague Castle further north and to create vast representative gardens in the manner of Renaissance landscape gardening, under the guidance of Italian experts, above the border of Jelení příkop. The gardens, called Royal, were gradually enlarged and further modified. Pietro Mattioli, a famous botanist, who was employed in Prague as Ferdinand's personal doctor, planted among other things also the first tulip bulbs, which were purchased at the king's request in Turkey. It was from here that the plant set out on its triumphant mission

through Europe – from Prague it spread to other countries of the continent, for instance to Holland, which was later so famous for it.

In the course of the 16th century, especially during he reign of Rodolph II, many buildings appeared in the Gardens – apart from the Royal Summer Palace, which we describe separately, there is the Great Mičovna (Hall for the ballgame), the Lion Court menagerie, fig tree conservatory, orangery, aviary, a firing range, various ponds and playthings including a maze. Only the Baroque reconstruction following French style principles in the 1st half of the 18th century definitively eliminated the damage caused by the Thirty-years War. The Gardens were given a symmetrical strictly axial appearance with regularly located ponds, flowerbeds and hedges and also an extensive sculpture decoration.

In 1861–1862 a section of the area was modified as a natural landscape park. Among the garden buildings the Great Mičovna is standing out, a beautiful Renaissance building by Bonifác Wohlmut and Ulrik Aostalli from 1567–1569 with a lavish graffito decoration on the façades, reconstructed after a fire in May 1945. There is also a Renaissance house for the gardener, a greenhouse from 1820, sculptures by Bernard Jiří Bendl and Matyáš Bernard Braun, in the front section there is the former private presidential residence, created by enlarging a Baroque house in the years 1937–1938.

Along the southern front of the Prague Castle above the Lesser Town there stretches a narrow strip of architectonically conceived gardens, called the Southern Gardens. Their present-day visual aspect is the work of Josip Plečnik from 1920–1924. They were formed by linking the Paradise Garden (Rajská zahrada) and Na Valech Garden, originating from the Renaissance period. In the gardens we can find a number of pavilions, observatory terraces, staircases, statues, fountains etc. Besides a pleasant walk the Southern Gardens can also offer spectacular views of Prague.

A FALL WITH A HAPPY ENDING

On 23 May 1618 the so-called second Prague defenestration took place in Louis's Wing of the Old Royal Palace, in the course of which rebel leaders of Czech Protestant estates lead by Jindřich Matyáš Thurn threw the Catholic proconsuls Vilém Slavata and Jaroslav of Martinic along with the scribe Fabricius out of the window. They survived, having fallen on a rubbish dump – they only suffered grazes and bruises in the defenestration. This incident marked the beginning of the rebellion of the Czech Estates and subsequently also the Thirty-years War, which set Catholics against Protestants in the whole Europe. When visiting the Southern Gardens we can see two sandstone obelisks below the Louis's Wing, which were placed there by king Ferdinand II, to mark the place where the defenestrated officials landed.

Left: a view of the Castle from the Royal Gardens

TO A WIFE
WITH LOVE

THE ROYAL SUMMERHOUSE

THE SINGING FOUNTAIN

In the garden in front of the Royal Summer Palace there is a lovely Singing Fountain. In 1546 the Czech ironmaster and bell founder Tomáš Jaroš cast it according to a sketch by the court painter Francesco Terzio from 1562 and a wooden model by woodcarver Peysser. It owes its name to the sound of drops of water falling on the lower bronze tank, which resembles soft singing. You can hear it if you lean closer. According to a story it is a water fairy imprisoned in the bronze by the fountain's creator. Tomáš Jaroš did not live to see gratitude for his work. He claimed the guaranteed reward – one thousand and four hundred florins – in vain. The king eventually solved the situation cleverly: to get rid of Jaroš he sent him to Košice to cast cannons. The ironmaster died shortly afterwards, without being paid one single florin.

Love is a mighty enchantress – it is as true today as it was centuries ago. Even rulers experienced warm human feeling in the past, although for couples of high social standing it was rather exceptional. It is said that Czech king Ferdinand I was hit by cupid's dart. Although his marriage to Anna Jagello was first and foremost a marriage of convenience, since the Czech estates conditioned the acquisition of the vacant throne with it, Ferdinand loved his Anna deeply. It was for her that he had the beautiful Summer Palace built in the eastern part of the Prague Castle Royal Gardens. That's why it was also called Queen Anna's Summer Palace. The official name is the Royal Summer Palace, although the most often used but incorrect name is Belvedere. Experts consider it to be the most beautiful and the purest Renaissance building outside of Italy. The design was developed by the Italian architect and stonemason Paolo della Stella, who is also the creator of the beautiful sculptures on the arcades. The construction began in 1538; when Prague Castle suffered a catastrophic fire three years later, it had to be interrupted and all the funds and building capacities had to be invested into the reparation of the damages incurred. The forced interruption lasted for quite a long time, until 1556, and Paolo della Stella did not live to see the construction continued. Architect Bonifác Wohlmut took charge of the task and by 1564 had constructed the first floor and the roof shaped as an upside-down keel. At that time queen Anna had already been dead for a long time (1547), and Ferdinand, who died the same year it was completed, did not live long to enjoy it, either. The more was the building used by their successors, especially Rodolph II, who often stayed there and placed here a part of his art collection.

In 1648 the richly furnished residential rooms were looted by the Swedes. They took away a bronze sculpture of Mercury and Psyche by Adrian de Vries, among other things. Today the statue is in Louvre in Paris. In the times of Joseph II a military laboratory was

hanging in the balance again in 1989 – on 21 July, during reconstruction works a fire broke out while the copper roof was being fitted. After the damage had been repaired the Summer Palace was again opened for public on 12 July 1991.

It is worthwhile to walk around the arcade gallery, which frames the rectangular building on all sides, and to have a look at the fine reliefs set between the arcs. The conception is purely Renaissance, full of life and its joys. There are historical and hunting scenes, genre scenes, and of course motifs from antique mythology.

Above: a statue by Jan Štursa at the Summer House
Above left: *sculpture decoration of the arcades*

established in the Summer Palace, and the soldiers were only evicted in 1836. After a reconstruction the building has served for exhibition purposes since 1955. Its fate was

A HEAVEN FOR
THE AMBITIOUS

HRADČANY SQUARE (HRADČANSKÉ NÁMĚSTÍ)

Above: Tuscan Palace
Opposite page above: *The Archiepiscopal Palace*
Opposite page below: *Martinic Palace and house No 7*

Since the very beginning of its existence there have been three entrances into the Prague Castle. The main road came from the west, through the outer ward, which served as an agricultural background. In 1320 the castle burgrave Berka z Dubé established the third Prague town, called Hradčany, in its place. It was a small town, very small, perhaps a stone's throw from one end to the other. Besides the rectangular square-marketplace, in the east adjacent to the castle moat and bulwark, it was made up of two short westward streets. It neither became a town with a significant burgher representation nor did its square fulfil the function of a busy trade centre. The houses surrounding it burned down in 1420

during the fights between Hussites and emperor Sikmund's army, in 1541 they were again turned to ashes during the great fire of Lesser Town, Prague Castle and Hradčany. Afterwards most of the building plots were bought by rich aristocrats and church dignitaries, who gradually replaced the burned-out burgher houses by spectacular palaces. It was crucial for the most powerful Czech aristocracy to have a residence in Prague in the immediate proximity of the Prague Castle – the more visible and close at hand they were to the ruler the greater a chance there was of lucrative posts and benefice. In the course of the 17th and 18th centuries the square acquired a predominantly Baroque charac-

ter, the palaces with lavishly structured and decorated façades tried to create a dignified counterpart to the Castle, with which they visually merged into one unit after the Theresian reconstruction in 1753–1775. Today we can find buildings here from the Renaissance, Baroque, Rococo and Classicism periods. Closest to the Castle complex there is the Archiepiscopal Palace, which was purchased by king Ferdinand I in 1562 for the re-established Prague Archiepiscopal. The building later went through several reconstructions. Its present-day appearance was most notably influenced by Rococo, or, to be more exact, by the architect Jan Josef Wirch, who designed of the profusely decorated façade from 1764–65 with sculptures by an influential late Baroque sculptor, Ignác František Platzer. The Tuscan Palace is a monumental Baroque building, exactly opposite Prague Castle, closing up the whole western side of the square. It is a two-storied building with a long façade and two entrance portals, having all the hallmarks of buildings by Jean Baptiste Mathey of Burgundy. It was built in 1689–1691 as per order of count Thun, since 1718 it belonged to Tuscan dukes and since 1848 it was a personal property of Austrian emperor Franz Joseph I. In its proximity there is an interesting Renaissance Martinic Palace from the 16th–17th centuries, whose façade is decorated with valuable figural graffito. One of its owners was Jaroslav Bořita of Martinice, one of the two Catholic proconsuls thrown out of the Prague Castle Czech Chancellery window in 1618. The emperor rewarded his loyalty with a magravial title, numerous estates and prestigious posts. In return Bořita zealously involved himself in persecution of non-Catholics and confiscation of their property.

CZECH ELL ON THE DOOR

Hradčany Town Hall (Hradčanská radnice) is small but charming. Its founders did not find a place for it in the square, but pushed it out to its very end, around the corner to the end of Loreta Street (Loretánská ulice). Later it became clear that standing in the corner can have its advantages. In the course of the great fire in 1541 most buildings of Hradčany were reduced to ashes, and one of the few buildings that were spared was the Town Hall. Its present-day appearance originates in the late Renaissance reconstruction from 1601–1604, when the graffito "letter" façade decoration appeared. We can find the emblem of Hradčany and the Austrian two-headed eagle here. The inconspicuous narrow metal stripe on the door represents the official gauge from the 19th century, the so-called Czech ell, 0.59m long. In the past these gauges were located in places accessible to public, so that people buying cloth at the market could measure the goods and assure themselves that the seller was not cheating.

OLD EUROPE
IN FULL VIEW

ŠTERNBERK PALACE

There's a short and narrow street leading from Hradčany Square (Hradčanské náměstí) to the entrance gate of the Šternberk Palace, which is located somewhat aside, behind the main line of the buildings of the Square at the edge of the Deer Moat (Jelení příkop), with the main façade facing the garden. Its predecessor was the Renaissance palace of Kryštof Popel of Lobkovice, emperor Rodolph II's courtier and a confirmed enemy of Protestants. It was built towards the end of the 16th century. This building completely disappeared after 1698, when it was bought by count Wenceslas Vojtěch of Šternberk who had it replaced with a splendid family residence, one of the most impor-

The palace consists of four wings around a square courtyard, and a massive oval body – a segmental bay, is integrated into the main wing, which faces the garden. It rises high above the palace roofs and there is a large hall on its first floor, called Rotunda. The interior is excellently decorated with painting and stucco. The Šternberks owned the palace until 1811, then it was used by various institutions, for some time by the National Museum, then it was made into a lunatic asylum and during the Protectorate it served the army. In 1947 the National Gallery acquired the building and opened a permanent exhibition in the palace. Today we can see here a collection of old European art – icons, Italian art from 14th to 16th centuries, Dutch painting from the 15th and 16th centuries, German and Austrian painting from the 15th–18th centuries, works of high Renaissance, Venetian school, German, Flemish and Dutch painting from the 17th century, among other things.

Here we can come across many famous names, such as Lucas Cranach, Albert Dürer, Hans Holbein, El Greco, Francesco Guardi, Peter Paul Rubens, Rembrandt van Rijn, Anthonis van Dyck, Francisco de Goya and many others. Among the most admired works are Dürer's *Feast of the Rose (photo opposite page, © 2010 Národní galerie v Praze)* from 1506, Rembrandt's A Scholar in his Study from 1634, El Greco's *Head of Christ (photo below, © 2010 Národní galerie v Praze)* from 1590, Cranach's *Adam and Eve* (around 1538) amongst others.

tant buildings of the secular high Baroque style in Bohemia. The author of the design is unknown, but according to the experts it could probably have been Giovanni Batista Alliprandi. Despite the remarkable typological design and the great artistic value of the building it is a mere torso – originally, more buildings, oriented southwards, all the way to Hradčany Square, were supposed to be connected to the existing northern section. After the builder died in 1708 the work was discontinued.

A REMINDER OF THE BLACK DEATH

From time immemorial the Black Death has been the scourge of mankind, being mainly the deadly bubonic plague, but also other infectious diseases that caused epidemics which struck Europe from time to time. They left tens of thousands of dead because doctors at that time did not know an effective cure. The so-called plague columns are a reminder of these epidemics, built mainly as an expression of gratitude by those who survived, for the end of the outbreak of the epidemic, or possibly because the plague missed the town and its citizens. One of the most handsome and artistically valuable plague columns in Prague can be found in Hradčany Square (Hradčanské náměstí). It was created between 1726 and 1736 and its designer is the important Baroque sculptor Ferdinand Maxmilian Brokof. At the top of the Corinthian column, rising from an ornamental two-storey pedestal, is a statue of the Virgin Mary (today a copy). Figures of eight other saints decorate the lower part of the sculpture. The Hradčany emblem can also be seen here.

Left: the garden and courtyard of Lobkowitz Palace

A PALACE DRESSED
IN LACE

SCHWARZENBERG PALACE

THE TOWN HALL STEPS

The atmosphere of the historical centre of Prague is highlighted by its numerous outdoor staircases. Their construction was needed because of the rugged, hilly landscape of the city, especially on the left bank of the River Vltava. One of them is the Town Hall staircase from the second half of the 17th century beneath the Schwarzenberg Palace, leading up from the upper end of Neruda Street (Nerudova ulice) to the former Hradčany Town Hall (Hradčanská radnice) in Loreta Street (Loretánská ulice). It passes through a dark narrow vacant space, closed in by the high walls of the houses on each side. It has 127 steps. At the foot of the staircase is a statue of St. Johanes Nepomucensis by Brokof (1709) and a sculpture by an unknown artist. In the semicircular arbour, above the staircase, has been preserved the brickwork of the Hradčany fortification from the 14th century.

The Schwarzenberg Palace in Hradčany Square (Hradčanské náměstí) is one of the most beautiful Renaissance buildings in Prague, a great example of the so-called Czech Renaissance – a mixture of Italian art and the native tradition. Originally, it was called the Lobkowitz Palace, after the wealthy Czech aristocrat and senior Prague burgrave Jan Popel of Lobkovice Jr., who had it built to replace several burnt-down burgher houses after the mid-16th century. The wealth and power of the owner were projected into the appearance of the palace, a splendid building rather resembling a castle, whose impressive appearance and dominant position are particularly appreciable from below, from the River Vltava. The main two-storied building with a T-shaped ground-plan was completed in 1567. Along with the western wing and the two-storied southern wing it encloses a square courtyard in the direction of Hradčany Square, from which it is separated by a wall with an entrance gate. All the buildings are crowned with richly decorated graded gables and the main building has a prominent attic cornice with lunettes. The most attractive feature of the Schwarzenberg Palace, though, is the graffito decorating the façades, which resembles fine lace, veiling the building from

head to toe. Squared-stone rustication is predominant – little rectangular squares diagonally divided. For its resemblance to a postage envelope it is called letter graffito.

The interior is decorated as lavishly as the exterior. The ceilings of the four first-floor halls are decorated with paintings on canvas, stretched onto a wooden construction. They date back to time around 1580 and de-

pict motifs from ancient myths – the trial of Paris, the kidnapping of Helen, the conquest of Trojan and the escape of Aeneas. The palace was built and decorated by Italian artists, who in the 16th century came to Bohemia in droves and worked on commissions for the royal court, rich aristocracy and burghers. The natives often mispronounced their names and generally called them "Vlach" – the Old Czech expression for an Italian – instead of using their complicated surnames. The builder of the Schwarzenberg Palace is one of the few Italian artists of that time whose original name is known. He was Agostin Galli, nicknamed Augustin Vlach by the Czechs. Towards the end of the 16th century the Lobkowitzs found themselves in emperor Rodolph II's black book. He confiscated the palace in 1593. From 1719 it belonged to the Schwarzenbergs, after whom it was named.

Since the 1950's the collections of the Army History Museum were placed here. Since 2008 the richly decorated rooms have been used by the National Gallery.

Left: the view of the palace from the Petřín lookout tower
Above: the arcade loggia
Below: original exhibition of the Army Museum

THE MOST RENOWNED
PLACE OF PILGRIMAGE

LORETA

The so-called loretas, fairly exact copies
of a building called Holy House (San-
ta casa) in the Italian town of Loreto, were
typical of the European Baroque of the 17th
and 18th centuries. According to legend this
house was the original house of the Virgin Mary of Nazareth, in which Archangel
Gabriel's annunciation of the birth of Christ
took place. When destruction from pagans
threatened the house in the 13th century, angels carried it to a new, safe place in Loreto. About fifty such Holy Houses were built
in Bohemia, although the one in Prague
is undoubtedly the most famous and most
frequently visited. It also gave its name to
the present-day place of pilgrimage, Loreta,
which was built, in several stages, until the
mid-18th century.

The actual Loretan chapel, today standing in the middle of a courtyard *(photo below)* was built in 1626–1627 by the Italian architect Giovanni Battista Orsi, having
been commissioned by the aristocratic Lobkowitz family. In the following years it was
surrounded by cloisters with seven chapels,
serving as a shelter for the pious pilgrims

who soon started to arrive in great numbers,
often from distant places. In 1664 Italian
artists created a rich stucco decoration with
biblical scenes on the outer walls of the Holy House. All seven chapels in the cloister –
and the cloisters themselves – are decorated
with wall paintings by Felix Antonín Schef-
fler from the mid-18th century and altars by
Matěj Wenceslas Jäckel. In one of the chapels, closed by a glass door and dedicated to
Virgin Mary the Grievous, there is a popular statue of St. Starosta, a saint rarely depicted, whose face is "adorned" with a thick
black beard. According to legend it was
God himself who made the beard grow at
her own wish, when there was a danger that
this daughter of the Portuguese king and secret Christian would have to marry a pagan
suitor against her will. The groom refused
the bearded bride, and the angry father, at
whose request the marriage was supposed
to have taken place, had his disobedient
daughter crucified.

In 1721–23 Kilián Ignác Dienzenhofer created a building facing the Loretan Square,
according to his father Kryštof's design. It is

THE LOVELY SOUND OF BELLS

On the picturesque tower above the entrance façade of the Loreta is the famous Loretan glockenspiel, the work of Prague watchmaker Petr Naumann. Altogether it has 27 bells of various sizes, which were cast by Klaudius Fromm in Amsterdam in 1694. Always on the hour they chime the familiar Marian song Tisíckrát pozdravujeme tebe (A Thousand Times We Greet Thee). The glockenspiel is also provided with a clavier, so any melody can be played. There is legend that explains why these bells not only ring but also play. Once upon a time there was an old widow with many children living at Hradčany. Her only possession was a string of silver coins which she was given by a rich godmother. When the plague epidemic broke out in Prague, her abode was not spared. One child after another died, and each was accompanied on its last journey with the sound of Loretan bells. The unfortunate widow had to pay for each with one silver coin. Finally the last child died and the last coin was gone. Then the mother fell ill and, as death grew closer, she realized she had no coins left with which to pay for the sound of the bells on her own journey to Heaven. Then, the story says, the bells started to ring by themselves, and not only to ring but to play a melody of breathtaking beauty.

an outstanding work in high Baroque style with an exceptionally structured and decorative façade *(photo above)*. On the eastern side of the cloister is the Baroque Nativity Church (1734–1735), perhaps also the work of Dienzenhofer, decorated by first-class Baroque artists, including the painters Wenceslas Vavřinec Reiner, Antonín Kern, Jan Jiří Heinsch, woodcarver Matyáš Schönherr and sculptor Richard Jiří Prachner.

Today, Loreta is managed by the Capuchins from the neighbouring monastery. Its grounds are open to the public – we can see the actual Holy House, walk through the cloisters, and visit the pilgrimage church and the treasures of the Loretan treasury. If we time the visit right, the lovely sound of Loretan bells will ring above our heads…

ČERNÍN PALACE (ČERNÍNSKÝ PALÁC)

LIKE IN BETHLEHEM

In the lower section of the Loretan Square behind a high wall are the unpretentious grounds of the Capuchin monastery. Built from 1600–1602, it is the first monastery of this order in Bohemia. Its simple buildings and the church without opulent decorations are typical of the Capuchins, who believe in modesty. However, at Christmas time there are long queues in front of the church, which is dedicated to the Virgin Mary Angelic. The reason or this is the Nativity scene, which is unique in the Czech Republic. It dates back to 1765 and has 43 life-sized figures, made of straw, textile and paper, which was then dipped in glue and painted. The figures "occupy" a separate room, which a perfectly depicts the Bethlehem landscape.

The monumental façade of the Černín Palace (Černínský palác), one of the largest and most important Baroque buildings in Prague is a dignified counterpart to the pilgrimage site of Loreta. Actually, the intention of the owner, the ambitious Count Humprecht Jan Černín of Chudenice, was much greater – he wanted his residence, built on a raised promontory, to create an optical counterpart to Prague Castle itself. He could afford it; he was one of the richest and most powerful people in Bohemia of his time. He was employed at the imperial court in Vienna and between 1660–1663 served as an imperial envoy in Venice. The palace, especially its main eastern façade, 150m long and divided by thirty continuous semi-columns *(photo below)* is clear proof of the founder's megalomania. It was built between 1669 and 1682. The designer was Francesco Caratti, an Italian architect of the early Baroque period working in Bohemia. After Humprecht's death his son Heřman Jakub continued with the construction of the building, but the work – especially

the opulent decoration – was completed only by the founder's grandson František Josef in 1723. Among the painters, sculptors and stuccoers who gave the interiors their final appearance were illustrious foreign as well as native artists, including Giovanni Bartolomeo Cometa, Giovanni Battisto Allio, Wenceslas Vavřinec Reiner, Petr Brandl, Matyáš Bernard Braun, Tommaso Soldatti, Ondřej Filip Quitainer and many others. Even for the exceptionally well-off Černíns the construction of the palace was a big investment and it swallowed a large chunk of the family wealth. During the wars for the Austrian inheritance in 1742 and 1757 the palace suffered considerable damage and from 1777 it was not permanently occupied and it deteriorated, later even becaming a shelter for the poor of Prague. Since 1851 it was in the possession of the army and used as a barracks; during reconstruction the interior decoration suffered considerable damage. Between 1928–1934 the building was adapted for the residence of the Foreign Office (and still serves this pur-

pose today). The broad terrace in front of the building and other modifications of the Loretan Square come from the same period.

The wings of the palace surround two arcade courtyards. The central room is a large hall, three storeys in height. The terraced palatial garden, adjacent to the beautiful northern façade, is also remarkable. It is shaped as an isosceles triangle. In one vertex there is a garden pavilion dating from 1744 to 1746 and the area is complemented by two ponds.

Above: Reiner's ceiling fresco, The Battle of the Titans

THE CORNER WHERE
TIME STOPPED

NEW WORLD (NOVÝ SVĚT)

If you were blindfolded and somebody brought you to New World (Nový svět), you would hardly recognize that you were still in Prague. A narrow, winding street, quaint, small, low houses and, behind a fence, gardens that create the atmosphere of the countryside. Somewhere at the end, further than the eye can see, is the overgrown upper part of the

Deer Moat (Jelení příkop), part of the medieval fortifications of Prague Castle and Hradčany. It is hard to believe that modern life of the 21st century pulses just a few dozen meters away.

New World Street used to be the backbone of the suburbs of Hradčany, was founded in the mid-14th century and after 1360 included into the new town fortifications. It was rebuilt

THE SMALLEST HOUSE

Several "applicants" compete for the title of the smallest house in Prague. The red-hot favourite for the title is the corner mini-house No 6. One of its walls faces the New World, another is in Černín Street (Černínova ulice), and the others are connected to the walls of the bigger and taller neighbouring buildings. The interior, in which there is barely enough room for a somersault, is illuminated by a single window. The door is only drawn in the plaster and the actual entrance is from a neighbouring house. The quaintness of the whole building is emphasized by its hollow tile roof, from which a high chimney points out like a finger.

At the turn of the 16th century two important European astronomers, Tycho de Brahe (1546–1601) and Johannes Kepler (1571–1630) were employed at the court of Emperor Rodolph II. In 1600 Brahe lived in one of the New World houses. However, from 1599 until his death in 1601 he spent most of his time in the so-called Kurz Summer Palace at nearby Pohořelec, where Kepler worked with him for some time. Remains of the summer palace were discovered and uncovered at the beginning of the 20th century in the grounds of a present-day grammar school. Both famous scholars are commemorated by a statue erected in 1984. Brahe died probably of a kidney disease, and was buried in Týn Cathedral (Týnský chrám) in Prague Old Town. Claims that his bladder burst during a heated discussion with his students, or while watching the eclipse of the sun, or at a banquet given by Petr Vok of Rožmberk, are false. Kepler lived in Prague until the year 1612. Here he articulated his famous laws concerning the motion of the planets on their elliptical orbits, laws which were included in the most famous astronomical work of all time, Astronomia nova, which was published in 1609, thanks to the support of Rodolph II.

after the fires of 1420 and 1541. Its name also dates back to this period. Its inhabitants were rather poor as is evident in the appearance of the houses. Neither their size nor their artistic sophistication is exceptional, but they have kept their indisputable charm and quaint character, some still being adorned with the original house sign. Many of the houses made up for their lack of splendour with their names, most of which have gold in them. Today this romantic setting is used mainly by artists, but in the past some of the abodes were associated with the fates of eminent people.

Golden Gryphon House, Number 76, was occupied by the astronomer Tycho de Brahe in 1600. Golden Acorn House, Number 79, belonged to the Santini family at the beginning of the 18th century, one of whom was an important Czech Baroque architect. In Number 90, Golden Plough House, the violinist František Ondříček was born in 1857. In Number 77, Golden Pear House, is a well-known period restaurant. Number 78, Golden Grape House *(photo right)* on the corner of Capuchin Street (Kapucínská ulice) has a fine oriel with a stone sculpture of a shark. Quaint suburban Baroque houses can also be found in the adjacent Černín Street (Černínská ulice – *photo left*). At its end you can find a remarkable thatched roof cottage called U Raka (Crayfish Cottage – *photo above*), the only well kept timbered house in Prague. In the 18th century there were stables for abattoir animals, in the second half of the 18th century the Libický family built another house here and transformed the stables into apartments. Today the house serves as a luxury hotel.

WHERE THE PREMONSTRATENSIAN HEART STILL BEATS

STRAHOV MONASTERY

A FAMOUS LIBRARY

The Library of Strahov has become world famous. In the 1780's the Premonstratensians even built a separate building for it and changed it into a public beneficial research establishment. Because of this the monastery was spared during the abolition of monasteries during the reign of Emperor Joseph II. The Philosophical Hall, built from 1728–1784, is the artistic gem of the library. It is decorated with a beautiful fresco by the influential Viennese painter Franz Anton Maulbertsch. Its theme is the Influence of Divine Wisdom on the Spiritual History of Mankind. The fresco, created in 1794, was one of the last works by this artist and an excellent "full stop", concluding the monumental paintings of the Central European Baroque era. Strahov Library includes 900 000 volumes, 16 inucabula among them. The oldest manuscript entitled Strahovský evangeliář dates back to the 9th and 10th centuries.

The Strahov monastery one of the oldest and largest in Prague, was founded in 1140 by the Czech ruler Vladislav II at the request of the Archbishop of Olomouc, for the order of Premonstratensians. Even at the time of its establishment its size and daring architecture were astonishing. It was one of the most sophisticated building complexes in Europe. Most of its original Romanesque buildings have survived, despite later changes, some of them covered in Baroque plaster.

The heart of the monastery is an unusually large paradise garden, surrounded by cloisters. Each side is 40m long. The capitular hall is enclosed by ten vaulting spans, something never seen before in Bohemia.

The abbatial Church of the Assumption of the Virgin Mary (chrám Nanebevzetí Panny Marie) has a clear prominence in the com-

plex. A Romanesque basilica, completed in 1182, it has three naves, a transept, three apses and a pair of towers on its western side. A large hospital, farm buildings and a mill also form part of this massive complex. In the garden, a little to the side, is also the abbatial residence. The Strahov Monastery was meant to be a burial place for Czech kings and other important people, but in the end it was only Vladislav II, his wife Gertruda (Judita) and the co-founder, bishop Zdík, who were buried here.

Over the course of the centuries the Premonstratensian complex of buildings was reconstructed several times, mostly after a fire or war damage, for example after the bombardment by the Prussian army in 1757. Its appearance was influenced by both Gothic and Renaissance styles, although its present-day visual aspect is mainly Baroque. In

1627 the remains of St. Norbert, the founder the Premonstratensian order, were secretly brought here from Magdeburg, which was at that time occupied by the Swedish army. Today they can be found in the abbatial church at the altar in the Chapel of St. Voršila's. The Baroque reconstruction was the work of outstanding architects, sculptors and painters.

In the first courtyard, not far from the main gate, stands Gothic-Renaissance style St. Roch Church built from 1602–1612 at the expense of Emperor Rodolph II as an expression of gratitude for avoiding the plague. In 1950 the monastery was confiscated by the Communist regime, the monks were evicted and the rooms were adapted for the needs of the Museum of National Literature. In 1990 the original owner, the Premonstratensian order, returned to Strahov.

The monastery is surrounded by gardens, the Convent Garden, Abbatial Garden and mainly the large Great Garden of Strahov,

through which a pleasant promenade path meanders. The most beautiful vistas of Prague reputedly open out in front of you from this path.

Above: the Theological Hall
Left: Church of the Virgin Mary

GREETINGS FROM
MR EIFFEL

PETŘÍN

Petřín is not only a distinct, landscaped hill above the left bank of the Vltava, interwoven with a dense web of neat paths and tracks, providing a favourite place for dates and quiet walks, but also the remarkable site of buildings of various ages and purposes, which serve only to increase its attractiveness. Until the Thirty-Years War grapevines were grown on the hillsides and there were small vegetable gardens, later replaced by orchards and eventually parks, which included some of the older palatial and convent gardens. The oldest surviving building is the Hungry Wall, stretching from Újezd

THE HUNGRY WALL

When during the 1360's "the father of the country" Charles IV ordered the Lesser Town area to be enlarged and newly fortified, he also included the eastern part of Petřín. The Hungry Wall, which has survived to this day, dates from that time. It is 1179m long, 7.5–8 m high and almost 2 m wide, has a terrace and battlements and is completed by prismatic towers, a crossbow shot apart. Crossbow and bow makers lived in the towers and performed sentry duty. In the 19th century the wall fell into disrepair and some said that it should be pulled down so that it would not disgrace Prague. Fortunately that did not happen, the wall was repaired and today it is the longest surviving section of original medieval town fortifications. The origin of its name – the Hungry Wall – is interesting. According to a story Charles IV had it built mainly to provide work for the poor during a bad harvest and famine to save them from the threat of starvation.

across the top of Petřín to Strahov Monastery. It was part of the Lesser Town fortifications, dating from 1360–1362. The Church of St. Lawrence (kostel sv. Vavřince) has a long history too. The original Romanesque building from the 12th century was from 1737–1770 gradually replaced by a Baroque church. The legend, depicted on the painting of the vestry ceiling, says that the church was founded in 991 by Bishop St. Vojtěch. The World Exhibition in Paris in 1889 inspired the organizers of a similar, although much smaller, Regional Jubilee Exhibition in Prague in 1891 and indirectly caused great building work on Petřín. The Petřín lookout tower *(photo left)* was built as a free copy of the Eiffel Tower. It is 60m high, five times smaller than the Eiffel Tower, although, unlike the Eiffel Tower, it does not stand on flat ground, but on a hill quite high above river level, which erases the height handicap and magnifies the view. At the same time a 396m long cable railway was built *(photo above)* so that visitors of the exhibition who wanted to ascend the tower would not have to walk to Petřín. It worked on the unusual, but for its time very progressive principle of water overbalance. In 1932 it was extended all the way behind the Hungry Wall to

the length of 510m and rebuilt to be electrically powered. In 1965 a section of the waterlogged slope came off and damaged the railway body. After a costly reconstruction between 1983 and 1985, the operation was renewed and the cable railway given two new wagons with a capacity of one thousand four hundred persons per hour. One way takes about three minutes.

When listing the interesting features of Petřín, the Mirror Maze must not be left out. Czech tourists found one of the pavilions at the Parisian exhibition, a copy of the Bastille fort, so fascinating, that one pavilion in the Regional Jubilee Exhibition was conceived as a copy of a defunct Vyšehrad gate called Špička. After the exhibition, the building was moved to Petřín and the Mirror Maze installed inside it in 1893. There are 45 mirrors in the Maze and they are complemented by a dioramic painting, "The Battle between Praguers and Swedes on the Charles Bridge in 1648" (11 x 10m). The Štefánik Observatory built in 1927–1928 is also a frequent destination. During the 1970's it was extensively reconstructed and modernized. It is equipped with several refractors, the largest of which magnifies six hundred and eighty times.

Above: Myslbek's statue of Karel Hynek Mácha in the Petřín orchards

A BAROQUE
FAIRYTALE

NERUDA STREET

The street that bears the name of Jan Neruda, an important Czech poet, writer and journalist, is one of the quaintest streets in Prague. It is part of the former Royal Road, which rises from the upper end of Lesser Town Square to Prague Castle. The name is

NERUDA AND HIS WORLD

Probably the most famous house in Neruda Street (Nerudova ulice) is No 233, named after its pretty sign, Two Suns House. Between 1845–1857 it was occupied by the writer Jan Neruda, whose father had a grocery store on the ground floor. There little Jan used to sit on sacks of flour, peeled barley or some other foodstuff and listen to his neighbours' stories, which he later used in his writing, mainly in *Stories of the Lesser Town*. After his father died in 1857 he moved into No 225, Three Black Eagles House, across the street. After his mother died and was buried in the Lesser Town cemetery in 1869, he left Lesser Town altogether and moved to the other bank of the Vltava, to 28 Convict Street (Konviktská ulice) in the Old Town, where he wrote his best-known works. His books of short stories, verse collections and newspaper sketches are still part of the treasury of Czech literature today.

tini also designed the façade of the nearby Church of the Virgin Mary "U kajetánů". The spacious Renaissance house No 244, with a Baroque façade, called Donkey and Crib House, is the setting of Neruda's short story A Week in a Quiet House. The Rococo Bredfeld Palace, dating from after 1765, is across the street and was the setting of the famous balls given by Josef of Bredfeld. Among the guests were Wolfgang Amadeus Mozart and the renowned adventurer Giacomo Casanova. Golden Horseshoe House No 220 belonged to the architect Oldřich Aostalis in the 16th century. In 1749 the first pharmacy at Hradčany was opened here. Later it was moved next-door, to Golden Lion House, No 219. The pharmaceutical display of the National Museum, which had been here for years, was moved to the Czech Pharmaceutical Museum at Kuks in 2000.

definitely deserved. After all, Neruda, who lived here, described the unmistakable atmosphere of the Lesser Town, its charms, its secrets and, most of all, the often unusual fates of the people who lived there, better than anyone else. The street is a living textbook of Baroque style, its appearance formed not only by the anonymous architects of burgher houses, but also by the great architects of that time, who built several artistically valuable palaces here. The houses are decorated with lovely, ornately-shaped gables and, in places, with pretty portals (photo left), although it is the house signs, some of the most beautiful in Prague, that are admired the most.

Every building could tell a story about the extraordinary lives of its owners, including famous people. House No 209 was owned at the end of the 16th century by the painter Bartolomeus Spranger, who painted Greek gods on the façade. House No 210 is adorned with one of the most famous house signs of all, three violins, to commemorate the fact that from 1667 to 1748 it was occupied by three families of violin-makers in a row. From 1795–1723 house No 211, called Valkounský, belonged to the outstanding High-Baroque Czech architect Jan Blažej Santini-Aichl, who designed the two neighbouring palaces. These were No 214, Thun-Hochstein Palace, decorated with impressive façade and sculptures by Matyáš Bernard Braun, and No 256 opposite, named Morzin Palace, decorated with beautiful statues by Ferdinand Maxmilian Brokof (photo above left). San-

Left: the most beautiful house signs in Neruda Street (from top) – Three Violins, Golden Wheel, White Swan

SOUL OF THE
LESSER TOWN

LESSER TOWN SQUARE

THE TRAGIC FIRE

When you take a look at the façade of Šternberk Palace *(photo below)* in Lesser Town Square, it is clear that the building was formed by connecting two formerly separate buildings. Its upper part, which is somewhat behind the main line of the neighbouring buildings, as if ashamed of its existence, is a house formerly known as Bašta, which made an especially tragic mark on the history of the Lesser Town. On 2 June 1541 a fire broke out here, which could perhaps have been extinguished, had the owner not locked the gate, supposedly out of fear of thieves, on people who were bringing water and were willing to help. The domestic staff were not able to fight the red rooster and soon it spread its ominous wings. Burning shingles, carried by the wind, set neighbouring roofs on fire before the fire spread uncontrollably still further. Very soon all the houses in the Square and in the adjacent streets were ablaze, as the fire spread throughout the Lesser Town. In the evening it spread to Prague Castle and Hradčany. In the course of the catastrophe, one of the worst in the history of Prague, more than 50 people died, many children among them, and 197 houses turned to ash.

The second oldest Prague town, the Lesser Town, was founded in 1257 by King Přemysl Ottocar II in the former settlements round Prague Castle. Its rectangular, slightly inclined square is its heart and soul and one of the most beautiful open spaces in Prague. The burgher houses and aristocratic palaces that surround it were built mostly in Renaissance and Baroque styles, after the great fire of 1541, and many of them retain their medieval cores. We can have a closer look at some of them, because nowadays they are occupied by many period restaurants, pubs, wine bars and cafés.

The higher western side of the square is taken up by Liechtenstein Palace (Lichtenštejnský palác), an early Baroque building dating from early 17th century, rebuilt in 1791 in Classicist style. Prague Post resided here from 1742–1790, from 1848 the Prague army headquarters was located here and at present it is used by the Academy of Music, Drama and Fine

Arts. On the northern side are also mainly palaces. Smiřicky Palace (No 6) is a Renaissance-style building with corner oriels dating from 1603–1613. Šternberk Palace (Šternberský

BLOODY COUNT LIECHTENSTEIN

The owner of Liechtenstein Palace (Lichtenštejnský palác), Count Karel of Liechtenstein, was a dark figure in Czech history. After the rebellion of the Czech estates was defeated on White Hill (Bílá hora) in 1620 the emperor named the count, who was a loyal Catholic, proconsul and charged him with the investigation and punishment of the rebel leaders, as well as with the administration of the following re-Catholization. It is his name that historians associate with the execution of 27 Czech noblemen and burghers in the Old Town Square in 1621, and with the severe repression that followed the White Hill defeat. Through confiscation of Protestant properties, often unscrupulous, the count accumulated enormous wealth. He died in 1627, just as investigation of his strange, often evidently illegal methods was about to commence. His descendants own the Liechtenstein Principality and they are conducting a legal action against the Czech Republic, concerning their past Czech and Moravian property, confiscated by the decree of President Beneš in 1945.

palác) (No 7), originally two Renaissance houses, became one unit during a Baroque reconstruction at the beginning of the 18th century. On the lower, eastern side stands the former Town Hall (No 35), a late Renaissance building with a fine portal, which served its purpose until the merger of the Prague towns in 1784. Also Kaiserštejn Palace (No 37), a beautiful example of Baroque architecture from the period after 1700, built from a design by Giovanni Battista Alliprandi. The bust on the façade commemorates Ema Destinová, the world-famous soprano, who is said to have spent the happiest years of her life here from 1908–1914. On the southern side of the square the high Baroque Hartig Palace (No 259) is found, although quaint burgher houses also remain. Among the most beautiful houses are No 272, U Petržílků, decorated with a Renaissance oriel, as well as the only purely Renaissance house, Golden Lion (No 261), housing the famous Patron Wine Bar (U mecenáše). In the upper section of Lesser Town Square is the Trinity Plague Column, a beautiful work, richly sculptured from a de-

sign by Alliprandi. It was created in 1715 in gratitude for the end of the plague epidemic. Afterwards the lower part was completed with fountains, and a balustrade with sculptures by Ignác František Platzer.

Above: Lesser Town Hall
In the middle: Trinity Plague Column
Below: the painting on the façade of House No 36

THE GEM OF
CZECH BAROQUE

ST. NICHOLAS'S CATHEDRAL

St. Nicholas's Cathedral in Lesser Town Square, with its massive cupola and slender bell tower being prominent features of the city, is considered to be the most beautiful Baroque building in Prague, perhaps even in the Czech Republic. This monumental building, whose construction lasted for more than 50 years, is the work of the renowned Dienzenhofer family, who were commissioned by the Lesser Town Jesuits.

At first, from 1703–1711 Kryštof Dienzenhofer built the cathedral aisle *(photo left)*, a complex hall with side chapels. Its ground plan consists of intersecting ellipses, and its stately, 40-meter-high forefront is a typical example of the so-called radical or dynamic Baroque. Its bulging curves create the illusion of swelling undulating matter, giving the impression of movement. When the nave was completed the construction was

THE CURIOUS JESUIT

If we take a careful look at the extensive fresco stretching across the aisle vault of St. Nicholas's Cathedral we can see a man's face, peeking from behind a column. The story goes that before he started work, the creator of the fresco, Jan Lukáš Kracker, had insisted that no one disturb him while he was painting and that the work be viewed only when completely finished. However, one of the Jesuits was too curious and could not resist, so he secretly sneaked into the cathedral and, hidden behind a column, watched the painting progress. However the painter saw him and, with the help of a mirror, quickly sketched his features before immortalizing his face in the fresco.

discontinued for about a quarter of a century. Then Kryštof's son, Kilián Ignác Dienzenhofer, continued the work. Between 1737–1752 he designed and built a chancel. Above the chancel is a massive cupola, 20m in diameter and 80m in height. The newest section of the building is a slender prismatic bell-tower, constructed between 1751–1756, in late Baroque (Rococo) style, by K. I. Dienzenhofer's son-in-law and pupil, Anselmo Lurago. The decoration of the cathedral's interior is as opulent as the building itself, created by first-class artists from the turn of the high and late Baroque periods. In 1752 František Xavier Palko painted the impressive 75 square metre fresco, celebrating the Trinity, in the cupola. The fresco on the nave vault is newer but more conservatively conceived. It was painted by Jan Lukáš Kracker in 1761–1762 and integrates several periods of the life of

St. Nicholas. Both painters created frescoes in other parts of the cathedral as well, and, apart from their work, there are also paintings by other artists, including Josef Hager, Josef Kramolín and Ignác Raab. In the tribune there is an older cycle of paintings by Karel Škréta. Most of the statues (main photo) are the work of Ignác František Platzer, though there are also sculptures by Richard and Petr Prachner and Jan Bedřich Kohl. Wolfgang Amadeus Mozart played the cathedral organ, which dates from 1745–1746, during one of his visits to Prague. After his death in 1791 Rosseti's Requiem was played here as a tribute. It involved 120 musicians and Mozart's friend, Josefína Dušková, sang the solo.

Above: typical outline of the cathedral with its tower and cupola
Below: Reiner's fresco in the cupola

ST. THOMAS'S CHURCH

The Church of St. Thomas in the Lesser Town used to be one of the most important churches. Originally it was a part of the Austin Friar Hermit Monastery, which is a treasury of Czech Baroque art. The build-

ing is a little in the shade of the neighbouring houses, just its high spire rising above them, and only the entrance frontage is accessible. The church was built gradually, between 1285 and 1379, in early and high Gothic style. During the Hussite Wars it was the main sanctuary of Catholics in Prague. After the fire of 1541 it was rebuilt in Renaissance style, its main portal coming from this period. Most of the Gothic and Renaissance details disappeared during the course of an extensive Baroque reconstruction designed by Kilián Ignác Dienzenhofer between 1723 and 1731. The body of the church and the design of its ground plan have been preserved, as well as the asymmetrically placed Gothic prismatic tower with its corner abutments. Dienzenhofer's undulating façade, divided by massive cornices, columns and pilasters in the extremely dynamic Baroque style, looks impressive *(photo left)*.

However it is the interior of the church that reveals the greatest treasures. The wall paintings of the legend of St. Hedvika in the

BEER FROM ST. THOMAS'S

The brewery, first mentioned in 1352 and supposedly the oldest establishment of its kind in Prague, was one of the farm buildings of the Gothic Austin Friar Monastery in the Lesser Town. Austin Friars definitely knew how to brew beer. At the beginning it was meant for their own consumption only, but the rumour of its quality soon spread outside the monastery walls and eventually the frothy beverage became established all over the whole bank of the Vltava. Even Czech kings found it on their table regularly. During the wars the brewery was closed down and was only reopened around 1656. It brewed stout exclusively and quickly re-gained its splendid reputation. Prague sculptor and woodcarver Jan Antonín Quitainer even had a greater part of his remuneration for the decoration of St. Thomas Church paid in liquid kind, namely, in St. Thomas's beer. To this day the brewery building with its Renaissance core, later rebuilt in Baroque style, stands in 12 Letná Street (Letenská ulice). Beer has been brewed here until the 1950's. Today the building is part of a new luxury accommodation complex Hotel The Augustine; the black Thomas beer is offered here as well.

sacristy are Gothic, dating from 1353–1354, although most of the decoration is the work of prominent Baroque artists. The magnificent frescoes in the nave, in and below the cupola and in the chancel, were created between 1728–1730 by the greatest Czech fresco painter, Wenceslas Vavřinec Reiner. The altar paintings are the work of Karel Škréta, Antonín Stevens of Steinfels, František Xaver Palko and the mannerist painter of the Rodolphine period Bartolomeus Spranger. The main altar is decorated with two large canvases depicting the martyrdom of St. Thomas and St. Augustine, the work of the famous Peter Paul Rubens. Today only copies can be seen here. To see the originals one has to go to the National Gallery. The statues of the saints were sculpted by Jan Antonín and Ulrico Filip Quitainer, Ferdinand Maximilian Brokof, etc. Several prominent figures in the history of Prague art are buried in the church, including builder Ulrico Aostali de Sala, sculptor Adrian de Vries and the English poetess (Elizabeth Jane Weston).

Opposite page below right:
one of the side altars
Main picture above:
a fresco by Reiner
in the main aisle

A DREAM OF POWER
AND FAME

WALLENSTEIN PALACE AND GARDEN

BEAUTY HIDDEN
BEHIND A WALL

The lovely Wallenstein Garden (Valdštejnská zahrada), built at the same time as the palace between 1623–1630, is surrounded on all sides by a high wall, part of which belongs to farm buildings. This garden, one of the most beautiful in Prague, is open to the public. At the entrance is a magnificent sala terrena with three arcades, decorated with ceiling stucco and paintings of the Trojan War *(main photo)*. The space in front of it is occupied by a square giardinetto which consists of a marble fountain and a bronze fountain with a statue of Venus and Amor (1599) by Benedikt Wurzelbauer. It is the only reminder of the splendid original sculptures. Adrian de Vries created most of the sculptures, depicting antique gods and horses, between 1626–1627. In 1648 the Swedes took them away as war loot and later they were placed in the Royal Gardens in Drottningholm. Venus and Amor was returned in 1890, the other statues were later replaced by copies created in 1914–1915. There are also numerous grottoes with artificial stalactites, aviaries, a pool with an artificial island and a riding hall, the latter now used as an exhibition hall *(photo above)*.

General Albrecht Wenceslas Eusebius of Wallenstein (Valdštejn), the commander of the imperial army, was one of the greatest personalities of the Thirty-Years War, but also one of the most controversial figures in Czech history. A careerist, unscrupulously pursuing wealth and political posts, he was at first an indefatigable commander and the indispensable guardian of Habsburg and Catholic interests in Europe, but gradually he lost the trust of the Emperor and became a threat to him. Wallenstein's dream of power and fame, and perhaps even the Czech crown, ended in 1634 in Cheb, where he was murdered, together with his loyal generals, at the emperor's order. In Prague he is commemorated by the palace in Wallenstein Square (Valdštejnské náměstí), a monumental and exceptionally vast building in a prominent position at the foot of the castle hill. Wallenstein Palace (Valdštejnský palác) was the first secular Baroque building in Prague, although there are elements of the retreating late Renaissance mannerism. The residence, which replaced 22 Lesser Town houses, consists of one- and two-storied buildings surrounding five courtyards. On the southern side there

is also an opulent palatial garden with a sala terrena and a riding hall. It was created between 1623–1630 under the guidance of Italian architects Andreas Spezza, Niccolas Sebregongi and Giovanni Pieroni. In the main wing, the façade of which is facing Wallenstein Square *(photo right)*, there is the ceremonial Knightly Hall (Rytířský sál), which occupies two floors and is richly decorated with paintings and stucco by the Italian painter Baccio del Bianco. The central ceiling fresco depicts Albrecht of Wallenstein as the god Mars riding in his triumphal cart *(photo below)*. The same artist decorated other rooms of the palace, including Wallenstein's circular study, the presence chamber, and the Astronomical-astrological Hallway. Wallenstein invested vast sums of money in improving the palatial interiors. He purchased furnishing of the best artistic quality bought in several of European countries. It was mainly inlaid furniture, Brussels tapestry, oriental carpets, upholstery, paintings, statues, chandeliers and other objects. Hardly anything remains, though, because

most of these priceless treasures were stolen by the Swedes in 1648.

Although in 1634 Wallenstein was charged with treason and all his wast property was confiscated, the emperor complied with his widow's wishes and allowed her to keep Wallenstein Palace. In 1639 Albrecht's cousin Maxmilian of Wallenstein bought the building, and it remained in his descendants' possession until it was confiscated by the Czechoslovak state. Today it is the seat of the Senate of the Czech Parliament.

THE PALACE OF INDEPENDENCE

Parliament Street (Sněmovní ulice), on both sides surrounded by Baroque palatial buildings, runs into Wallenstein Square (Valdštejnské náměstí). Historically the most valuable of these buildings is Thun Palace (No 4), the seat of Czech Parliament. This institution owes its residence above all to the great fire of 1794, which severely damaged the opulently decorated and furnished seat of the Thun family. They did not want their destroyed residence and in 1801 sold it to the Czech estates, who had it rebuilt into the Royal Czech Estate Regional House (Královský český stavovský zemský dům). The building has a long front. It was given a somewhat gaunt Classicist façade, the interior being reconstructed to suit the needs of the assembly. During the first Republic it was the seat of the Senate of the National Assembly, which forever dethroned the Habsburgs in its first session. After extensive modifications the Palace now serves as the seat of the Lower House of the Parliament of the Czech Republic.

BEAUTY IN THE SHADE
OF PALACES

GARDENS BELOW PRAGUE CASTLE

THE STAIRCASE
FROM A SONG

The most beautiful view of the Palatial Gardens below Prague Castle is from the lookout terrace near the eastern castle gate, Na Opyši, at the upper end of the Old Castle Staircase (Staré zámecké schody). There is a famous song that caught on quickly about these 101 steps, the most famous and picturesque in Prague, which lead from Klárov to the area of a long-ruined Renaissance fore-gate. They were built in 1683, to replace an old path leading up to the castle from the east from the former ford crossing the Vltava. Especially in summer they are frequently used by tourists, who find their way between dozens of stalls of artistic (and not so artistic) objects.

Above: sala terrena in Lederburg Garden
Right: Lederburg Garden's terraces

Next to the northern side of Wallenstein Square (Valdštejnské náměstí) and Wallenstein Street (Valdštejnská ulice) is a line of former aristocratic palaces. Behind them, hidden from the curious eyes of passers-by, is a remarkable complex of palatial gardens, one of the real wonders of European landscape design. It is a graphic proof of the life style and taste of the aristocracy, but above all of the creative ingenuity and feeling for beauty of the first-class artists of the Baroque period. The five intimate Palatial Gardens below Prague Castle were, during the course of the costly reconstruction and regeneration of 1988–2000, interconnected into one tourist circuit. They represent the Italian-type garden, built on a sloping terrain and made up with architecturally conceived terraces,

abutment walls, staircases, arbours, lookouts, fountains, sculptures and small buildings. The westernmost Ledeburg Garden (Lederburská zahrada), adjacent to Ledeburg Palace (Lederburský palác), is the work of an unknown Baroque artist from the first half of the 17th century. It was modified between 1787–1797 by Ignác Jan Palliardi. In the lower level section, the pit, there stands a magnificent sala terrena with five arcade arches, decorated with paintings of antiquity motifs by Wenceslas Vavřinec Reiner. The terraced section is formed by a system of terraces and staircases with balustrades, which lead up to the highest octagonal arbour. The sloping section of the Ledeburg Garden is adjacent to a utilitarian Small Palffy Garden (Malá Pálffyovská zahrada) which consists of terraces and fruit trees, (its present-day appearance dating back to 1751). To the east above Palffy Palace (Pálffyovský palác) is Great Pallfy Garden (Velká Pálffyovská zahrada) from the same time, reconstructed in Classicist style at the beginning of the 19th century. It has seven terraces; with an observatory loggia on the highest. The staircases leading up to it use tunnels to pass through the thick abutment walls. A plaque in the upper section commemorates the participation of the Prague Heritage Fund Foundation in the reconstruction of the gardens, which took place under the patronage of President Wenceslas Havel and His Royal Highness Charles, Prince of Wales. The adjacent Kolowrat Garden (Kolovratská zahrada), which consists of seven terraces connected by a staircase, also used to have a purely utilitarian character. The lower terrace is decorated with a fountain that includes a gargoyle shaped as a human head. Perhaps the most beautiful of the five Palatial Gardens is Small

Fürstenberg Garden (Malá Fürstenberská zahrada), created by an unknown Baroque artist, and modified and reconstructed by Palliardi in an ornamental, artistically impressive Rococo style from 1784–1788. From the pit, which has two fountains, a fresco-decorated staircase gloriet runs up the terraced section of the garden. The staircase leads up to the dominant feature of the whole area, a tower-like observatory arbour, from which it is possible to walk through to the Southern Gardens of Prague Castle. A visit to the gardens, open in summer, is a special experience.

The year 2008 marked the opening of the sixth and largest garden, Great Fürstenberg Garden (Velká Fürstenberská zahrada) (1.5 hectares), surrounding Fürstenberg Palace (Fürstenberský palác), the Polish Embassy residence. Its flat section provides the background for the Embassy employees, the upper sloping section, divided into ten terraces, with a pavilion accessible by a double-flight of stairs, is in the possession of the Czech Republic. Originally there was a vineyard here, in the 18th century it was modified into a garden, romantically arranged around 1860. Before that, since 1822 the Fürstenberks had used it as a utility area – there had been a timber storage, for example.

Above left: paintings decorating the sala terrena
Above: the fountain in Small Fürstenberg Garden
Below: Small Fürstenberg Garden

THE MOST BEAUTIFUL
OF ALL

VRTBA GARDEN (VRTBOVSKÁ ZAHRADA)

ATLAS, THE RESCUER

From the dark, somewhat grim courtyard of Vrtba Palace (Vrtbovský palác) one enters a garden through a gate guarded by a statue of Atlas, the strongman bearing the Earth on his shoulders. Along with the other statues in the garden it is the work of Matyáš Bernard Braun. The story goes that this stone guard put the Earth down for a short moment. It happened when in the street outside a frightened team of horses was racing straight at a little girl who did not realize the danger she was in. Atlas jumped off the gate, ran into the street and stopped the horses. Then he returned to his place, where he has been standing to this day, indifferent and unconcerned.

So much charm in such a small area can hardly be found anywhere else in Europe. Vrtba Garden, named after the palace of the lords of Vrtba to which it originally belonged, is a classic example of the aristocratic garden of the Italian type, which was born in the Renaissance, but reached perfection only in the Baroque period. This type of garden preferred sloping terrain, which made it possible to construct abutment walls, terraces and outdoor staircases, all in accordance with a strict axial system. The eastern side of Petřín hill offered ideal conditions, which explains why several gardens of this type were created here. However, Vrtba Garden is the most beautiful and artistically challenging of all. The important Czech Baroque architect František Maxmilian Kaňka created it around 1720 for Count Jan Josef of Vrtba in place of a former vineyard. During the course of

he reconstruction and regeneration of monuments of 1990–1998 an entrance section,
with a ticket-office and sanitary facilities, was
added.

When we enter through the inconspicuous
gate from Karmelitská Street into the narrow,
dark courtyard, there is no indication that just
a few dozen meters away a tiny world of singular beauty will open up in front of us. And
as we ascend the staircase, it opens up with
each step. The endeavour of the builder, who
succeeded in including everything that landscape design of that time knew and demanded, into such a limited space (0.31 hectares),
is worthy of our admiration. The display be-
gins at the bottom. The level pit at the foot of
the palace includes a pond and a putti statue,
and is adjacent to a stately sala terrena decorated with a fresco of Venus and Adonis by
Venceslas Vavřinec Reiner. A double-flight
staircase connects this area with the first ter-

race, the ground plan of which resembles
a butterfly with spread wings. At its end is the
massive abutment wall of the second terrace,
again with a double-flight staircase. This terrace is inclined, topped with a gloriet with
lavish sculptural decoration, a relief of mer-
maids being its dominant feature. The front
wall was originally decorated with a fresco
by Reiner, which unfortunately disappeared
in the ocean of time. The narrow, steep staircase inside the building leads to the very top
of the gloriet, the highest place in the garden.
The observatory platform offers a magnificent
view of the neighbouring Lesser Town palaces, dozens of Prague spires and above all of
the stately structure of St. Nicholas's Cathedral (photo left). Especially from here, with
a bird's eye view, we appreciate the architectural conception of the garden, the lace-
like tangle of paths, shaped flowerbeds and
hedges, banisters with skittle balustrades,
statues and stone vases. The Baroque sculptural decoration is the absolute highlight of
the garden.

Above: Braun's sculptures
*Below: frescoes in the sala
terrena*

BAMBINO
DI PRAGA

THE CHURCH OF VIRGIN MARY
THE VICTORIOUS

my armies. Gifts from grateful believers grew as the number of fulfilled wishes increased. The Bambino was given not only large sums of money, but also its own altar *(main photo)*, the epithet 'graceful', gold crowns, an orb and even, from one of its benefactresses, an entire estate in Solnice. Yet chiefly its wardrobe has enlarged; up to the current time both individuals and organizations across the whole world have provided the Bambino with nearly fifty different frocks, chemises and rochets *(photo left)* which are changed to suit particular religious celebrations. And they are not ordinary dresses! Adorned with pearls, gold and diamonds, their value is incalculable. One piece of the Bambino's garment was sewn and decorated by Empress Marie Thérése herself. The sculpture has reached high eminence, especially in traditionally Catholic countries, where it is known under the name of Bambino di Praga. Visitors can acquaint themselves not only with the Bambino, but also with its museum, which was recently opened.

MUMMIES IN THE BASEMENT

The basement of the church also attracts attention. In the large catacombs the bodies of deceased White Friars and their benefactors were buried in the 17th and 18th centuries. Owing to the dry environment and air circulation the bodies did not decompose, but underwent a process of natural mummification.

When German Lutherans built their church dedicated to St. Trinity at the base of Petřín Hill in the Lesser Town in 1611– 1613, they had no idea they would be using it for such a short period of time. The church was the first religious building in Baroque style in Prague. After the defeat of the Czech Estates army on White Hill (Bílá hora) the church was taken over by the Catholic Church, who assigned it to the order of White Friars in 1624. They rebuilt it with a tower and dedicated it to Virgin Mary the Victorious to honour the Catholic victory *(photo right)*. The interior boasts valuable decorations. Paintings by Petr Brandl, sculptures by Jan Jiří Bendl can be found here. There is even a copy of the 'miraculous' painting of the Virgin Mary, under which the Catholic League army reputedly fought on White Hill. Yet in terms of popularity none of these works of art can compete with the Prague Bambino, a sculpture of the infant Christ famous throughout the Catholic world for its miracles. The 45cm high wax sculpture was made in Spain in the 16th century and brought to Bohemia by Maria Maxmiliana Manriques de Lara who was married to Vratislav of Pernštejn. Eventually the Bambino became, through the intricate paths of destiny, the property of the White Friars of the Lesser Town who displayed it in their church. Even here the sculpture continued to perform miraculous acts of supplication; restoring people's sight and hearing, helping them gain lucrative office, helping them conceive, providing protection against epidemics or ene-

A MONUMENT TO
PRIDE AND GREED

MICHNA PALACE – TYRŠ HOUSE

DESTINATION SARAJEVO

There is only a simple and unobtrusive Classicism façade on the frontage of Chotek Palace (Chotkovský palác) in 1 Hellich Street (Hellichova ulice). It was built between 1804–1848 and served as the Chotek family residence. Countess Sofie Chotková, who married the successor to the Austro-Hungarian throne Franz Ferdinand d'Este in 1900, came from this family. He was so much in love with his wife that he could not bear her being constantly humiliated and slighted by the Viennese imperial court. Despite the fact that Sofie came from an ancient aristocratic family (already mentioned in the 14th century), their marriage was considered unequal in terms of social standing. She never became a fully-fledged member of the Habsburg family, as was made clear to her by an array of humiliating restrictions concerning court etiquette ordered by Emperor Franz Joseph himself. In 1914 both Sofie and her husband were victims of the Sarajevo assassination, after which World War One broke out. Its consequences led to the division of the Austro-Hungarian monarchy.

The turbulent events of the rebellion of the Czech Estates had a significant impact on the history of the palatial building in Újezd Street in the Lesser Town. Originally there stood a Renaissance house and

summer palace, from 1616 owned by count Jindřich Matyáš Thurn, one of leaders of the rebellious Czech Estates. In 1620, after the defeat of the revolt, he was forced into exile. He carried on fighting against the Habsburgs in the protestant army. His wife had remained in Prague and as it was her dowry, she managed to keep the house from confiscation. However, she became heavily indebted and was eventually forced to sell the house well below its real value in 1624. Pavel Michna of Vacínov, the new owner, was an unscrupulous man, infamous for his greediness, callousness and dishonesty. Through servility to the reigning Habsburgs, which included spying, informing on people and betrayal, he worked his way up from being a humble burgher's son, a secretary in the imperial court, to a peer. In 1627 he was knighted, then promoted to lord and finally to count. He helped himself to enormous wealth by violent looting, and nothing could stop him. He owned large estates in different

ends of the country and was the second richest aristocrat in Bohemia after Wallenstein (Valdštejn). According to contemporaries not a fraction of his property was acquired honestly. To make a display of his newly acquired status he had the small original buildings at Újezd converted into a pompous Baroque palace (above), the buildings of which surround three courtyards. His son Wenceslas later continued the construction. The designer of this stately building with its richly ornamented and adorned façades and interiors, all in the same elaborate style, remains unknown. The name of Francesco Caratti has often been mentioned, and it is clear that the stuccoes, masonry and paintings must be the work of Italian artists. However the proverb that pride comes before a fall applies even to the Michna of Vacínov family. As a result of their extensive investments and highly extravagant lifestyle these post-White Hill nouveaux riche exhausted their resources and could not complete the reconstruction. In 1670 Michna was declared bankrupt and the property sold up. The new owners, the Schwarzenbergs, at first endeavoured to complete construction of their half-finished residence, but eventually they settled for the building of a riding hall and stables. In time they lost interest in the palace, called Michna Palace after its builder. In 1767 it was sold to the army and an armoury was established there. In 1921 the Czech Sokol organiza-

tion bought the neglected building. They altered it to suit their purposes and called it Tyrš Palace after the founder and first chief of the Physical Education Organization Sokol, Dr. Miroslav Tyrš. Between 1950 and 1990 there was the Museum of Physical Education and Sport. Nowadays it is used once again by the Sokol organization.

Opposite page above: an embossed entrance gate
Opposite page below: a courtyard within the Renaissance heart of the palace
Left: statue of Dr. Miroslav Tyrš

UNDER THE MALTESE CROSS

GRAND PRIOR SQUARE

JOHN LENNON'S WALL

After the death of Beatle John Lennon in 1980, one of his fans painted a large portrait of the singer-songwriter on the wall of Grand Prior Garden (Velkopřevorská zahrada). As time went by various graffiti has appeared around the portrait. This wall, later called John Lennon's wall, used to be a meeting place for young people, who on various occasions protested against the communist regime. The police often acted against them. The wall was recently repainted, but it still exhibits paintings and graffiti by anonymous painters. Even Yoko Ono, Lennon's widow, signed her name and wrote a few messages here upon her visit to Prague in December 2003.

The knights of St. John of Jerusalem, later called the Maltese Knights after their main seat on the island of Malta, were one of the so-called knight orders active in Bohemia. They had been in Prague since the 12th century and their monastery called "komenda" was built on the left bank of the River Vltava, near the end of a stone-built Judita Bridge on the left bank of the Vltava. The monastery observed its own law independent of the laws of the land. It kept this privilege even after it became surrounded on three sides by the newly established Lesser Town. In 1420 the St. John "komenda" was burned down by the Hussites and was only reconstructed 100 years later. During the 17th century it became a seat of the highest members of the order, the Grand Priors. Between 1725–1731 a spectacular reconstruction in high Baroque style was carried out. Old Romanesque and Renaissance buildings have been preserved in this large edifice, nowadays known as Grand Prior Palace (Velkopřevorský palác). Its oblong courtyard is surrounded by four wings. Both main frontages facing Grand Prior Square (Velkopřevorské náměstí) and Spa Street (Lázeňská ulice) boast richly decorated façades with

Right: Grand Prior Palace with the Church of the Virgin Mary under the Chain

mbossed portals. During World War Two he Maltese Knights were ousted from their seat by the Germans and the palace was used by the German University. Six large Brussels tapestries made around 1730 used to adorn the capitular hall, but were stolen by the then Minister of Foreign Affairs, Joachim von Ribbentrop. Nowadays the palace is again a property of the order, whose chief activities include social work, health care and charity.

The Church of the Virgin Mary under the Chain (kostel Panny Marie pod řetězem), originally a large Romanesque basilica from the second half of the 12th century, forms part of the monastery. Conversion into a Gothic style building commenced in the second half of the 14th century but was interrupted by the Hussite Wars and has never been completed. Only bare peripheral walls and a hall containing two massive towers have remained of the unfinished nave. The former early Gothic presbytery, dating from the 13th century, was rebuilt in Baroque style. Nowadays it is used as a church. Altar paintings by Karel Škréta and Antonín Stevens of Steinfels, as well as sculptures by Jan Jiří Bendl are listed among its valuable inventory.

Grand Prior Square (Velkopřevorské náměstí) is complemented by the monumental frontage of Buquoy Palace (Buquoyský palác), built from 1736–1748 in late Baroque

style. Nowadays it houses the French Embassy. The adjacent Small Buquoy Palace (Malý Buquoyský palác – *photo above right*), is a building with a Renaissance core, later altered in Baroque style. In the Renaissance Palace of the Mettychs of Čečov from the 16th–17th centuries composer Josef Bohuslav Foerster was born in 1859.

FAMOUS HOTELS

In the neighbourhood of Grand Prior Palace, on the corner of Spa and Saxon Streets (Lázeňská and Saská ulice, respectively) is Spa House (V lázních) (No 7). Since the 17th century it has been a famous hotel where many great personalities have stayed, including the famous Russian commander Alexander Vasilievich Suvorov in 1799, in 1833 the French king Charles X and poet François-René de Chateaubriand, and the Prussian chancellor Otto von Bismarck in 1866. The hotel in Golden Unicorn House (U zlatého jednorožce) across the street (No 11), was very famous as well, composer Ludwig van Beethoven *(photo left)* staying there in 1776.

55

PRAGUE
VENETIA

KAMPA

THE LAUNDRETTE CHURCH

When we approach Kampa from the south we cannot miss one the oldest remaining sights of the Lesser Town – the early Gothic Church of St. George's also called The Launderette Church (Na prádle) *(photo above)* mentioned as early as 1142. Its sanctum nave dates from reconstruction in mid-13th century. The renowned lawyer Viktorin Kornel of Všehrdy was buried here in 1520. The name and history of the church reminds us of the 'Prague Venetia' banks being crowded by comely laundresses. Even Emperor Rodolph II's laundress used to come here to do the washing. The church was closed down and converted into a launderette in 1784, only re-opening as a church in 1935.

Kampa is a quiet, romantic spot full of greenery, washed from one side by the waters of the River Vltava and from the other by an artificially constructed canal, Čertovka (the Devil's Canal). The canal flows along a picturesque cluster of houses on the northern tip of this remarkable area, a striking nook also known as the Prague Venetia. Its name may have been derived from the Latin word "campus" (a flat field) or from the name of Tychon Gangsel of Camp, a man who made a fortune growing tulips and built a house here in the 17th century. The Italian word "campo" also means an island garden, and Kampa has always been an island of gardens. Kampa was mentioned for the first time in 1169. At that time it was called simply The Island, but from 1770 the name Kampa began to be used officially. The profile of the island changed because of the ground washed away during the course of floods. However, its shape leveled off after the Lesser Town fire of 1541, the material from the destroyed houses being used to reinforce of its banks.

The artificially constructed branch of the canal that separates Kampa from the Lesser Town. The name is supposedly connected to a lady who owned a house in Maltese Square (Maltézské náměstí). Six infernal creatures were portrayed on the wall of her house with the inscription beneath them: Seven Devils House. The name began to be commonly used and everybody could work out who the seventh devil was; that lady had a glib tongue, no one could measure themselves against her, and because she often washed her laundry in the Gully, the canal began to be called the Devil's Canal (Čertovka).

Originally only the fruit gardens of the burghers and nobility were on Kampa. Only in 1948–1949 were the walls surrounding these gardens knocked down and the current-day large park created in an area covering 2.65 hectares. The park was inspired by English landscaping style, with prome-

Kampa is connected with many famous personalities. The poet Jan Neruda left his footprints here, while walking home Anna Holinová, whom he had met at dancing lessons. Upon parting he handed her a book of poetry. At home she noticed that some words had been thinly underlined. When she put them together she read a declaration of love. A week later she returned the book to him, the happy student reading his longed-for answer from the words she had underlined. However, although Neruda saw Anna for many years, he was not willing to marry her, and there was no wedding in the end. Painter Adolf Kašpar and writer František Langer lived and worked on Kampa, too. And let us not forget house No 501. Count Bedřich Jan Nostic had the garden house adapted for Josef Dobrovský. The outstanding Slavist scholar suffered from a mental illness, but found peace there while gardening. Between 1929 and 1940 Zdeněk Wirth, a respected authority on the history of Prague, also lived in No 501. Poet Vladimír Holan lived there between 1948 and 1968. The first floor was then occupied by the actor, writer and playwright Jan Werich who lived there until his death in 1980. Nowadays there is a bust commemorating him *(photo above)*. Two connected houses, numbers 500 and 543, stand nearby, in the lower one the well-known painter Jiří Trnka lived and worked.

nades along the Vltava and Čertovka. Beautiful vistas of the river, Charles Bridge, the Lesser Town Bridge Tower and the Old Town open up from here. For a long time the gardens had not been open to the public, and when the Prague councillors agreed to the construction of the first houses, the owners were charged with the care of Charles Bridge. The first inhabitants were stonemasons, bricklayers and joiners, later on followed by craftsmen whose workshops were huddled under the arches of the bridge. Then smiths and blacksmiths moved in. Potters offered their wares here for the first time around the turn of the 16th and 17th centuries. They originally brought their products to Pohořelec, but in 1599 the plague epidemics broke out on Hradčany, so they moved to Kampa and have remained there to this day. The tradition of the pottery markets has been preserved and pottery from Kampa is a sought-after souvenir. The quaint square

(photo opposite page below), encircled by beautiful houses, is called The Potter's Spot (Hrnčířský plácek).

One of the dominant features is Lichteinstein (Kaiserstein) Palace (Lichtenštejnský or Kaiserštejnský palác), a Baroque structure built from 1684–1696, later reconstructed in Classicist and Neo-Renaissance styles. On the Vltava bank are the Sova Mills (Sovovy mlýny). Across Čertovka we can see Michna Palace, also called the Tyrš House (Michnův palác or Tyršův dům). The mills on Čertovka should be mentioned as well. There is a nice view of Smeltery Mill (mlýn Huť) with its original millwheel, the Grand Prior Mill (Velkopřevorský mlýn – *photo above*) with its huge millwheel is famous too, being mentioned as early as the 13th century when it was the property of the knights of St. John. Nowadays it is considered to be the most picturesque corner on the whole Kampa.

FIRST IN
PRAGUE

SOVA MILLS (SOVOVY MLÝNY)

The first Prague mill delivering flour even to Prague Castle used to be on Kampa. According to legend, an old oak had to be cut down before of the mill could begin. An owl, a sacred bird in pagan times, flew out of the oak's hollow. Due to this propitious sign the mill was called the Owl Mill (Soví mlýn). However, the reality is less romantic. Towards the end of the 15th century the mill was owned by an Old Town citizen Wenceslas Sova ('owl' in Czech).

The St. George's Mill (mlýn sv. Jiří) existed here as early as the 13th century. The present-day, originally Renaissance-style building dates from 1589, but was altered in Neo-Gothic style between 1836–1862. Because of their location the Sova Mills suffered frequent flood damage and they were not spared by fires either. The mills changed owners quite frequently. At one time there was a saw mill and a grinding shop under burgomaster Pavel Severín. Eventually the entire site was taken over by the Lesser Town municipality which rented it to experienced millers on the so-called "third groschen". It meant the lessee kept one third of the proceeds, the town getting two thirds. Costs were divided in the same manner.

KUPKA WORTH A MILLION

The gallery in the Sova Mills *(photo above)* boasts an exceptionally valuable collection of 215 paintings by František Kupka (1871–1957). Their estimated value is 14 million dollars. The famous Czech painter, illustrator and graphic designer lived in Paris from 1906; that his work was brought to Prague is the credit of Meda Mládková, who loaned the family collection to Prague in exchange for using the Sova Mills. Between 2000–2001 she instigated a reconstruction of the whole site. The cost exceeded one hundred million Czech crowns. Placing a huge glass cube on the original building raised many objections among experts as well as from the public *(photo opposite page above)*. Nowadays Prague is getting used to this new feature and the public has been able to admire Kupka's paintings and other works of art since September 2003.

During the Thirty-Years War in 1648 the Swedes chose this area as the location for their artillery. The Old Town citizens shot back and the Sova Mills were left in a state of ruin. However they were later reconstructed and Josef Mysliveček (1737–1781) apprenticed here, at that time having no idea that he would become an excellent composer, known in Italy as "il divino Boemo" (the divine Czech). In the 19th century the Odkoleks arrived, reconstructed the mill yard and built a new residential two-storey wing in English Gothic style according to a design by architect Josef Zítek. But during the night of 29–30 January 1896 another huge fire broke out. Fire-fighters had to break the ice on the Vltava in order to get to the water. Crowds of curious people were watching; these standing on the frozen river having an unexpected bath when the heat melted the ice. The building complex then went to ruin until the town bought it and used sections as apartments or workshops. In 1920 the eastern wing was pulled down. After World War Two it became a seat of several institutions, including the Of-

fice for Study of Czech Theatre, the Czechoslovak Academy of Science and the Institute of Czech and World Literature. At the turn of the second and third millenniums there was an extensive reconstruction and nowadays it houses the Kampa Museum.

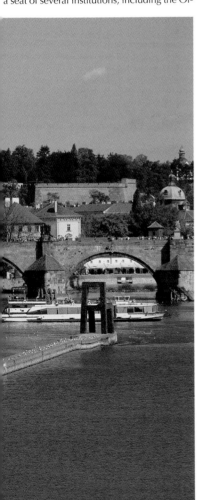

A LOST CHAIR

The Sova Mills could hardly be spared by the devastating flood at the end of summer 2002, this location clearly being among the most threatened. The water toyed with the iron benches in the yard, turned them into rams and broke a glass sculpture by Wenceslas Cígler. It even washed away a huge wooden chair, perched on the lock, the singular and admired work of Magdalena Jetelová. Fortunately the most valuable works of František Kupka, Otto Gutfreund and Jiří Kolář were deposited on the upper floors of the building, which the water did not reach. As the flood waters subsided people immediately started working on the reconstruction. It is interesting to note that even the employees of the nearby American embassy, including Ambassador Craig Stapleton himself, helped. Nowadays the Sova Mills serve as a gallery and the gigantic chair is back in its place (main photo).

A SILVER RIBBON
IN THE HAIR

THE RIVER VLTAVA

ISLANDS BIG AND SMALL

There are nine islands interspersed on the River Vltava in the Prague area. There used to be many more. In some places, Karlín, for instance, there were whole clusters of islands, interconnected by footbridges, but later they disappeared in the course of stream regulation and riverbank alternations. The ones that have remained to this day are pleasant oases of greenery and quiet, places for a stroll and relaxation. This is completely true of Slavic Island (Slovanský ostrov), Shooter Island (Střelecký ostrov), Children's Island (Dětský ostrov), Kampa, and partially true of Štvanice and Imperial Island (Císařský ostrov). The latter, situated between Trója and Bubeneč, is the largest island in Prague, almost 3 km long. The tiniest is Petržilkovský Island, the location of which is hardly known by any Praguer. It is found at the Smíchov side of Jirásek Bridge (Jiráskův most). The Renaissance tower of the Lesser Town waterworks on the island *(photo above)* is only a small reminder of a once large island, removed before World War Two when a sluice was built.

The river Vltava winds trouhg Prague like a silver ribbon. It is the longest and most famous Czech river. Dividing the city in two parts, today it is once again clear and covered with silvery foam. Without it, Prague would not be Prague, and probably would not exist at all. One reason for the emergence of the local settlement was a ford, the only one for miles around, which made it relatively easy to cross. For that matter, according to experts even the name Prague (Praha) is related to the Vltava, being derived from the word "práh" (Czech for "sill"), after the sills in the broad riverbed.

The source of the Vltava lies in the Šumava, and after 430 kilometers, at Mělník, it surrenders all its water to the Elbe (Labe). Who knows why our ancestors gave priority to the Elbe in this "marriage of rivers" and used its name for the river after the confluence. After all, the Vltava is much longer and before the confluence it is also bigger and has more water.

Wherever you look from, the river is always different. It is slender and deep in the narrow rocky valleys where it enters and

leaves the city, and wide and lazy in the city centre, wherein its flow is confined by several weirs. It looks different in spring, when its banks and island are veiled with a shawl of white flowers; in summer, when the little rowboats and steamboats crisscrossing its surface are watched with envy by swans; in autumn, when it wears colourful clothes of fallen leaves and sometimes modestly hides behind a misty veil; and in winter, when it sparkles with icicles and the glitter of snowflakes on the embankment walls. Only the statue of Bedřich Smetana on its bank by the Old Town weir never changes its expression, as if replaying in its mind the tones of the famous symphonic poem he named after the river…

The dozens of water mills that used to skirt

FROM WOOD TO CONCRETE

For centuries Prague managed with only one single bridge across the Vltava, at first the Romanesque Judith Bridge (Juditin most), then the Gothic Charles Bridge (Karlův most). Only between 1841–1845 was a second bridge built, named after Franz I (František I). The bridge floor was fastened with massive chains hung on high towers. It has since been replaced by Legion Bridge (most Legií), which is just a little younger than Negrelli Viaduct, built between 1846–1850 for railway transport and, at 1110 m long, still the longest of all bridges crossing the Vltava. Trains cross it even today, not surprisingly, as a real expert supervised its construction, namely Alois Negrelli, who was also involved in designing the Suez Canal. And suddenly there were suddenly many bridges: bridges made of stone, iron, concrete and ferroconcrete, serving road, railway and tram transport. Currently there are seventeen bridges crossing the river. The youngest is Barrandov Bridge (1978), but who knows how long it is going to keep this title. Allegedly a new bridge is being born under the hands of designers.

both riverbanks have been silent for a long time now. The ferrymen's boats, and the rafts bringing timber from the woods of the Šumava and Czech-moravian Highlands have also disappeared. The river surface does not freeze over anymore to offer pleasant amusement for ice-skaters or subsistence to the ice-men who used to take care of the refrigeration of beer in brewery cellars.

Once in a while the river lets us know she has her whims and spills over the banks. What she showed in 2002, though, was closer to apocalypse than to a whim. Possessively she took upwhole Prague areas in her arms, transformed streets and squares into lakes and paralysed the life of the city. Such catastrophe Prague experienced for the first, and hopefully for the last, time.

Opposite page below: statue
of Bedřich Smetana
Main photo: the Vltava with
Charles Bridge
Above left: Slavic Island
(Slovanský ostrov – Žofín)

LEGACY OF THE FATHER
OF THE NATION

CHARLES BRIDGE

SECRETS IN THE TOWER

At the end of the indoor staircase in the Old Town Bridge Tower (Staroměstská mostecká věž) is a statue of a 14th century tower-watchman, for its time a unique portrait of a common, anonymous person. The sculptor probably made the statue for his own pleasure, without commission. From the gallery there is an amazing view of the city. The Catholic victors of the Battle of White Hill used the tower for a rather morbid purpose. Here on iron hooks they impaled the heads of 12 of the 27 noblemen and burghers, leaders of the estates anti-Habsburg rebellion, executed in Old Town Square in 1621. The head of Jáchym Ondřej Šlik was redeemed by his relatives in 1622, the remaining heads being kept here until the Saxon invasion of 1631–1632, when Czech Protestants removed them and respectfully buried them in Týn Cathedral.

In earliest times the Vltava was crossed in the Prague area by a ford, and later by a wooden bridge, which stood somewhere in the area of present-day Klárov. The first stone bridge across the river was for its time a very advanced Romanesque structure with hardly a parallel in Europe. King Vladislav I had it built between 1160–1172 and named it after his wife Judith. A flood in 1342 damaged the bridge so severely that it could not be repaired, so Emperor Charles IV, whom Czechs in gratitude called the Father of the Nation, had a new bridge built in its place. Originally it was called Prague Bridge or Stone Bridge, but since 1870 it has been called Charles Bridge. The work, conducted by the famous architect and sculptor Peter Parler, commenced in 1357 and was completed after Parler's death at the beginning of the 15th century. The bridge is 515m long and 9.5m wide, has 16 arches and is made of sandstone blocks. Its fate has also been influenced by floods, perhaps most significantly in 1890, but damaged or torn down sections have always been successfully repaired.

The entrance to the bridge from the Old Town is guarded by the gate of the Old Town Bridge Tower (*photo left*), often called the most beautiful medieval tower in Europe. Besides its defence function it also had a symbolic purpose, confirmed by the rich sculpture decoration. On the side facing the square we see valuable Gothic statues of seated sovereigns Charles IV and Wenceslas IV, a sculpture of St. Vitus, the patron of the bridge, between them and on the second floor the figures of Czech patron saints, St. Vojtěch and St. Sikmund. Above the arch of the gate there are the emblems of Charles IV's lands and a motif of a kingfisher in a veil, the emblem of his son Václav. The other side of the tower used to boast similar decoration, but

was destroyed by Swedish gunfire during the siege of the Old Town in 1648. The present-day shape of the roof dates from 1874 to 1878 when the building was renovated.

At the Lesser Town end of the bridge there is a gate situated between two towers of differing ages. The lower tower, called Judith Tower, was built at the beginning of the 12th century as part of the fortification of the left-bank settlement. Later it was joined to Judith Bridge and, after that was destroyed, to the Charles Bridge. While its core is Romanesque, the tower was modified in Renaissance style in 1591. The higher Lesser Town Bridge Tower was, in 1464, converted from

an older, perhaps also Romanesque building. Its design is a continuation of Parler's Old Town Bridge Tower. The gate arch between the towers dates from 1411. The bridge is one of the oldest and most significant structures of its kind in Europe.

THE EARLIEST SCULPTURE

On the eastern side of Judith Tower the first floor is a relief which, dating from around 1170, is the oldest surviving secular sculpture in urban Prague. It depicts a young man kneeling and a torso of another man, perhaps sitting, a sovereign according to some interpretations. What it really depicts has been a matter of controversy among experts for many years. To see the relief we have to enter the building of the former Lesser Town Custom House in 1 Bridge Street (Mostecká ulice), adjacent to the tower; from its balcony we can enter the chamber with the sculpture.

Above: major sights of the Old Town
Photos below from left: *excursion boats near Charles Bridge, a portrait as a keepsake, the view from the Old Town Bridge Tower*

AN OPEN-AIR
GALLERY

CHARLES BRIDGE

GOATBEARD

On the Old Town embankment wall a sculpture of Goatbeard (Bradáč – *photo above*) is incorporated. It functioned as a water-level indicator. When the water reached the Goatbeard's chin, the city was in danger of a catastrophic flood.

Photos below from left:
Vincenc Ferrarský
and St. Prokop,
St. Francis Xaverius,
St. Johanes Nepomucensis,
the Vision of St. Luitgarda
and Bruncvík

Charles Bridge is renowned for its sculpture decoration, a unique gallery of statues situated outdoors, on the upper part of the bridge's pillar columns. It consists of thirty statues and sculptures variously dating from the 17th to the 20th centuries. Among the most valuable are the works of the high Baroque period from the first quarter of the 18th century, created by first-class artists of the time. The oldest statue is St. Johanes Nepomucensis (1683), sculptured by Heroldt according to a sketch by Mathey and a wood model by Jan Brokof. According to legend artificially created by the Jesuits, the statue stands in the place where Vicar-general Jan of Pomuk was thrown into the river in a sack to be drowned on the order of King Wenceslas IV. Later the Vicar-general was associated with St. Johanes Nepomucensis. This incident is commemorated in a metal relief on the bridge balustrade. The sculpture the Vision of St. Luitgarda by Matyáš Bernard Braun (1710) and the statue of St. František Xaverský by Ferdinand Max-

milian Brokof (1711) are considered by experts to be the most valuable statues on the bridge. However Brokof's sculpture of St. Jan of Matha, Felix of Valois and St. Ivan is the most popular. The former pair were founders of the order of St. Trinity, which specialized in rescuing captive Christians from Turkish bondage. The figure of a Turk, guarding captives in a cave, in the lower part of the sculpture, earned the whole sculpture the name "Prague Turk". Other sculptors whose work appears on Charles Bridge include Matouš Wenceslas Jäckel, Jan Oldřich Mayer, Michal Jan Brokof, Jan Bedřich Kohl, brothers Josef and Emanuel Max and Karel Dvořák, who sculpted the the most recent addition, Konstantin and Metoděj, which was placed on the bridge in 1938. On the tenth pillar column from the left beneath Brokof's sculpture of St. Vincenc Ferrarský and St. Prokop, is a statue of the mythical Bruncvík, who allegedly brought a tame lion back to Prague from one of his journeys. The lion then found its place in the Czech emblem. Only the pedes-

tal has been left from the original late Gothic statue of Bruncvík of the late 16th century, which the Old Town councillors placed
here as a sign of their right to the bridge and

which was destroyed by the Swedes in 1648.
A new statue by Ludvík Šimek was placed
on the pedestal. Since 1965 all statues have
gradually been replaced by copies.

A JEWISH APOLOGY

If we walk on the bridge
coming from the Old Town, the
third sculpture on the left is
Calvary with the statue of the
crucified Christ. We can see
there a distinct gilt Hebrew
inscription, encircling the arm
of the cross. Its origin dates
back to 1696. One of the
Prague Jews was walking by but
unlike other passers-by who
respectfully took off their hats
at the cross, he kept his hat on
and uttered some blasphemous
words. He was punished with
a fine, and furthermore had to
arrange the inscription at his
own expense. Translated into
English it says: "Holy, holy, holy
the Lord of the multitudes",
which are, according to the
Scriptures, the words of praise
that angels sing to God in
Heaven.

THE MONASTERY OF THE CROSS

The Order of the Cross with the red star, founded in 1237 by Pope Gregory IX, is the only purely Czech religious order. Since 1252 the order have had a residence at the Old Town end of Judith Bridge, where they built a monastery with a hospital. Besides taking care of the poor and the old, their duty was also to guard the safety of the bridge and levy customs and fees. Because of their origin and charitable vocation the order enjoyed great respect and esteem in Czech religious circles. Its superiors, called grand masters and, at the same time, generals, were between 1561 and 1694 elected bishops of Prague. The monastery went through a series of reconstructions, and, after being damaged by the Swedes in 1648, in the second half of the 17th century it was newly built in Baroque style, from designs by Carlo Lurago and Giovanni Domenico Orsi. The early Gothic tower that used to be the entrance to Judith Bridge was also incorporated into the building. In 1846 the generalate was significantly reconstructed, and its capitular hall decorated with ceiling paintings. In 1909 the convent, rectory and brewery were pulled down and replaced by a new building, which successfully continues in style of the old buildings through the application of Classicist, Baroque and Art Nouveau elements. The monastery's art exhibition is open to the public.

The Church of St. Francis of Serafin, dating from the turn of early and high Baroque styles, the main façade of which faces Square of the Cross (Křižovnické náměstí), is a distinct feature of the monastery and from an artistic viewpoint the most valuable building. It was built by Jean Baptista Mathey from Burgundy between 1679–1685. The cathedral nave is covered with a massive cupola, decorated with an exceptional fresco depicting the Day of Judgment by painter Wenceslas Vavřinec Reiner (photo below). The cathedral interior forms a small gallery of first-class works by some of the best Baroque painters and sculptors (photo above left).

Underneath the sanctum, in the area called the lower church, are uncovered fragments of the original medieval cathedral brickwork dating from the 13th century.

CHARLES AND CHARLES

In Square of the Cross (Křižovnické náměstí) in front of the Church of St. Francis there is a Neo-Gothic monument of the most important Czech sovereign, Emperor Charles IV. The upright figure is holding the rolled up deed of foundation of Prague University. The pedestal is decorated with allegories of the four faculties of the university. Above them there are statues of three archbishops of Prague and architect Matyáš of Arras. This monument of iron and bronze was cast in Nürnberg according to the design of Dresden sculptor Ernst Julius Hähnel. It was ceremonially unveiled in 1848 on the occasion of the 500th anniversary of the foundation of Charles University. It may be interesting to compare the relatively new likeness of the emperor with the appearance his contemporary Peter Parler gave him on the Gothic statue situated nearby, on the Old Town Bridge Tower. It seems that Hähnel must have copied Parler's work a little, as both faces have very similar features…

Main photo: the Church of St. Francis near Charles Bridge

SYMBOL OF JESUIT POWER

THE KLEMENTINUM

During the post-White Hill counter-reformation, the Jesuits gradually assumed the leading position among religious orders and became the main organizers of the Habsburg re-Catholization effort in Bohemia. They became the unrestricted rulers of spiritual life, deciding matters of faith, upbringing, education, culture and science. On the outside, their absolute power, supremacy and expansionism was symbol-ized by a number of monumental and opulent buildings. The most prominent among these was the Old Town Jesuit College called the Klementinum, which is the largest Jesuit building in the Czech Republic. Thirty-two houses, three churches, a monastery and two gardens were removed to make room for this complex of two-storied buildings surrounding three courtyards. The oldest section next to Street of the Cross

A TOWER DEDICATED TO THE WEATHER

High above the Klementinum buildings rises the observatory tower, built in 1721–1723 by F. M. Kaňka and rebuilt in 1748 by Anselmo Lugaro. The top of the dome is decorated with a leaden statue of Atlantos (1727) from the workshop of Matyáš Bernard Braun. At first it served as a lookout, but later the astronomer Josef Stepling established an astronomical observatory in the tower, which was equipped with refractors and other devices, first-class for their time. Today it houses one of the Czech Hydro Meteorologial Institute weather stations. Observing the weather has a long tradition; data concerning temperature, air pressure, precipitation levels and other phenomena have been recorded here continuously since 1775.

Below right: the library

(Křižovnická ulice) seems rather severe and ascetic. It was built after 1653 in early Baroque style. At the beginning of the 18th century it was completed by František Maxmilian Kaňka, whose work included the wings surrounding the third courtyard, the gate to Marian Square (Mariánské náměstí – *photo below right*) and the observatory tower. After the Jesuit order was abolished in 1773 these buildings became the residences of cultural institutions. Nowadays the Klementinum is used by the National Library of the Czech Republic.

The interior decoration is the work of prominent Baroque artists. Among the best preserved rooms are the former refectory and the Mirror Chapel (nowadays an exhibition and concert hall), above which is the hall of the former Jesuit library, with an illusive painting of a cupola *(photo left)*, Mozart's hall with Rococo paintings and several Mozart's manuscripts, a mathematical hall and a music hall.

Two churches also form part of the complex. The Church of St. Salvator *(photo above)* near Square of the Cross, has a Renaissance core from the turn of the 16th and 17th centuries, but was rebuilt between 1638–1655 in early Baroque style. The other one is the Church of St. Kliment near Charles Street (Karlova ulice), designed between 1711–1715.

THE RESIDENCE
OF LADY MUSIC

THE RUDOLFINUM

On the right bank of the Vltava there stands the Rodolphinum, one of the most handsome Neo-Renaissance buildings in Prague. Today it is known mainly as a seat of music, a place where many prestigious cultural events are held, especially the international music festival Prague Spring (since 1946). Originally it was a multi-purpose cultural establishment, built between 1876 and 1884 according to a design by Josef Zítek and Josef Schulz, a design which won the competition and beat eight others.

The building is richly decorated with sculptures, including the work of Ludvík Šimek, Tomáš Seidan, Bohuslav Schnirch and Antonín Wagner, amongst others. The statues on the attic represent great figures from the world of music and fine art. Although the construction was financed by the Czech Savings Bank (Česká spořitelna), there is not one single Czech artist among them. The name of the building has nothing to do with art-loving Emperor Rodolph II, but with the Austrian descendant to the throne, Crown Prince

AWAY WITH MENDELSSOHN!

During World War Two the Rodolphinum was adapted to the needs of the German Philharmonic Orchestra. The Reich's Vice-Protector Reinhard Heydrich inspected all sculptures of people in the building, and ordered Mendelssohn-Bartholdy to be removed because of "non-Aryan origin from father's side". Workers of the Czech firm entrusted with this task made a mistake and took the sculpture of Hitler's favourite, Richard Wagner, instead. The mistake was discovered in time so there was no reprisal. The sculpture of the "non-Aryan" composer was not destroyed, as was the order, but carefully placed inside a wooden box and hidden in the attic. There it survived the war without damage, afterwards being returned to its original place.

IN MEMORY OF
JAN PALACH

In November 1989 the square in front of the Rodolphinum was renamed Jan Palach Square. After 1945 it had been called Krasnoarmějců after the Soviet soldiers who died liberating Prague and were temporarily buried in the local park. Now it commemorates the 21-year-old student who burned himself to death in protest against the occupation of Czechoslovakia by the Warsaw Pact armies in Wenceslas Square on 16 January 1969. There is a memorial plaque with Palach's death mask by sculptor Olbram Zoubek at the Faculty of Arts, where he was a student.

Rodolph. After completion the building was used as a concert hall and exhibition hall. The Music Academy, the Union for the Improving of Music in Bohemia, the Arts and Crafts Museum and other institutions resided here. Between 1918–1939 it became the residence of the Lower House of the National Assembly of the Czechoslovak Republic. In September 1938 a large demonstration against the cession of the border areas to Germany was held in the square in front of the Rodolphinum. Since 1946 the building has served music almost exclusively. For a time after World War Two it was called the House of Artists, but nowadays the original name is preferred. During renovation in 1990–1992 part of the building was adapted for art exhibitions, and a vast underground parking space was developed beneath the adjacent square.

The columned Dvořák Concert Hall is the heart of the Rodolphinum. Hundreds of outstanding ensembles and dozens of eminent Czech and world conductors have played here, including Antonín Dvořák, Petr Ilyich Tchaykovski, Johannes Brahms, Edvard Grieg, Jan Kubelík, Rodolph Firkušný and Wenceslas Neumann.

In May 1944 Jan Kubelík Memorial Hall was opened here.

Opposite page above: stairway to the gallery
Main photo: façade from Palach Square (Palachovo náměstí)
Above left: Dvořák Hall
Above right: statue of Dvořák near the Rodolphinum

IN PRAISE OF
SKILFUL HANDS

THE ARTS AND CRAFTS MUSEUM

**KOTĚRA-STYLE
MODERNISM**

Not far from the Arts and Crafts
Museum in Curies Square
(náměstí Curieových) stands
the Faculty of Law of Charles
University, an architecturally
important structure, one of the
several Prague "visiting cards"
of an outstanding Czech
architect Jan Kotěra. It was built
after his death (1923) from
1926–1931 in late modernist
style of Kotěra with steep
hollow tile roofs and a distinct
triangular gable with relief
decoration above the façade.
The Graduation Hall is
decorated with a mosaic by
Max Švabinský. During the
German occupation, after the
forced closure of Czech
universities, it became the main
headquarters of the SS.

Above: a porcelain set
Right: the main façade
Main photo: a section of the
exhibition rooms

The Arts and Crafts Museum in Prague,
established 1885, is one of the best in
the world. Its extensive collections consist
of more than a quarter of a million objects,
about one fifth of which exhibited. However, not all of them are in the main Prague
building of the museum; many are found in
several Czech castles. The glass collection
is world-famous. Other collections are also
very valuable, including these of pottery, porcelain, applied graphic arts and photography,
furniture, objects made of wood, metal and
other materials, textiles, fashion and jewel-
lery, toys, miniatures, literature and, since
2000, art of the 20th century. A permanent
exhibition called The Stories of Materials represents Czech and European arts and crafts
from antient times to the present. A library
with a special department of books about
Prague history and topography also form part
of the Museum. Over the years it has been
used by a number of outstanding painters,
sculptors, historians, architects and writers.

The first attempt to establish the museum collections, which were to include the
most valuable artefacts, dates back to 1867.
At that time it was not successful. Nevertheless, it increased public interest in this area of
human activity, which was later boosted by
several successful exhibitions. The museum
was eventually founded in 1885 with part
of its collections placed in the new Rodolphinum. The number of valuable showpieces in its possession was increasing, though,
and soon it became clear they would have
to be placed in a new, much more spacious
building. The new building was erected between 1897–1900 directly opposite the Rodolphinum in 17 November Street (ulice
17. listopadu), in the neighbourhood of the
Old Jewish Cemetery. The architect José
Schulz conceived it in French Neo-Renaissance style, with a façade decorated with relief which has a crafts-theme.

THE OLDEST
IN EUROPE

THE OLD-NEW SYNAGOGUE

**TIME MEASURED
BACKWARDS**

The Jewish Town Hall on the corner of Maisel Street used to be the centre of the Jewish Town administration. The present-day building has a Renaissance core dating from 1570–1577. It was built at the expense of a rich primate Mordechaj Maisel, who used a vast amount of his wealth to improve the Jewish municipality and who allegedly even loaned money to Emperor Rodolph II. The original council hall on the first floor has been preserved. It is connected to the adjacent Council or High Synagogue, which is also a Renaissance building financed by Maisel. The present-day appearance of the Town Hall is the result of a decorative Rococo reconstruction in 1736. A small tower with a gallery and a green copula featuring a clock rises from the roof. The Prague Jews earned the right to build it when they courageously defended Charles Bridge against the Swedes in 1648. On the gable above the side façade is another clock, this one with Hebrew numerals. Hebrew, as you know, is read from right to left, and so the hands of this clock move counterclockwise and measure time "backwards".

Only a fraction has been preserved of Prague's Jewish Town, which, from the early Middle Ages, was situated on both sides of what is today Paris Avenue (Pařížská třída) as an isolated island surrounded on all sides by Old Town buildings. The everyday life of the ghetto and its inhabitants was full of injustice and discrimination, but what is worse, many times the Prague Jews were the target of bloody pogroms, burning and looting. Significant relief came only in 1784 with the decrees of Emperor Joseph II. As a tribute to him the town was renamed Josefov. During the course of the 19th century most of the wealthier Jewish inhabitants of the former ghetto moved out, and the unsightly houses, lacking basic sanitary facilities, became in most cases the refuge of the Prague poor and the haunt of the underworld. So after 1890, during the so-called Prague Renewal they were pulled down and replaced by new houses. Only several synagogues, the Town Hall and the Old Jewish Cemetery were spared.

The most precious surviving monument of

the extinct Jewish Town is the Old-New Synagogue (Staronová synagoga) in Paris Avenue (Pařížská třída), built after 1270. It is the oldest surviving synagogue in Europe and one of the most artistically valuable early Gothic buildings in Prague. The Jews believed that it was brought to Prague from The Promised Land by angels and that it was built of stones taken from the ruins of the Jerusalem temple. In the course of its history it survived a number of pogroms and fires without suffering great damage, even when flames consumed all other buildings in the neighbourhood, the synagogue was allegedly untouched. The two-nave structure has an unusual type of vaulting, with five ribs in each vault span, born by two central pillar columns. The tympanum above the entrance is decorated with vine leaves and grapes growing from crooked branches. The leaf motif from the 13th century also fills the tympanum above the sanctuary, where the sacred scrolls of the Torah are kept in a recess behind a drape.

In the row of seats along the perimeter wall, the yellow star of David marks the place where, in the 16th century, Rabbi Löw used to sit. Among the valuable relics is the standard of the Prague Jews. In the 18th century the synagogue was extended with a new gallery, its small, high windows enabling women to at least hear the service.

For centuries, the legend was passed on that on the grounds of the Old-New Syna-gogue Rabbi Löw buried in great secrecy the proverbial artificial man, Golem. Rodolph II searched for it, and so did many after him. However, it was not permitted to enter the attic of the synagogue, Jews believing that if someone disobeyed they would die. Only the Jewish journalist Kisch managed to search the attic, but he found nothing except musty old temple curtains.

A UNIQUE MUSEUM

The collections of the Jewish Museum (Židovské muzeum) are concentrated in the surviving synagogues of the former ghetto (with the exception of the Old-New Synagogue). Paradoxically, the German Nazis assisted the birth of the museum. During World War Two they had valuable religious objects from the abolished Jewish communities and synagogues from Bohemia and Moravia brought to Prague to establish a museum of the "extinct race" as part of their perverse plan. The present-day collection of Jewish relics, which includes about forty thousand objects, is one of the most significant in the world. The library, which contains one hundred thousand volumes, possesses rare manuscripts and incunabula. The exhibition in the Maisel Synagogue (Maislova synagoga) is concerned with the history of the Jews in Bohemia and Moravia, in Spanish Synagogue (Španělská synagoga – photo above) with the period from the Enlightenment at the end of World War Two, in Klaus Synagogue (Klausova synagoga) with Jewish traditions and customs.

From left: interior of the synagogue, unusual Gothic vaulting, overall view

GARDEN OF
THE DEAD

THE OLD JEWISH CEMETERY

P rague's Old Jewish Cemetery (Starý
židovský hřbitov) at Josefov is one of the
most notable and oldest preserved Jewish
burial grounds in the world. Deservedly it
captures the attention of art and history en-
thusiasts all over the world. Founded, possibly, as early as the 14th century, it served
as the main cemetery of the Jewish Town for
about 350 years, from the mid-15th century to 1787, when Emperor Joseph II banned
burials in built-up areas. The cemetery ar
ea was delimited by boundaries of the Old
Town, so it could not be enlarged, although
the Jews had often requested it. Because o
the lack of space the dead were laid one
above the other, as many as twelve deep. In
this small area, less than one hectare, a hun
dred thousand people dream their eterna
dream. About twenty thousand headstones
have survived from the periods of early

RABBI LÖW AND GOLEM

Visitors to the Old Jewish
Cemetery (Starý židovský
hřbitov), should not miss the
grave of Rabbi Jehuda Löw ben
Bezalel *(photo above)*, the
famous scholar and founder of
the rabbinic learning institution.
His beautifully decorated
Renaissance tomb is full of little
stones, pebbles that people
have placed there in the Jewish
custom of expressing respect.
From time to time someone
throws a little note with a secret
wish into the slit between the
stone slabs of the tomb; it is said
that the wise rabbi, endowed
with miraculous abilities, did
not actually die, but that he sits
inside the tomb and reads old
books. His life is connected
with many legends, the most
famous seeing him as the
creator of the renowned Golem,
the artificial man, created with
the help of the four elements,
whose task it was to guard the
Jewish Town from Christian
intrigues. The rabbi was famous
for his excellent knowledge not
only of the Jewish religion but
also of astronomy and physics.
It is said that he even
demonstrated many of his
incredible tricks to Emperor
Rodolph II.

ments of his or her life. It is worthwhile having a closer look at the decorated headstones and most of all at the spectacular tombs, which were built above the graves of eminent persons in the early 17th century. The oldest headstone is that of the poet and scholar Avigdor Kar. Also among the most famous and frequently visited are those of of Rabbi Löw (1520–1609), primate and patron Mordechaj Maisel (1528–1601), writer and astronomer David Gans (1541–1613), astronomer and doctor Josef Dolmedig (1591–1655), and rabbi and collector of Hebrew prints, David Oppenheim (1664–1736). One of the most ornamented tombs comes from 1628 and covers the grave of Hendela Bassevi, the wife of the banker Jakub Bassevi, who was the first Jew to be given an aristocratic title. The language of the relief symbols on the tombs is also interesting, usually signifying the family the deceased belonged to and what their profession was. For example blessing hands represented the Cohen family, a deer the Hirsch family, a lion the Löw family, a fox the Fuchs family, scissors represented a tailor, a mortar represented a pharmacist, tweezers stood for the profession of a doctor and so on.

Gothic, Renaissance, Baroque and Rococo. They not only provide graphic evidence of the development of gravestone sculpture, but are often also an important source of information; the long Hebrew texts state not only the name of the deceased, but also the names of his or her closest relatives and the so-called "praises", which describe the profession of the deceased and the achieve-

THE LONGEST INSCRIPTION

The Pinkas Synagogue (Pinkasova synagoga) is the second oldest surviving synagogue in Prague. It stands on the grounds of the Old Jewish Museum (Staré židovské museum). Rabbi Pinkas founded it in 1479, although it was his grandson Aaron Meshulam Horowitz who rebuilt it and gave it the late Gothic appearance it still retains today. A hall with vaulting in Jagellon Gothic style is the heart of the building. A Renaissance hall with a gallery for women was added to it between 1607–1625. After World War Two the synagogue was converted into the Memorial to the Victims of Nazi Racial Persecution (Památník obětí nacistické rasové perzekuce). The names of all the Jewish people of Bohemia and Moravia who died in concentration camps are written on the walls. It is the longest gravestone inscription in the world, with exactly 77 297 names (photo above).

ART NOUVEAU ABOVE
THE VLTAVA

ČECH BRIDGE

A TRAVELLING CHAPEL

The early Baroque Chapel of
St. Mary Magdalene adjacent
to Čech Bridge (Čechův most)
below Letná *(main photo
below)* has an interesting
history. It is an artistically
valuable circular structure
dating from 1635 with
remnants of original paintings
within. During the Reforms of
Emperor Joseph II the chapel
was closed and used for various
purposes. It was renovated only
when Čech Bridge was being
built. In the May Rebellion of
1945 it was in danger of
destruction when SS forces
bombarded it from the Law
School on the opposite bank. It
was threatened again, ten years
later, when the traffic
interchange in front of the
bridge was being designed.
However it was decided that
the chapel, which was in the
way of the planned
intersection, should be moved
somewhere else, to a bastion
built specially for it thirty-one
metres upstream. The removal
took place at the beginning of
February 1955, using rails. The
chapel moved at the speed of
1 meter every 8 minutes, the
whole transfer taking two days.
It was the first case of a removal
of an entire building within the
boundaries of the former
Czechoslovakia.

Named after an important Czech poet
and writer Svatopluk Čech, Čech Bridge
holds several titles. At only 169m in length,
it is the shortest one of the bridges that cross
the the River Vltava. It is the only bridge in
Prague, and one of very few in the world
built in Art Nouveau style. It is also the first
bridge built in Prague in the 20th century.
The reason for its construction is a little curious: supposed to be part of a wide boul
evard leading from Wenceslas Square (Vá
clavské náměstí) via the Old Town (Star
město) across the Vltava to Letná, it woulc
mercilessly sweep away all that the preced
ing generations of Praguers had put in its
way, including many precious monument
of cultural history. Fortunately, at the turn o
the 19th and 20th centuries, the modernising

city planners who decided to pull down and rebuild a large part of the city centre managed to execute only a small section of their plan, the "victims" of which were the Jewish Town (Židovské město) and several adjacent streets. The defenders of the ancient character of Prague (and of sound reason) managed to halt the so-called renewal at the edge of Old Town Square (Staroměstské náměstí).

Čech Bridge, which connects Paris Avenue (Pařížská třída) with Edvard Beneš Embankment (nábřeží Edvarda Beneše), was definitely the most positive feature of these changes. The work of architects Jan Koula and Jiří Soukup, between 1906–1908, it is the only arch metal bridge in Prague, with three arches of unequal span and finely decorated in Art Noveau style by contemporary Czech artists. Bronze figures of the four goddesses of

victory, the Victorias, and bronze statues of linkboys and six-headed hydras are its dominant features. The goddesses are situated, in pairs, on high columns at each end of the bridge. Sculptured elements are also found on the balustrade, bridge pillar columns, lantern stands and so on. In the columns bases are the stalls of the former toll collectors. The road was originally paved with hard Australian wood, later replaced by oak cobbles and finally with asphalt. The Austro-Hungarian sovereign Franz Joseph II himself attended the ceremonial opening of Čech Bridge.

Above: *a detail of the decoration of the bridge pillars*
Below: *a statue of the Goddess of Victory*

IN THE TURMOIL
OF HISTORY

OLD TOWN SQUARE

THE PRAGUE MERIDIAN

A metal strip is embedded in the paving near the statue of Hus, showing the direction of a meridian crossing the Prague area. It is not an important meridian from a geographical point of view, but it has played a significant role in the life of the city. This role is explained by the Czech and Latin inscription: "The meridian according to which, in the past, time was set in Prague."

Below: decoration of the façade of Štorch House by Mikoláš Aleš

Many important chapters of the history of Prague and the Czech nation were written in a relatively small rectangular space in the middle of the Old Town. The present-day Old Town Square (Staroměstské náměstí) is a magical place, with an unmistakeable atmosphere, perhaps because it is as old as the city itself. Originally it was a busy marketplace on the right bank of the Vltava, around which a settlement slowly grew. As early as the 12th and 13th centuries it was surrounded by spectacular stone houses. After the establishment of the Old Town (Staré město), enclosed within a circular bulwark, the square became its natural centre, the location of the Town Hall and the main town church. During the course of the centuries many important events, often tragic for the Czech nation, took place here. In 1437 Jan Roháč, the last Hussite commander, was hanged here on a massive three-storey gallows, together with almost sixty of his co-fighters. In 1621 executioner Mydlář beheaded 27 Czech noblemen, knights and burghers, leaders of the anti-Habsburg rebellion, in front of the Old Town Hall. In 1902 Praguers demon-

strated here for the universal right to vote and in 1918 for an independent Czechoslovak Republic. During the May Rebellion o 1945 the square witnessed heavy fightin between the rebels and the German occu pants. In February 1948 Prime Minister Kle ment Gottwald announced from the Goltz Kinsky Palace balcony the "final victory o the working class", which was followed b more than forty years of the totalitarian com munist regime.

In the middle of the square is a monumen of Master Jan Hus. One of the few monu mental Art Nouveau sculptures, it was cre

culminates in a distinct cupola and a pair of spires. The sculptor was Antonín Braun. The houses around the square have Romanesque or Gothic cores, with the façades usually from the Renaissance, Baroque or Romantic periods. White Lamb House (No 551) retains its pretty Renaissance portal. Unicorn (White Horse) House (No 548) has a late Gothic portal and a gateway with beautiful ribbed reticulated vaulting; in 1848 composer Bedřich Smetana established a music school here. The interesting roof arbour of Red Fox House (No 480) catches one's eye, providing its owners with a pleasant place to sit down, relax and escape the summer heat.

In the so-called Little Square (Malé náměstí), separated from the main square by a block of town hall buildings, we find Rott House (No 142), with a façade decorated by Mikoláš Aleš paintings and a Romanesque underground room. In No 144 there is an original late Gothic room with a beautiful stellar vault from the 15th century. From 1353 the oldest pharmacy in Prague was located here.

ted by sculptor Ladislav Šaloun in 1915. he prominent figure of Jan Hus is surrounded by a crowd of Hussite fighters and post-White Hill exiles. The most admired feature f the north-western section is the massive church of St. Nicholas (kostel sv. Mikuláše) esigned by Kilián Ignác Dienzenhofer beween 1723–1735, one of the most remarka-le high Baroque buildings in Prague, which

Above: façade of a house on the southern side of the square
Main photo: the view from the Town Hall tower

THE OLD TOWN HALL

THE STONE INHABITANTS OF THE ASTRONOMICAL CLOCK

The little statues that perform a regular show are a remarkable feature of the astronomical clock. The main focus of the spectators' attention is Death, represented by a skeleton situated at the edge of the horolog. He symbolizes the transience and impermanence of life, which is emphasized by the hourglass he turns in his hand. He is paired with the Turk who shakes his head and symbolizes cruelty and treachery. The pair on the other side consists of a Vain Person, looking in the mirror, and a Miser, based on the original concept of a medieval usurer. To the sides of the calendarium we can see three figures of burghers and an angel. They do not lack symbolic meaning either, representing a fair rule over the city. The figures of the apostles are fairly recent, being created in 1948 by sculptor Vojtěch Sucharda as a replacement for the old ones, destroyed in the Town Hall fire of 1945.

The Old Town Hall (Staroměstská radnice), the main feature of Old Town Square, is one of the most important, popular and frequently visited buildings in Prague. It was founded in 1338 as a privilege by King Jan of Luxembourg. What is quite unusual is that it was not built "on a green-field site", but by joining and rebuilding original burgher houses. The first two houses, of Wolflin of Kámen and shopkeeper Kříž, were in 1458 joined to house of furrier Mikš and, much later in the 19th century, Rooster and Minute Houses. The councillors had a 69.5m high town hall tower, completed in 1364, added to Wolflin's house. A beautiful Gothic chapel, with an oriel jutting out into the square, was established on the first floor. The whole block was opulently rebuilt in late Gothic style; Wolflin's house next to the tower was given a spectacular ornamental portal and a new window, in the style characteristic of the important builder and stonema-

Above: Gothic interiors
Above left: the Town Hall building, including the tower and the astronomical clock

on Matěj Rejsek. Kříž's house was expensively rebuilt in Renaissance style, the large rectangular window with the Old Town emblem *(photo below right)* coming from that period. Minute House *(photo opposite page below left)* stands out because of the beautiful Renaissance graffito on its façade as well as the stone sculpture of a lion on the corner. At the southern and northern ends of the Town Hall complex two Neo-Gothic wings were built between 1838–1848. During the May Rebellion of 1945 they were set ablaze by gunfire from German tanks. Part of the buildings, together with the valuble decoration and archival records, either burnt or were damaged in the fire. In the post-war years the historic buildings were reconstructed, the architecturally not very interesting Neo-Gothic wings were pulled down to be replaced by lawns.

The most popular part of the Old Town Hall, and its pride, is the astronomical clock *(photo opposite page above left)* in the lower section of the tower. Unique in Europe, it was created around 1410, at the end of the 15th century it was improved. Each hour two windows open in the upper part of the astronomical clock, and the figures of the 12 apostles parade in them, the stone statue of Death pulls a rope and the production ends with the crowing of a rooster. The middle section of the clock consists of an astronomical sphere and a dial, which, representing the movements of the Sun and the Moon, is based on the mistaken medieval concept that the Earth was the centre of the universe. The dial measures three kinds of time, Old Czech, contemporary and Babylonian. The lower part of the astronomical clock is the most recent. It consists of a calendarium and symbols of each month and scenes from the life of rural people, set in actual Czech landscapes, painted by painter Josef Mánes in 1866.

A FAIRY-TALE
BACKGROUND

GOLTZ-KINSKY PALACE

A CHILD BURIED IN THE FOUNDATIONS

One of the numerous medieval superstitions was the idea that it was possible to ensure that a building would be solid and long-lasting if a living child or a young virgin-girl was immured in its foundations. A child's skeleton was reputedly found in the foundations of Goltz-Kinsky Palace. Allegedly the builder kidnapped a child and offered it to the devil, who, not in favour of the construction, had methodically thwarted the builder's work.

THE PALACE AND ITS PEOPLE

The history of Goltz-Kinsky Palace is associated with the lives of two interesting personalities. In 1843 the Austrian writer and pacifist Bertha Suttner-Kinsky was born here. The first Nobel Peace Prize was awarded to her in 1905. For some time the Prague German Grammar School, where writer-to-be Franz Kafka studied between 1893–1901, resided in the building. At that time his father had a little shop on the ground floor of the palace.

The gorgeously decorated Rococo façade of Goltz-Kinsky Palace occupies most of the eastern front of the Old Town Square. A Romanesque house stood here until the first half of the 13th century at the latest, the remains of which have been preserved in the basements. Later at least two Gothic houses were built here, and, being in the possession of aristocratic families most of the time, they were probably large and expensive buildings. In one of them King Sikmund accepted the vow of loyalty from Prague councillors in 1436; in the other part of the legation of the Turkish Sultan to king Mathias were accommodated in 1615. In the course of the 16th century they were joined into one complex and expensively rebuilt in Renaissance style. Everything changed after 1755, though, when both buildings were bought by count Jan Arnošt Goltz, who had a palace built in their place over the next ten years. Anselmo Lurago, son-in-law of the famous architect Kilián Ignác Dienzenhofer and one of the most important builders of the Czech Rococo, designed it. Count Goltz did not have much time to enjoy his new residence.

He died shortly after its completion and th palace was then bought by Duke Františe Oldřich Kinský, whose family were there ur til 1945. In the first half of the 19th century th Kinský family had the interiors rebuilt in Em pire style, as well as having a new staircas built and three wings added to the buildin on the courtyard side. After World War Tw the building was confiscated, in accordanc with the Beneš Decrees, and handed over t the National Gallery, which stored its collec tions of drawings and graphic design her Since the end of 2010 a permanent exhibitio The Art of the Old World (Asia and Ancier Mediterranean) has been presented here. Th palace is one of the best works of Anselmo Lu rago. The main façade facing the square ha two entrance portals lined by columns. On th first floor there are two triangular gables wit relief decoration connected by a balcony, an between them an attic with allegorical stat ues. The shaped and open plan gables, typic of Rococo, above the windows are comple mented by rich stucco relief. The outstand ing personality of Prague late Baroque, Igná František Platzer, created the decoration.

A SURPRISE BENEATH
THE PLASTER

STONE BELL HOUSE

When the renovation of Stone Bell House (No 605) in the Old Town Square commenced in 1980, hardly anyone expected the secret it would reveal. It soon became clear that a palatial high Gothic burgher house, almost in its original shape, was hidden beneath the plain Neo-Baroque plaster, which comes from 1899. The façade of the house is without parallel, not only in the Czech Republic, but also in the whole area east of the River Rhine. Among the rubbish stored in the cellars builders discovered about 12 000 original Gothic segments, including window linings, traceries, portals, cornices, vault ribs and other elements, most of which they either managed to piece back together and return to their original locations or make copies of. Gothic paintings were also found in the interiors, and perfectly renovated during the reconstruction. The origin of the house dates back to the second half of the 13th century. During reconstruction in the first half of the 14th century it was given the appearance of a monumental urban palace. The experts believe that it might have belonged to Queen Eliška Přemyslovna. It is probable that it was here

Above: the tower-like section
of the house
Below right: the painted
timberwork ceiling in the
interior

that her son, Crown Prince Charles, who later became Czech King and Roman Emperor Charles IV, stayed after he came to Bohemia in 1333. Prague Castle was at that time damaged by fire, and the sovereign-to-be, who was entrusted with control of the country during his father's absence, had to find accommodation in one of the burgher houses, a fact he himself mentions in his autobiography. ▶

685 the original Gothic building was covered by a great Baroque reconstruction, during which the Gothic segments on the façade
and elsewhere were cut off and placed in the
cellars, or possibly re-used as building materials. The reconstruction from 1980–1987 gave
back the house its original appearance. The
house sign that gave the house its name, the
stone bell dating from 1413, was once again
hung on the corner; according to a story the

KAREL ŠKRÉTA, PAINTER

Short and narrow, Týn Lane
(Týnská ulička) goes along
Stone Bell House and leads into
a tiny square. On the left-hand
side is a Neo-Gothic Black
Deer House (No 628), which
dates from 1894. A medieval
Black Deer House used to stand
in its place. As you can read on
the memorial plaque, Karel
Škréta was born here in 1610.
He was the most important
Czech painter of the early
Baroque period, and his
paintings are found not only in
the National Gallery, but also in
a number of Prague churches.
He is one of the greatest artists
in Czech history and his works
became the model for many of
the other stars in the Baroque
sky, especially Petr Brandl and
Wenceslas Vavřinec Reiner. He
came from a wealthy
aristocratic Protestant family,
the Škréta Šotnovský of
Zádveřice. His widowed
mother refused to convert to
Catholicism after the Czech
estates rebellion was defeated,
preferring to go into exile with
her children. Karel studied
painting in Venice and Rome.
In 1638 he converted to
Catholicism and returned to
Prague, where he worked until
his death in 1674.

bell fell off the tower of Cathedral of the Virgin Mary before Týn (chrám Panny Marie před
Týnem). The tower-like section on the edge of
Old Town Square is the most spectacular. Its
façade has a strictly geometrical composition.
On the first and second floors are three pointed windows with traceries, and between them
there are niches where Gothic statues originally stood. The torsos of four of them, representing the king, the queen and two men-at-arms,
were found in the Baroque brickwork. Lower
wings are adjacent to the tower-like section,
surrounding a rectangular square. Since 1988
the house has been used by the National Gallery of Prague, which organizes occasional
exhibitions in the renovated medieval building. Classical music concerts are also given in
the large hall on the second floor.

Main photo: details of the
decoration of Stone Bell
House
Above: Gothic hall with
entrance

IN THE NAME
OF THE CHALICE

TÝN CATHEDRAL

The Cathedral of the Virgin Mary before Týn, shortened to Týn Cathedral, was the main church of the Old Town and one of the most important in Prague. Its spires rise high above the houses on the eastern side of Old Town Square, unmistakably dominanting the square. The construction began around 1350, but the church only acquired its final shape in 1511 when the southern tower was completed. In 1420, when the construction was interrupted by the Hussite Wars, the perimeter walls of all sections stood without roof frames. Even in this provisional state it served its purpose, becoming the religious and ideological centre of the Prague U traquists. The important preacher Jakoubek Stříbro and the Hussite archbishop Jan Roky cana, representatives of a moderate Hus site wing seeking rapprochement betwee the Ultraquists and the Catholic Churcl preached here. In the great fire of 1689 th cathedral suffered significant damage. Th Gothic vaulting in the nave and the chance was ruined and had to be pulled down. was replaced by new, Baroque vaulting, and the cathedral roof was also set a little lowe at that time. The church is a classic Gothi basilica with three naves. The outer walls ar

CHALICE VERSUS HALO

A tall statue of the Virgin Mary, surrounded by a golden halo, looks down on the city from the upper part of the gable above the main frontage of Týn Cathedral (Týnský chrám). However, this statue is not the original. In the 15th century a statue of King George of Poděbrady stood there, above it a large golden chalice, the symbol of Hussitism. It is said that storks made a nest inside it and brought many frogs and snakes, which often fell on the square, causing confusion. Hussites had a simple solution to the problem; they waited for the storks to migrate to warmer regions and then covered the chalice with a large board. The Hussite motifs stayed on the cathedral frontage until the 1620's, when students of the Jesuit seminary pulled them down. They replaced King George with the Virgin Mary, had the chalice melted and a halo cast from the acquired material.

divided and strengthened by abutment pillar columns. The magnificent six-part window in the entrance frontage is framed by two towers and crowned with a steeply rising triangular- shaped gable. The side entrance portal, accessible from Týn Lane, differs markedly from the fairly modest and demure outer decoration. It is probably the work of Peter Parler's building and sculpting workshop from around 1390. Its tympanum is filled with a three-part relief depicting the Ordeal and Crucifixion of Jesus Chris, one of the best Czech Gothic sculptures.

The importance of Týn Cathedral is mirrored by its exceptionally valuable interior decoration. We find nineteen richly carved altars here, mostly in early Baroque style, with paintings by Karel Škréta, Jan Jiří Heinsch, Michael Wenceslas Halwachs and František Xaver Palko, and sculptures by Jan Jiří Bendl, Jan Oldřich Mayer and Ferdinand Maxmilian Brokof. There are also late Gothic sculptures and reliefs, including the Týn Madonna dating from around 1420, the Gothic stone pulpit and the late Gothic canopy

by Matěj Rejsek, painted in 1493. The tomb of the famous astronomer, Tycho de Brahe, is situated in the Cathedral, along with those of other outstanding historical figures.

In the past there were doubts concerning the exact position of Tycho de Brahe's grave. When experts examined the marked tomb some time ago, a small particle of metal, covered in green verdigris, helped to positively identify it. It is a well-known fact that Tycho de Brahe got into a fight when he was a hot-headed young man, and, though not seriously wounded, he was still scarred for life, his adversary cutting off the tip of his nose. The astronomer replaced the missing part of his face with an artificial prosthesis made of copper. Another interesting feature of the church is the grave of a ten-year-old Jewish boy Simon Abeles, who got baptized secretly. When his father found out, he had his son cruelly tortured before murdering the boy himself. The body of the child reputedly did not decay for many years.

Main photo: view of Týn Cathedral from the Old Town Hall Tower
Above: side entrance with a relief in the tympanum
Below: the gravestone of Tycho de Brahe

IN THE FOOTSTEPS
OF A SAINT

THE CONVENT OF ST. AGNES
(ANEŽSKÝ KLÁŠTER)

THE GEMS
OF CZECH GOTHIC

An exhibition of 19th century Czech art was the first to be displayed when the National Gallery opened the reconstructed Convent of St. Agnes. Today it houses a permanent exhibition of the medieval art of Bohemia, including the best works of Gothic and early Renaissance art. The exhibition also includes paintings by Master Theodorik, Vyšší Brod altar Master, Třeboň altar Master, all examples of the so-called beautiful style from the reign of Wenceslas II, sculptures by Peter Parler and his workshop, as well as art of Austrian or German origin, notably by Lucas Cranach and others.

Above: St. Francis church
Below: Street of St. Agnes (Anežská ulice) leading to the convent
Above right: the Ressurection of Jesus Christ (photo © 2010 Národní galerie v Praze)

The gothic style entered Bohemia for the first time through the gate of the Convent of St. Agnes of Bohemia, founded around the year 1231 by king Wenceslas I., although the initiative was his sister's. Her name was Anežka and she decided, after a series of disappointments in life, for a religious vocation. She invited nuns of the St. Claire order, a women's branch of the Franciscan order, to the convent and became its first abbess. The monastic community was under the personal protection of Wenceslas I. and the pope, who both gave it numerous privileges. Besides the St. Claire nuns, a hospital confraternity of St. Francis also worked on the grounds of the convent, which after the year 1237 became a separate order, called the Order of the Cross with the red star, which after the 1st half of the 13th century built its own monastery in the present Street of the Cross (Křižovnická ulice). The abandoned hospital was turned into a smaller Franciscan monastery, which disappeared during the Hussite wars. The construction of the complex, which included three churches, continued until the year 1270 approximate-

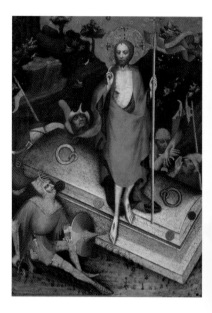

ly, one hundred years later it was enlarged and re-decorated. The Hussites expelled the St. Claire nuns and turned the convent into an armoury and a mint, in the 16th century the neglected buildings were used by

Above: St. Salvatore church
Below: Master of the Třeboň altar – Jesus Christ on the Mount of Olives (photo © 2010 Národní galerie v Praze)

the Dominican order. The St. Claire order returned here in the year 1626, but it never reached its former glory again. The great fire of the Old Town in the year 1689 damaged some of the buildings, the most severely St. Barbara church. In the year 1782 emperor Joseph II. abolished the convent, then it was offered in an auction and turned into an abode for the Prague poor, a storehouse and workshops. In the 19th century the neglected complex went to ruins, part of the buildings either collapsed or was deliberately damaged. In the course of the Old Town renewal plan it was supposed to be pulled down, but fortunately that did not happen. On the contrary – already in the year 1900 the res-

cue works began, which were supposed to give the convent back its original form. With breaks they lasted until the year 1963, when the National Gallery acquired the buildings. The last phase of the renovation, completed in the year 1986, modified the rooms for the needs of art exhibitions.

The early gothic paradise garden with a cloister is the heart of the former convent of the St. Claire nuns, named after its first abbess Convent of St. Agnes of Bohemia. There are other parts of the convent adjacent to it, such as the capitular hall, refectory, dormitory and kitchen, which also come from the 13th century. Only parts of brickwork are left from the defunct Franciscan monastery.

A CHURCH FULL
OF SECRETS

ST. JACOB'S CATHEDRAL

THE THIEF'S HAND

When we enter the Church of St. Jacob (chrám sv. Jakuba) and immediately look up to the right, we see a strange thing: a mummified human hand hangs there. A story explains this. A long time ago, a certain thief had his sights set on the jewels with which people adorned the late Gothic statue, the Pieta of St. Jacob's, in gratitude for its miracles. The statue can be found in a niche on the main altar. The thief secretly allowed himself to get locked in the church and during the night attempted the deed. As soon as he touched the string of pearls around the Virgin Mary's neck, the saint moved and seized the thief's hand with such strength that he could not free himself. And that was how the Minorites, coming from service, found him. They could not free him either. In the end they had to send for the executioner, who cut the unfortunate man's hand off. Only then the grasp loosened and the hand fell to the floor. The Minorites then hung it on the wall near the entrance partly as a reminder of this miracle, but mainly as a warning.

Above: *sculpture of Madonna*

No other church in Prague is so connected with mysterious legends as St. Jacob's Cathedral, which is part of the Minorite monastery in the Old Town. It may be the influence of the splendid decoration and imposing size of the building, which is, after St. Vitus's Cathedral, the second longest church in the capital. Despite later modifications and reconstructions it has kept much of its original Gothic mysticism. The oldest part of the church is the 30m high presbytery, built between 1291 and 1308.

BURIED ALIVE

Experts consider the sculpture decoration on the tomb of Jan Wenceslas Vratislav of Mitrovice in the Church of St. Jacob to be one of the most beautiful works of Czech Baroque sculpture. It was created by Ferdinand Maximilian Brokof in 1714–1716. A truly horrible story is connected with it. After the Lord of Mitrovice, the highest Czech chancellor, died and was buried, strange sounds were heard from the tomb. People believed that the chancellor's soul had not found peace in its tomb and ardently sprinkled it with holy water. They were pleased when the terrible wailing and banging ceased within a few days. The real cause of these sounds was only credibly explained several years later. When another member of the family died, the tomb was opened and the dreadful truth revealed: Jan Wenceslas Vratislav of Mitrovice had mistakenly been buried alive, and when he had come to, had tried to get out of his tomb. He had managed to break open the lid of the coffin, but, being unable to move the heavy stone slab covering the tomb, had tried to attract attention by yelling and banging. In vain. In the end he gave up and waited for actual death to come. The terrible grimace on his face indicated what the waiting was like.

which was after a longer delay in the second half of the 14th century complemented by a spacious, high Gothic triple nave with a pair of frontage towers. The church survived the Hussite period without suffering much damage, but the Old Town great fire of 1689 proved calamitous. The fire ruined the roof, the front wall and the towers. The vaulting collapsed because of the heat. Only the perimeter walls were left standing. The subsequent Baroque reconstruction, while preserving the Gothic body of the church, completely replaced the façades and changed the shapes of the windows and the interior. Only one of the two towers was rebuilt, the other being brought down to the level of the new Baroque frontage gable. Between 1695–1701 the space above the three Baroque entrance portals was decorated with extensive stucco mezzo-relievo (photo below) by the sculptor Ottavio Mosto. The interior was fitted with Baroque barrel vaults in the nave. Ceiling paintings from the Marian cycle were added by František Voget in 1736.

The decoration and furnishing of the cathedral, among the most lavish and artistically precious in Prague, are as imposing as the size of the church itself. We find twenty-three altars altogether and on them the works of true masters, including painters Hans von Aachen, Petr Brandl, Wenceslas Vavřinec Reiner, Michal Wenceslas Halwachs, Jan

Kryštof Liška and Jan Jiří Heinsch, sculptors Matouš Wenceslas Jäckel, Richard Jiří Prachner, Jeroným Kohl and Ignác Michal Platzer and woodcarver Matyáš Schönherr, amongst others. As the acoustics of the church are excellent, concerts are often given here.

In the adjacent Minorite monastery many original Gothic sections have been preserved, such as the northern and eastern wings of the cloister, with their Gothic arches and crossed vaults, the northern refectory and the sacristy. In 1311 the wedding feast of King Jan of Luxembourg and Eliška Přemyslovna was held in the refectory.

Main photo opposite page:
the cathedral nave
Above left: *the cloisters of the Minorite monastery*

A HAVEN FOR FOREIGN MERCHANTS

TÝN COURTYARD

SCHOOL WITH A TRADITION

Týn gave its name also to the nearby school, which stands on the south-eastern corner of the Old Town Square in front of Týn Cathedral. It is one of the few houses in Prague that have retained its original Gothic arcade, which dates from the late 13th and early 14th century, and is arched with ribbed vaulting. In the 16th century pretty embowed gables in the style of the Venetian Renaissance were added. The school has a remarkable tradition. Renowned architect of late Baroque style, Matěj of Prostějov, was one of the teachers here. Because he taught "rejsování" (technical drawing), he was nicknamed Rejsek. The adjoining White Unicorn House (No 603) also has a Gothic arcade dating from around 1330.

B ehind Týn Cathedral and Malá Štupartská Street is a large, beautifully renovated complex of buildings, called Týn or Ungelt. Its origin dates back to the 11th century at the latest. The name Týn refers to an Old Czech word meaning "fortified". Originally the area was a fortified duke's courtyard incorporating a church, hospital, accommodation and inns, which served as a centre of commerce and customs office. Every foreign merchant coming to Prague had to declare his goods and pay the custom duty, called "ungelt", which went in the duke's, and later in the king's, treasury. However, Týn was also a place where merchants could find shelter. It offered safety and peace, accommodation and entertainment and during an illness also medical care. Entrance was only allowed to those without arms, which had to be left at the gate, where they were kept for the duration of the foreigner's stay. As the town expanded and trade gradually developed, Ungelt ceased to be sufficient as the only customs house. It served its purpose until 1774, when

Above right: the eastern gate leading into the courtyard
Right: a detail of the painting on Granovských House

94

Like other Prague places, Týn also has its spook. On dark, moonless nights a young man wearing a turban and carrying the severed head of a girl with a long plait appears here. There is an astonishing story about his origin. Among the many foreign merchants, who came to Prague to trade, was a handsome young Turk, who fell in love with the beautiful daughter of a Týn innkeeper. The girl loved him too, and agreed to marry him. Unfortunately they were not of the same faith. Hoping to solve the problem, the young man decided to return home to the Ottoman Empire and ask permission for the marriage, promising to come back to his beloved. The girl kept waiting for many years. She missed him at first, but with passing time her love faded. Then a merchant's son from the neighbourhood asked her for her hand, but unfortunately shortly after the marriage the Turk returned. When he found out what had happened, he begged her to meet him just once. That was the last time she was seen alive, disappearing without the slightest trace, together the lovesick suitor. After many years a housemaid working in the house in which the foreign visitor had stayed got a shock, discovering the severed head of the unfortunate young woman. People, alarmed by her screams, started digging at that spot, and found the rest of the body as well. What had actually happened, then? The Turk killed his ex-sweetheart, put her head into a valuable casket, bringing it with him on his journeys. After some time, his conscience started to bother him, so he secretly returned to the Prague Týn and left her head in the place where he had committed his terrible crime. However, he still could not find peace, not even after his death. Therefore his ghost has to wander around every night, carrying the dreadful burden in his hand.

Above: Týn courtyard with Granovský House

ts buildings were turned into apartments, offices, workshops and storehouses. Through neglect they became run-down, especially after World War Two. The situation improved in 1977, when plans for the restoration of Ungelt were completed, funds were found and long-term reconstruction commenced. Completed in the 1990's, numerous shops, restaurants and cafés are now established in the restored buildings, attracting attention from both Czech and foreign tourists.

The Týn area has retained its form; a closed courtyard with two gates around which there are burgher houses dating from the 14th century. The most beautiful and at the same time most precious building is the Renaissance-style Granovský House (No 639),

which was built in the place of an old Ungelt house in 1559–1560 by duty collector Jakub Granovský of Granov. On the first floor there is a lovely arcade loggia, the wall above it decorated with chiaroscuro paintings. The neighbouring house, No 640, is also built in Renaissance style and dates from around 1569. It belonged to the family of the emperor's archivist, Strada, whose daughter, Catharine, was a lover of Emperor Rodolph II, by whom she had several illegitimate children. Later this house became the renowned Old Ungelt Inn. The other buildings in the courtyard have mostly Gothic cores, although their outer appearance is predominantly Baroque; the façades of some decorated with sculptures and house signs.

THE ART NOUVEAU GEM
OF PRAGUE

MUNICIPAL HOUSE (OBECNÍ DŮM)

THE DEFUNCT
RESIDENCE OF KINGS

Municipal House (Obecní dům) stands in the place of a once important building called King's Court (Králův dvůr), which for a hundred years, from the 1380's to 1483, was the main seat of Czech sovereigns. It was built at the request of King Wenceslas IV, who felt that here he would be closer to the everyday joys and worries of Prague's citizens. After him, Sikmund, Ladislav Posthumous, George of Poděbrady and Vladislav Jagellonský resided here. The latter, however, out of fear for his own safety, moved his seat to Prague Castle in the turbulent times, in which the bloody conflict between Hussites and Catholics broke out again. King's Court went to ruins. In 1635 an Episcopal seminary was established there, which was later replaced by military quarters and a cadet school. After several reconstructions, realised mainly because of fires, the buildings lost their Gothic character, as well as their original decoration. In 1903 they were pulled down completely to make place for Municipal House.

Prague is valued not only as a city of Gothic and Baroque, but also of Art Nouveau. And deservedly so. It was in Prague that Art Noveau, at the beginning of the 20th century, attempted to replace the outdated and rathe sterile historicism. In so doing, it left very sig nificant marks, but was short-lived, and wa soon replaced by styles that were new an

Right: the façade of the house with the Tribute to Prague mosaic

modern in form as well as content. Prague's Municipal House, sometimes called Representative House, is a gem of Art Nouveau style. It is an important cultural centre, with banqueting, exhibition and conference halls, as wel, as a large concert hall. It was built between 1906–1911 according to a design by architects Antonín Blšánek and Osvald Polívka. Prominent Czech artists of the time were involved in the decoration, including Alfons Mucha, who painted the allegories in the Mayor's Hall, Max Švabinský, who painted the portraits of national revivalists in Rieger Hall, Jan Preisler, who created the paintings for Palacký Hall, Mikoláš Aleš, who created the colorized drawings decorating the basement rooms, as well as sculptors Čeněk Vosmík, Ladislav Šaloun and Josef Wenceslas Myslbek. Above the main entrance, in the semicircular gable in front of the colossal cupola, is the large Tribute to Prague mosaic by Karel Špilar. Smetana Hall is the heart of the building, its largest space and a place where great concerts are held, such as those on the occasion of the Prague Spring festival. Visitors can use the local restaurants and cafés, also decorated in the remarkable Art Nouveau decoration.

The Municipal House also witnessed an event crucial to the Czech nation. On 28 October 1918 the independence of the Czechoslovak Republic was declared in Smetana Hall *(photo above right)*. The first sessions of the newly established Czechoslovak government and parliament took place here as well.

This event is commemorated by a memorial plaque, on which are inscribed the names of five politicians, members of the National Committee, who formed the government of the newly established state of Czechs and Slovaks. During the "Velvet Revolution" Municipal House played an important role again. On 26 November 1989 the first negotiations between the delegation of the defeated Communist government, led by the then Prime Minister Ladislav Adamec, and the delegation of the newly organized Civic Forum (Občanské fórum), led by Wenceslas Havel, later President of democratic Czechoslovakia. In the 1990's Municipal House was extensively reconstructed and became an important cultural centre of Prague.

Below: a painting by Alfons Mucha

OLD TOWN'S
"VISITING CARD"

GUNPOWDER GATE (PRAŠNÁ BRÁNA)

THE ORIGIN OF POTATOES

In the 17th century an Irish Franciscan monastery stood on the current day site of Hibernian Palace (palác U Hybernů), opposite Gunpowder Tower (Prašná věž) and Municipal House (Obecní dům). The monks were called Hibernians, after the Latin word for Ireland, Hibernia. In 1786 Joseph II abolished the monastery and three years later a Czech theatre, evicted from a wooden building, called the Shack (Bouda), in what is today Wenceslas Square (Václavské náměstí), moved in. The head of the theatre was the writer, translator and actor Wenceslas Thám. Between 1808–1811 Jiří Fischer reconstructed the whole building in Art Nouveau style, and made it into a customs, finance and censorship office. Since reconstruction in 1940–1942 the building has served for exhibition purposes. But to get back to the Hibernians. In the monastic garden they grew a crop unknown in Bohemia at that time, called "ground apples". From here potatoes quickly spread all over the country and became one of the main foodstuffs.

An important Czech Gothic monument, one of the most famous features of Prague, stands in the neighbourhood of Municipal House. Its predecessor, one of the towers of the municipal fortification, was called Mountain Gate (Horská brána) because the road from the town of Kutná Hora (Mine Mountain in Czech) led through it. After 1348, when the newly established New Town (Nové Město), which had its own fortification, surrounded the Old Town (Staré město) on three sides, the Old Town fortifications lost their purpose, became neglected and Mountain Gate went to ruins. The councillors had it pulled down, lest it bring shame on the town, and replaced it with a new tower. Its defensive function was to be minimal, but its representative character significant. It was supposed to become a spectacular "visiting card" for the Old Town and a dignified neighbour to the adjoining sovereign residence King's Court. Construction commenced in 1475 under master Václav. However, his work did not fulfil expectations, and three years later he was replaced by a builder and stonemason Matěj

Opposite page above: details
of the stonemasonry
decorating Gunpowder Gate
Opposite page below:
19th century stained-glass
windows
Above left: *Gunpowder Gate
with the Hibernian Palace
(Palác U Hybernů)*
Below: *statue by Matěj Rejsek*

Rejsek of Prostějov, a master of late Gothic decoration, perfect in form. He completed the tower-like gate, at least tentatively, decorating it with lavish sculptures. After King Vladislav Jagello left the Old Town and moved to Prague Castle, and then even further away to Hungarian Buda, the town representatives lost interest in its construction. Its removal was even considered; but in the 18th century it served as a gunpowder storehouse, which also gave it its name. The Prussian artillery, which bombarded Prague in 1757 did significant damage to Rejsek's decoration. The gate was given its present form, which was based on Old Town

Bridge Tower (Staroměstská mostecká věž), between 1875–86 during the pseudo-Gothic alteration carried out under the guidance of architect Josef Mocker. He had the damaged part of the original late Gothic sculptures removed and replaced with new decoration. The rebuilding concerned mainly the upper section and the roof of the tower, which was given its present-day "chisel-like" shape, as well as three small corner towers. The Gunpowder Gate is open to the public and the view that opens up from its gallery is beautiful. First, though, one must negotiate the 180 steps of its steep spiral staircase.

ON THE THRESHOLD
OF THE ROYAL ROAD

CELETNÁ STREET

INTERESTING FEATURES OF THE COURTYARD

The courtyard of Manhart Palace (Manhartovský palác) in Celetná Street is adorned with copies of two remarkable Baroque sculptures, a wooden statue of Hercules with a lion, from around the mid-18th century *(photo above)*, and the allegory Patience by the famous Matyáš Bernard Braun from his Virtues and Vices cycle, which is in Kuks Castle in Eastern Bohemia. In the gateway leading into Štupartská Street, several walled-in Gothic portals can be found. It is evident that originally they extended deep below the level of the present-day pavement. The explanation is simple: medieval Prague lay several meters lower than today. Because frequent floods, caused considerable damage, people defended their homes by building embankments. Gradually the whole terrain in the area was levelled with them. This also explains why there are spacious Romanesque rooms in the basements of many houses. In fact they were not originally cellars, but the ground floors of the earliest buildings, which later sank below the street level.

The so-called Royal Road (Královská cesta), crossing the town from the east to the west, is one of the oldest streets in the Prague area. Its route was established at the time of the first, spontaneous settlement of the area around Prague Castle. It began from the present-day Gunpowder Gate (Prašná brána), from there it lead through Celetná Street, Old Town Square (Staroměstské náměstí), Charles Street (Karlova ulice), across the stone bridge into Bridge Street (Mostecká ulice), across Lesser Town Square (Malostranské náměstí) into Neruda Street and finally onto Prague Castle (Pražský hrad). It was normally on this road that sovereigns ceremonially rode into the city. Coronation processions used this route too. At both ends there used to be a royal residence, Prague Castle and the now defunct King's Court.

If we walk from Square of the Republic (náměstí Republiky) through Gunpowder Gate, we find ourselves at the beginning of the royal route, in Celetná Street. In

the Middle Ages there were many bakeries in the street. Its name derives from the term for plaited rolls, called "calty" or "celty" that they made. The brickwork preserved in the cellars of many local buildings confirms that a row of stone buildings existed here as early as the Romanesque period. Today the street is lined with attractively built burgher houses and palaces which have Gothic cores, but are "dressed" in Baroque, Classicist and Rococo "coats". On the corner of Celetná Street and Fruit Market (Ovocný trh) stands the late Baroque New Mint (Nová mincovna) (No 578) dating from 1759, it is also called the Palace of the Pachts of Rájov (palác Pachtů z Rájova). During the period when Czech rulers resided at nearby King's Court, this building belonged to the queens. From 1539 to 1784 the Prague mint operated from here. The main entrance from Celetná Street is adorned with an imposing three-part portal, which is the work of Ignác František Platzer. Figures of ancient soldiers

AN UNFORTUNATE DEATH

From 1784 the Prague military headquarters was based in Palace of the Pachts of Rájov. A tragic event occurred here on 12 June 1848. On the order of the then military commander of Prague, Count Alfred Windischgrätz, the military confronted marching Praguers, the culmination of a turbulent demonstration called the St. Wenceslas Mass (Svatováclavská mše). About fifty protesters were injured in the bayonet charge and Windischgrätz's wife, Maria Eleanora, paid for the skirmish with her life. She moved closer to a window, drawn to it by the noise, and was hit by a stray bullet. It has been a mystery ever since whose gun the bullet came from; whether it was intentional or just an unfortunate accident. The clash triggered a rebellion, in which mainly young Praguers fought, defended by barricades against a numerically superior force. The death of his wife was probably the reason why Windischgrätz proceeded with unusual harshness against the rebels, not hesitating to issue orders for the city to be bombarded by cannons.

bear the balcony on their shoulders like Atlas. On the opposite corner, by the end of the Fruit Market, is a large building called Black Mother of God House (dům U Černé Matky boží – *photo above right*), after the statue at its corner; a black Madonna, one of the most important examples of Czech Cubist architecture created by Josef Gočár in 1911–1912. One of the prettiest buildings in Celetná Street is Manhart Palace (No 595). Its present-day appearance is Baroque, dating from the 18th century, although it includes the preserved brickwork of several medieval houses. Artistically the most valued building is the Hrzáns of Harasov Palace (No 558), the work of architect Giovanni Battista Aliprandi (1702–1704) including sculptures by Ferdinand Maxmilian Brokof. Three Kings House (dům U Tří králů) (No 602) *(photo opposite page left)* near Týn Cathedral is also worth one's attention. It has kept its Gothic form from walls to roof gables and roof frames. The famous writer Franz Kafka lived here from 1896 to 1907.

And let's notice one more house, almost directly across the street. Number 556 has been called Black Sun House (dům U Černého slunce) since early times. Josefína Dušková, a famous opera singer in her time, lived here from the age of 15. The musical genius Wolfgang Amadeus Mozart was a guest of the Dušeks each time he visited Prague; it being no secret that he was completely besotted with lady Josefína's elegance and beauty.

Left: a house sign in Celetná Street

ALMA MATER ABOVE
THE VLTAVA

THE KAROLINUM

A DRAMATIC HISTORY

In pre-Hussite times Master
Jan Hus served two terms as the
Chancellor of Prague
University. From his position,
and together with other
professors, he openly protested
the vices and dogmas of the
Church. In 1419 King
Wenceslas had the ratio of
votes at the university changed
– three were granted to the
Czech nation and only one to
foreigners. In 1622, after the
defeat of the rebellion of the
Czech estates, Jesuits seized
Prague University, connecting
it with Klementinum College;
from 1654 it was even called
Charles-Ferdinand University.
Only in 1881 was the university
divided in two, a Czech section
and a German one. The name
Charles University was restored
in 1920.

Above: statue of Master
Jan Hus
Above right: the honorary
yard
Right: a Gothic oriel

In 1348 King Charles IV, who took care of
the well-being of the Czech Kingdom and
its capital in many ways, established Prague
University, the oldest university in Central Europe. The university consisted of four faculties, arts, medicine, law and theology, but did
not have its own building. Lectures took place
in all kinds of temporary places, and the accommodation for both professors and students was unsatisfactory. Gradually the university at least acquired several colleges, the
most famous being the Charles College (Karlova kolej). In 1383 King Wenceslas IV bought
a splendid house from a rich Prague burgher, master of the Rotlev mint, had it adapted
to suit the needs of the university and gave
it to Charles College. There were auditori-
ums, apartments for the masters, an armoury,
a prison, a large amphitheatre for ceremonial
assemblies, and, after 1390, the Chapel of St.
Kosma and Damian. In 1611 the other dor-
mitories were closed and the whole university concentrated into this building, now called
the Karolinum. During the course of the fol-

lowing centuries, other houses in Fruit Mark
(Ovocný trh) and Celetná Street were grad
ally added to it, and structurally connecte
into one complex. To this day the original u
ban palace of master Rotlev is the heart

this vast complex. The greater part of its vaulted rooms on the ground floor *(photo below)* have survived, as well as the oriel of a former chapel on the southern façade, an outstanding example of the work of Parler's building workshop. Although in 1718 the Karolinum was reconstructed in Baroque style, its medieval character has been preserved. After World War Two the interior was reorganized and an entrance building built from a design by architect Jaroslav Fragner. The brand new rectory wing with its honorary yard connects the historic building with the adjacent university buildings in Celetná Street and Fruit Market. The honorary yard contains a fountain with lions, the courtyard a statue of Master Jan Hus. The most prominent feature of the Karolinum is the great Gothic amphitheatre *(photo above)*, enlarged by Kaňka and, during the course of Fragner's modification, decorated with emblems of Czech lands, a tapestry depicting Charles IV kneeling before St. Wenceslas, a bronze statue of the emperor and others.

HIS PRAGUERS
UNDERSTOOD HIM

THE ESTATES THEATRE

The famous quote by Wolfgang Amadeus Mozart: "My Praguers understand me" gives a true indication of the relationship this musical genius had with the Czech capital and its citizens. The enthusiasm of the audiences, who received *The Wedding of Figaro* at the end of 1786, was boundless, and the composer encountered only words of praise the next time he stayed in Prague. So it was no wonder that he promised to compose an opera for the following Prague theatre season. It was *Don Giovanni*, later called the "opera of operas" by experts.

The Estates Theatre (Stavovské divadlo), the oldest permanent theatre of the capital, is closely connected with Mozart's success. It is also interesting from the architectural point of view, as it is one of the handsomest structures of Baroque classicism in Prague and one of the most beautiful theatres in Europe. Count František Antonín Nostic-Reinech, a favourite of Emperor Joseph II, had it built between 1781– 1783 at his own ex-

penses, according to the design by Antoní Haffenecker. This explains why the build ing was originally called the Nostic Theatre Originaly plays in the Czech language wer also staged, but the management dismisse Czech actors, when Prague Germans threat ened to boycott the theatre if "Czech patri ots" continued to perform in it. And the the famous day came. On 29 October 179 the theatre experienced the world premier of *Don Giovanni*. Mozart took part as wel conducting the theatre orchestra himsel The success was so great that the opera lef Prague for a victorious tour around Europe After Count Nostic died, representatives o the Czech estates, rich aristocratic families bought the building for 60 000 florins, and gave it a new name: the Estates Theatre. Be tween 1813–1816 composer Karl Maria vo Weber was the opera director of the thea tre. Czech plays were only staged again af ter 1824 and in 1827 the first Czech opera *Tinker (Dráteník)* by František Škroup ha

A THEATRE FOR
ONE CROWN

In Fruit Market (Ovocný trh) opposite the Estates Theatre (Stavovské divadlo) stands Kolovrat Palace (Kolovratský palác – *photo above*). An early Baroque structure with a handsome entrance portal and elegant dormers, it was created by Domenico Orsi around 1673. The Kolovrat family owned the palace until the beginning of the Communist regime, and again after restitution in 1990. Then they rented it to the National Theatre for the symbolic amount of one crown a year. After reconstruction the National Theatre established a studio theatre in the attic, housing the Kolovrat Theatre, a club and administration offices.

Right: side façade of the theatre

THE ONLY TOWER

Around 1232 the so-called Galus Town (Havelské město) was established in the small area between the present Fruit Market (Ovocný trh) and Coal Market (Uhelný trh). It soon merged with the Old Town and shared its fortification. Originally there were a number of houses with massive early Gothic prismatic towers, but these disappeared during later reconstructions, and only one was left, part of Blue Column House, 403 Knight Street (Rytířská ulice). Like other house towers it served accommodation and defence purposes. During the building of the neighbouring New Town (Nové město), its position also proved useful: the tower was used to aim the axis of Wenceslas Square (Václavské náměstí). Later it was given windows, a new Baroque façade and was adapted into apartments.

ts premiere here. On 24 December 1834, at the first night of *Fidlovačka* by Škroup and Josef Kajetán Tyl, the song *Where is my Home (Kde domov můj)* was heard in public for the first time. It proved so popular that later it became the official Czech anthem. The theatre was modified in 1859, and more significantly in 1882–1883, when safety directives (following fires in the Prague National Theatre and the Viennese Opera House) demanded a greater number of staircases, as well as their enlargement, and the construction of external fire-escapes. The last expensive reconstruction took place in 1983–1990, after which the theatre (in 1984 renamed the Tyl Theatre) returned to its original name Estates Theatre.

Above left: *a view of the auditorium*
Below left: *columnal portico above the entrance*

BEASTS FROM
A PORTAL

TWO GOLDEN BEARS HOUSE

The memorial plaque on Two Golden Bears House commemorates the journalist and writer Egon Ervin Kisch, who was born here in 1885. He was one of the prominent group of German-writing Jewish authors in Prague between the two world wars. His whole life was connected with Prague. He worked for the German newspapers Prager Tagblatt and Bohemia, and because of his uncompromising style became known as the "ferocious reporter". He confirmed his outstanding journalistic nose with several sensational disclosures that significantly affected the political scene of that time. In his books he also dealt with the fates of people on the periphery of society, and searched for themes in various countries of the world. He was a famous opponent of fascism, and fought in Spain. In 1939 he emigrated, spending the war years in Mexico. He returned to Prague in 1946 and resumed his career, which only ended with his death two years later.

Dozens, even hundreds, of historic Prague houses are decorated with beautiful entrance portals from the Gothic, Renaissance and Baroque periods. According to experts, the prettiest portal of all adorns Two Golden Bears House (dům U Dvou zlatých medvědů) (No 475) on the corner of Melantrich and Kožná Streets. The present-day Renaissance house, resembling a small urban palace, was established by connecting two older Gothic buildings between 1560 and 1570; the owner, printer Jan Kosořský of Kosoř, managed to get one of the outstanding artists of the court of Emperor Rodolph II to accept the commission. Reputedly it was court architect Bonifác Wohlmut himself – he had designed the completion of the Royal Summer Palace (Královský letohrádek) and the upper section of the Great Tower of St. Vitus's Cathedral at Prague Castle. This splendid portal was sculpted in sandstone and had very fine relief decoration which served the purpose of a house sign. In the upper section, separated by a cornice, two sculpted bears face two men, both of whom are sitting and holding sprouts in

Galus Town (Havelské město), around 1232 founded on a grid-like ground plan, was named after the Church of St. Galus, which is still the most dominant feature of Galus Street (Havelská ulice) with the well-known Old Town marketplace. It used to be one of the most important churches in Prague. During a high Baroque reconstruction in the 18th century it was given a remarkably dramatic undulating façade by Jan Blažej Santini and was decorated with statues of saints by Ferdinand Maxmilian Brokof. The artistically valuable and precious inventory of the church includes several outstanding paintings by the leading representative of Czech early Baroque painting, Karel Škréta, who is also buried here.

heir hands. Next to this Renaissance portal in the direction of the street corner is a fragment of its predecessor, a Gothic doorway dating from the beginning of the 15th century. The small courtyard inside, with its two-storied Renaissance arcades featuring Ionic and Doric columns, is also lovely. At the turn of the 17th and 18th centuries some sections of the house were reconstructed in Baroque style and later modified again in Classicist style. Beneath the buildings are cellars of Gothic origin; a story claims that all the underground passages of Prague led right here. Since extensive renovation in the 1970's Two Golden Bears House has been used by the management of the Museum of the Prague city.

Opposite page below: the courtyard arcades
Above left: the main entrance
Below left: a period shop in a nearby street

IN ROYAL
FOOTSTEPS

CHARLES STREET (KARLOVA ULICE)

The meandering shape of Charles Street, connecting Old Town Square and Charles Bridge, shows that it developed naturally, without urban planning. It was in existence by the 12th century at the latest. It used to be part of the Royal Road, an ancient route used by kings for coronation processions. It is lined with picturesque burgher houses and palaces. Their medieval cores are today mainly hidden by more recent Baroque, Rococo and Classicist façades. The quaintness of these buildings is in places emphasized by original house signs and stucco decora-

tion. Some of the houses in Charles Stree but also in the adjacent streets, have kep their original Romanesque rooms. The mo handsome is found on the corner of Hu Street (Husova ulice), in the cellar of hous No 156. A former Romanesque farmstea dating from the 12th century, including a ha with four sections of crossed vaulting on on central column, today serves as an exhib tion room. The original Romanesque groun floor was also preserved in Mansfeld Palac (No 147) on the corner of Charles and Jilsk Streets. It is a high Baroque structure datin

A SPOOKY HOUSE

The most beautiful house in Charles Street (Karlova ulice), and one of the finest in Prague is Golden Well House (No 175) by the end of Seminary Street (Seminářská ulice). This Renaissance structure has a high Baroque façade, with beautiful stucco relief of the patron saints who protected people from the plague. It is by Oldřich Jan Mayer, dating from 1701 and renovated between 1983–87 (photo above). Allegedly it is a haunt for spooks. The ghost of a young housemaid wanders the corridors. She drowned trying to find the source of a mysterious glow coming from the depths of the Earth. When they were pulling her body out of the well, they found a treasure at the bottom of the well. There is also a spooky couple, a headless knight and his equally headless wife. Allegedly the owner of the house killed them to get at their money.

rom 1736, in which Gothic halls with ribbed
aults can be found. Hegelein House (No
45) has Gothic origins although it was given
n arcade courtyard during a Renaissance re-
onstruction; a Romanesque room has been
reserved here as well. Three Pomegranates
House (U Tří granátových jablek) (No 146)
vas formed by joining two Gothic struc-
ures. On the ground floor there is a Gothic
all with crossed vaults. A pretty house sign
dornes Golden Serpent House (U Zlatého
ada) (No 181) on the corner of Lily Street
Liliová ulice), in which there used to be one
f the oldest cafés in Prague, run by an Arme-
ian merchant Deodat Damaján from 1714.
chönfeld House (No 184) was named af-
er the printing press owner and publish-
r Jan František of Schönfeld, who pub-
ished the Imperial Royal Postal Newspaper
c. k. Poštovské noviny) edited by Wenceslas
Matěj Kramerius. Pötting Palace (No 186) is
lso an important building, it is a Renaissance
tructure on Gothic foundations with a spec-
acular Baroque façade and an impressive

portal, atributed to Jan Blažej Santini. The "Ta
Fantastika" theatre resides here. The Renaissance French Crown House (U francouzské
koruny), from the period around 1600 was
once occupied by the German astronomer
Johannes Kepler. It was here that he completed the manuscript of his most important
work Astronomia nova. In the gateway of the
house there is a memorial plaque, as well as
a relief portrait and a composition of the motion of heavenly bodies, dating from 1971.
Colloredo-Mansfeld Palace (No 189), close
to Square of the Cross (Křižovnické náměstí)
is also an important piece of architecture. Its
Baroque street frontage is complemented by
a portal with sculptures.

*Main photo: the corner of
Charles Street and Hus Street*
Above: *at the height of the
tourist season*
Below: *the Romanesque
cellar of house No 156*

A PALACE GUARDED
BY HERCULESES

CLAM-GALLAS PALACE

IN LOVE WITH A STATUE

On the Marian Square
(Mariánské náměstí) side of the
wall encircling the garden of
Clam-Gallas Palace is a niche
which contains a small
fountain with a Classicist
statue, dating from 1812, by
Wenceslas Prachner *(photo
above)*. The naked sitting girl
pouring water from two jugs
represents the Vltava allegory,
but people renamed her
Therése (Terezka). Before the
duct was established, people
used to come here with pails for
water. The story goes that
a demobbed soldier fell in love
with the beautiful Therése,
visiting her every day and even
talking to her softly. Before he
died, he willed his estate, ten
thousand florins, to his stone
idol. However, his heirs took
the matter to court, and, and,
accepting their claims, the
court declared the will invalid.

One of the most impressive palaces in Prague, Clam-Gallas Palace, stands in Hus Street (Husova ulice) (No158). It is easily recognizeable: its two massive entrance portals being complemented, on either side, by a pair of muscular Herculeses, bearing the balcony on their shoulders *(photo below)*. These gems of Czech Baroque sculpture were created by the high Baroque master Matyáš Bernard Braun, whose work also inludes the sculpture of mythological gods in the attic and others on the main staircase. The palace designer, the Viennese court architect Jan Bernard Fischer of Erlach, was also indisputably a master in his field. In 1713–1729 the most senior Czech marshal Jan Václav Gallas de Campo had the monumental structure *(photo right)* built to replace earlier palatial buildings. As early as the 12th century a large Romanesque farmstead stood here, being replaced in the 14th century by the spectacular Gothic palace of the Moravian margrave, Jan Jindřich, the younger brother of Emperor Charles IV.

Vast cellars and parts of the brickwork on the ground floor have been preserved to this day. One of the later owners, Vilem Vchynský of Vchynice, was one of Albrecht of Wallenstein's generals and was murdered along with him, at the emperor's order, in Cheb in 1634. The palace was then confiscated and given to Count Mathias Gallas who had exposed Wallenstein's conspiracy. He did not take proper care of the building though, and it soon went to ruin and became uninhabitable. It was his nephew, Jan Václav, who decided upon radical change. He had the buildings pulled down and the magnificent residence we see today built in their place. However, on his death in 1719 the structure was still incomplete, and only the decoration of the completed section was continued. Still it is a vast complex with a main courtyard, three smaller courtyards and a garden encircled by a stone wall. The artistic high points of the palace are the spectacular staircase with Braun's statues of linkboys and stone vases and also the remarkable rooms on the second floor

AN IRON KNIGHT AND RABBI LÖW

The Prague municipality has its main seat in the New Town Hall (Nová radnice) in Marian Square (Mariánské náměstí), a late Art Nouveau building with magnificent sculptures. In the niches on the corners are two Art Nouveau statues by Ladislav Šaloun, the creator of the statue of Hus in Old Town Square (Staroměstské náměstí). They represent two figures from Old Town legends: the Iron Man from Platnéřská Street, a knight who killed his mistress in jealousy and was cursed by her before she died, so that he turned into iron; and the wise Rabbi Löw, the scholar from the Jewish Town of Prague and legendary creator of an artificial man, Golem.

Left: a staircase with Braun's statues
Below: one of the magnificent halls

which feature ceiling paintings by the famous Italian painter Carlo Innocenzo Carlon. After the death of the last Gallas, Filip Jakub, Countess Marie Anna became heiress to the family fortune. In 1757 she married Kristián Filip of Clam, both families joining under the name Clam-Gallas. The new owners turned the palace into a centre for artistic life of Czech aristocracy. Balls and concerts were held in the main hall, where even Wolfgang Amadeus Mozart and Ludvig van Beethoven peformed. Later, theater was played here. The Archive of Prague city was placed here in 1945.

A HIDDEN ROMANESQUE PALACE

THE HOUSE OF THE LORDS
OF KUNŠTÁT AND PODĚBRADY

A DOG WITH A TORCH

Above the doorway on the southern side of the Church of St. Jiljí, not far from the House of the Lords of Kunštát and Poděbrady, we see a dog with a burning torch in its mouth. It is an emblem of the Dominican order, which acquired the church in 1626 and built a monastery next to it. The original Romanesque church is mentioned in historical records as early as 1238. The present-day Gothic aisled hall was built by Bishop Jan of Dražice and Archbishop Arnošt of Pardubice between 1310–1371. Even Emperor Charles IV himself was present at the consecration, although the church had already been used before that, when in 1346 the famous reformer Jan Milíč of Kroměříž preached here in the Czech language. The Church of St. Jiljí was at its time one of the most collosal, being more than 30m high. In 1432 there was a fire in the church, but the building was soon repaired and given practically its present-day form (the northern spire never regained its original form). A Baroque reconstruction followed the Dominican acquisition of the church. The interior decoration comes from this period as well. The vaults are decorated with frescoes by Reiner. The stucco decoration was crafted by Spinetti. The sculptures by Brokof are also exceptionally valuable. Other masters who worked on the decoration include sculptors Weiss, Quitainer and painter Molitor.

At first sight the House of the Lords of Kunštát and Poděbrady in 3/222 Chain Street (Řetězová ulice) is one of the best preserved Romanesque buildings in Prague. The original vast Romanesque farmstead was built in the second half of the 12th century, its residential palace surviving in what today are the cellars. The original ground floor of the palace gradually disappeared under the surrounding terrain, earth being continually brought here as protection against the fre-

quent floods. Three vaulted rooms have sur vived *(main photo)*. The middle room has si: spans of ribbed vaulting. The rooms to th side are vaulted on one massive four-squar column with pilasters. Sections of hearth can be found in the corners. Also on th present ground floor (originally the first floor there are the remains of Romanesque brick work. The name of the palace's founder is no known. We only know that between 140 and 1438 the bulding was owned by the ser

Old Town records tell us that George of Poděbrady (1420–1471) took over the house from his uncle on 2 September 1451. Already by that time he had been through a lot. At the age of fourteen he participated in the battle of Lipany on the side of the moderate Ultraquists and Catholics, who defeated the radicals of Tábor and their allies. Ten years later he became the leader of united Ultraquism in Bohemia. During an unexpected night attack on 2–3 September 1448 he seized Prague and became the most powerful man in the country. In 1452 he became the regional regent and, after the death of Ladislav Posthumous in 1458, was elected Czech king. The ambitious aristocrat, who had no connections with the ruling families, he had a brilliant career in front of him. Even before he was elected, still living in his house, he negotiated the marriage of his daughter to the Hungarian King Mathias Korvín. It was also there that he prepared plans for a message of peace to European sovereigns, realised in 1463–1464. He was the first Czech ruler to seek a system of collective security. In 1465 he was confronted by Czech Catholic opposition, the so-called Green Mountain Union (Jednota zelenohorská). He also was opposed by the Pope, even a Crusade set out in 1468, led by the ambitious Mathias Korvín. In February 1469 the Czech army besieged Mathias and offered him a generous ceasefire. Mathias, though, did not keep the conditions of the ceasefire and waged war with intermittent success until 1471, when one of the most important European politicians George of Poděbrady died.

ior regional scribe Boček of Kunštát. George of Poděbrady lived here from 1451 until he was elected Czech king in 1458. Many years later an ordinary tenement house was built on the Romanesque foundations, and coal and junk were stored in the Romanesque cellars. During World War Two an air-raid shelter was established in a section of the cellar. Although it was clear that the cellar was not insignificant, the then owner would not give permission for a more detailed research. That took place between 1950 and 1952. It was only then that one of the most important historical buildings in Prague was definitively saved. In recent years the site has been modified for exhibition purposes.

Left: a motif from the courtyard

WHERE MASTER JAN PREACHED

BETHLEHEM CHAPEL

THE LARGEST MEETING PLACE

Bethlehem Chapel's (Betlémská kaple) deed of foundation, issued on 24 May 1391, makes it clear that there was no suitable place for sermons in Prague at that time. Those who wanted to listen had to go to preachers' private houses or assemble outdoors. According to contemporary records about three thousand people could meet in the new, simple chapel, making it the largest medieval indoor meeting place in Bohemia.

In Bethlehem Square (Betlémské náměstí) we find one of the most important structures of medieval Prague, associated with the reform efforts in Bohemia at the end of the 13th and beginning of the 14th century. Today Bethlehem Chapel is a national cultural monument, associated with the preaching of Master Jan Hus. It was built in 1391–1394 mostly on the property of a wealthy Old Town councillor. The actual founder was an influential courtier of King Wenceslas IV, Hanuš of Mühlheim. The chapel was designated for preaching the gospel in the Czech language. Master Jan Hus preached here from 1402 for more than ten years. Here he commenced the struggle for the reformation of Church and society. He understood his common listeners well, he spoke Czech, wrote books in his mother tongue, and even the first Czech hymns owe their emergence to him. At first he had the favour of both the archbishop and the king, even influencing King Wenceslas IV to issue the Deeds of Kutná Hora (Kutnohorské dekre-

ty), which gave decisive rights in Charles U[niversi]-versity to Czech students and professors. [In] time, though, Hus gradually lost the favour [of] those in power, especially when, in 1412, [he] opposed the undignified selling of indulger[c]-es, by the means of which the Pope finance[d] the war he waged against the King of N[a]-ples. The Archbishop of Prague banned H[us] from preaching in Bethlehem Chapel. H[e] did not obey and the archbishop declared [an] interdict. The Pope banned all church ser[v]-ices and practically all sacraments includi[ng] baptism, wedding and administering the l[ast] rights before death.

So Hus left Prague and started to prea[ch] in Czech rural areas. In 1414 he was su[m]-moned to the religious court in Konsta[nz] and, despite the earlier guarantees of E[m]-peror Sikmund, was sentenced to death a[nd] burned at the stake in July 1415. This sp[ar]-kled off the extensive Hussite moveme[nt.] Bethlehem Chapel remained the centre [of] radical followers of Hus led by Jakoubek

Above: the lane leading to the Convent
Right: the pulpit of Master Jan Hus

THE HOUSE
OF THE PREACHERS

Next to Bethlehem Chapel is the
Bethlehem Estate, part of which
includes the so-called House of
Preachers, restored in 1954. It
was precisely here that Master
Jan Hus lived and worked. The
neighbouring buildings of
Nazareth College were also
reconstructed. Today the College
houses the Gallery of J. Fragner,
named after the architect
Jaroslav Fragner who designed
the renovation of Bethlehem
Chapel in 1950–1952.

bro. In 1512 a German reformer Thomas
intzer tried to continue the work of his
at predecessor, but without significant re-
onse. Between 1536–1548 the chapel was
pensively reconstructed into a church, and
en a new vaulting, set on three rows of
agonal columns. In 1661 the church was
rchased by the Jesuits, who restored Cath-
c service in it. They wanted to rebuild the
urch but reconstruction never took place –
order was abolished in 1773. The build-
became neglected and in 1786, with its
llapse impending, it was decided to pull
church down. Only a section of the pe-
eter walls survived, being later used in
construction of a late Classicist house

in 1836–1837. Most of the inscriptions and
paintings were destroyed at that time. The
sacristy at the end of the chapel, which includes the room in which Master Jan Hus
used to live, has survived.

Between 1950–1952 the chapel was rebuilt according to its original design and
vedute. The present-day frontage, with two
high gables, is completely new; the other
three walls containing remnants of brickwork
form the original 14th century chapel. In the
large hall is a wooden ceiling, five windows
with pointed arches, and the reconstructed
old well. On the wall are fragments of original inscriptions from the beginning of the
15th century, and modern paintings.

Above: a medieval well
Above left: the main frontage
of the chapel

THE WHOLE WORLD
IN FULL VIEW

NÁPRSTEK MUSEUM

THE TEMPLAR AT ST. ANNE

In sight of Naprstek Museum in the back yard of the former Dominican convent in Anne Square (Anenské náměstí) is the Church of St. Anne (kostel sv. Anny). As early as the 12th century the Romanesque Rotunda of St. Lawrence (rotunda sv. Vavřince) stood there, later enlarged into a church. When that was pulled down, the current Gothic church emerged in the 1360's. This church, along with the convent, ceased to be used for religious purposes in 1782. In the 19th century it even served as a storehouse for paper, and being neglected, went to ruin. In 1956–1957 the foundations of the original Romanesque structure were uncovered. In 1553 the chronicler Wenceslas Hájek of Libočany was buried here, and between 1732–1736 Christoph Willibald Gluck played the organ. The ghost of a Knight Templar from the convent haunts Liliová Street by the church. Executed on the scaffold for some wrongdoing, he never confessed his guilt and so his soul is consigned to wander the earth. The templar appears every Friday after midnight. He rides a restless horse, wears a long white cloak and carries his head in his hand, unable to find deliverance until someone dares to catch the horse by the rein and run the unfortunate ghost through with a sword.

Main photo: *the museum courtyard*
Opposite page above: *the Native American collection*

The collections of the Náprstek Museum (Náprstkovo muzeum) in Bethlehem Square (Betlémské náměstí) include more than 95 000 exhibits from all over the world. We see prehistoric and ancient Egypt and the Near East here, and an exhibition dedicated to the Native cultures of North and South America. In 1992 the section dedicated to the culture of Australia and Oceania even received a prestigious international award: its exhibits include Mapucho ritual columns with stylised human heads, a naval map made of bamboo splinters and shells from the Marshall Islands. These and other interesting features are found in a large house named U Halánků after its owner *(photo right)*. The house was already in existence when people used to gather to

hear Master Jan Hus preach in Bethlehe Chapel (Betlémská kaple) across the street had a number of owners before a certain J Halánek from Jičín bought it in 1676. He w not very famous, and certainly more intere ing people occupied the house, so it is ha

Brewer Antonín Fingerhut had two sons. Ferdinand, the elder, went into the family brewing business, while Vojta, the younger son, went to grammar school at his mother's request. Even during his school days, he was already holding Czech cultural functions at the family brewery. He studied law in Vienna and, during the riots of 1848, encouraged active resistance to the Austrian government. A warrant was issued, and Náprstek had to escape to Hamburg and from there by ship to America. In America he had several jobs, at the same time organizing compatriot life and learning about the culture of Native Americans. Ten years later his mother succeeded in obtaining a pardon for him, and he returned home in 1858. He established an important centre of the Czech intelligentsia within the family brewery. He brought a refrigerator, a washing machine, a wringer and a sewing machine from America; he promoted these machines, relieving human toil in every way he could. Over twenty years he gave 475 lectures, to which he invited famous personalities. He founded the American Club of Czech Ladies, and organized outings. He was a founding member of the Czech Tourist Club and became its first chairman. Vojtěch Náprstek (1826–94) died after a short, serious illness and was cremated, according to his wishes. As there was no crematorium in Bohemia at that time, his body had to be taken to Gotha in Germany.

say why it is named after him. The large ‍ilding was formed by joining three small-‍ houses, one of them having strong brew-‍g tradition. In 1826 brewer Antonín Finger-‍ut bought U Halánků. His name caused him a little trouble. When the priest christened him, he automatically translated the Czech name Náprstek (Czech for thimble) into German, and it was not until 1880 that the Austrian government allowed the return to the original Czech name. The Fingerhuts successfully ran the brewery, as well as a winery. When Antonín Fingerhut died in 1832, his wife Anna continued in the business. Nine years later she bought the neighbouring Little Golden Shoe House (dům U Zlaté botky). She was well known for her good heart and no poor person ever left her house empty-handed. Anna's sister, Barbora Serafínová, helped her, and left her Black Eagle House (dům U Černého orla) in Na Poříčí Street. In 1862 Anna used the money she earned by selling Black Eagle House to help her son establish the Museum of Asian, African and American Cultures in 1862. Vojta Náprstek (relief in photo above right) dedicated his own library, as well as trophies from his travels, to the museum. His collections grew with contributions from his many explorer friends, including Emil Holub or Stanko Vráz. A library used to form part of the museum, where Náprtstek's erstwhile protégé Klára Špecingrová-Baušová (1880–1918) worked. She was probably the first Czech female librarian, as well as a translator from English, French, German and Russian. A new section was added to U Halánků House between 1885–1890, enlarging the museum into its present-day form.

AN AVENUE
AT THE BOUNDARY

NATIONAL AVENUE (NÁRODNÍ TŘÍDA)

A NEW STYLE

An aesthetic way of using various materials, a fluent waving curve giving the impression of easy movement on the surface, stylisation, ornamentation, these are the main elements of a new style, which initially emerged as a form of protest against historicism and eclecticism, before becoming influential at the end of the 19th and the beginning of the 20th centuries. We find the pleasant Art Nouveau style in National Avenue (Národní třída). The prettiest examples are two houses designed by Polívka in 1907–1908. Number 1011 is the Prague Palace, its façade decorated with relief by Šaloun. The neighbouring house (No 1010) is Topič's Publishing House *(photo above)* and has a rich stucco façade.

National Avenue is one of the busiest streets in Prague. It emerged in the place of the castle moat, which originally defended the Old Town, but later was levelled. In 1781 it was modified into a road, and when two lines of lindens were planted there seven years later, it was called New Alley or In an Alley.

In 1870 the name was changed to Ferdinand Street and, again in 1900, to Ferdinand Avenue. The reason is clear; the former Austrian Emperor Ferdinand V, called the Kind-hearted, used to enjoy walking here. Ferdinand was the last Czech sovereign to be crowned in Prague. In 1848 he was forced to abdicate, spending his retirement in Prague Castle until his death in 1875. The ex-emperor, whom people nicknamed Ferdie (Ferdáček), used to walk from Můstek to the Vltava, obligingly returning all greetings by raising his hat…

National Avenue separates the Old Town and the New Town (Staré and Nové Město, re-

spectively) and is lined with many importa buildings. Besides those to which we dedica separate chapters, we should also mentic the Church of St. Voršila *(photo below)*, sit ated sideways to National Avenue. The chur is the work of Canevallo from the beginni of the 18th century, its façades decorated wi sculptures by Preiss, Kohl, and Platzer, th latter creating the sculpture "Johanes Nep mucensis with Angels". The furnishing is B roque, with ceiling paintings by Steinfels, ar others by Liška, Brandl and Rys. The extensi convent of the Order of St. Voršila, founded 1672 and completed in 1721–1722, is adj cent to the church. Portheim (Wimmer's) Pa ace (Portheimský or Wimmerův palác) fun tions as a residential house with shops on tl ground floor. It was built around 1794 fro a design by Palliardi and replaced three old buildings (one of which had belonged to tl excellent Baroque sculptor Jan Brokof). Du ing the Napoleonic Wars, the Russian gener Alexander Suvorov stayed here in the wint of 1799–1800. Between 1923 and 1925 a r markable structure, known as Adria Palac was built in the style of Venetian Renaissanc palaces, designed by Janák and Zasch. Tl frontage is decorated with the sculptural grou Adria by Štursa, the creators of other scul tures include Guttfreund, Dvořák and Kafk The work of Eisler, Masák and Rajniš, M (Máj) was, at the time of its opening in 197 one of the largest department stores in Pragu

WHERE HISTORY REVOLVED

On the corner of Národní Avenue and Mikulandská Street is Kaňkovský House (No 16), also known as Schirnding Palace (Schirndingovský palác), a Baroque work by Maxmilian Kaňka dating from 1735–1740. The house has an arcade, a seemingly quiet corner in the very busy street. Everybody slows down when they walk here, and it is impossible to overlook the modest memorial and constantly burning candles. The plaque in the wall informs visitors that they are at the site where the police forces brutally attacked a peaceful student demonstration on 17 November 1989. The student action was organized on the occasion of the 50th anniversary of Czech universities closure by the Germans during the war. The massive procession got here, where the people were cornered and there was no way out. Shots of the confrontation between unarmed people and the special police forces were shown all around the world. The only answer to "Our hands are empty" were blows. This event triggered the so-called Velvet Revolution, which led to the fall of the Communist regime in the former Czechoslovakia.

he remains of a settlement called St. Martin's Domain (Újezd sv. Martina), which was in exitence before the New Town, were uncovered ere during archaeological research. A prominent building can be seen on the corner of Národní Avenue and Na Perštýně Street. Up o 1950 a Classicist-style house, dating from he end of the 18th century, was situated here. On the first floor there used to be the famous Union Café, where Czech artists, writers and ctors met. Another famous café, Slavie *(pho-* *to below left)*, can be found on the corner of Smetana Embankment (Smetanovo nábřeží) opposite the National Theatre (Národní divadlo). The café, which has been popular with writers, artists and actors from the very beginning, occupies the ground floor of Lažanský Palace, designed by Ulman and built in 1861–1863. In the first years of its existence composer Bedřich Smetana lived and worked here (composing the operas *Dalibor* and *The Bartered Bride – Prodaná nevěsta).*

Main photo: *contrasing architectual styles*

AN OWL ON
A PERCH

PLATÝZ

WIMMER'S FOUNTAIN

From 1797 Platýz Palace was the property of one of its most eminent owners, landowner Jakub Wimmer. He made his wealth from supplying materials for the construction of Terezín fort. Nevertheless, this wealthy man was well respected in Prague, not least because he invested part of his money into projects which benefitted the public, for example he founded Letná Gardens and Vinohrady Gardens. He also commissioned František Xaver Lederer, a first-rate sculptor of the Classicist period, to create a fountain *(photo above)*. Wimmer's fountain originally adorned the corner of National Avenue and Jungmann Street, but in 1895 it was moved to Bethlehem Square (Betlémské náměstí) and later to the park in front of the Central Railway Station (Hlavní nádraží). In 1951 it was moved again to Coal Market (Uhelný trh). It is a superb work, which today is situated not far from Wimmer's former home. A stylised tree trunk topped with a leaf plate grows from a square sandstone pool. A swan in its centre spouts water.

The small sculpture of an owl sitting on its perch had an important role; when its head was bowed, it meant that the yard and stables were fully occupied, when it was sitting upright, carters could drive straight in. Such "traffic lights" functioned in front of Platýz, an interesting palace, facing both Coal Market (Uhelný trh) and National Avenue. During the course of history it served various purposes, such as an inn for carters and their horses. The palace, which reportedly somewhat resembled a castle, was built around 1350 by Duke Frederic of Burgundy, who used to stay at the court of Emperor Charles IV. Lord Frederic liked to be surrounded by numerous staff. He grew fond of a young man in his entourage, the son of his caretaker. However, while they were abroad, a rich girl fell in love with the young man. Her parents did not approve, so the young couple fled to a certain rural castle in Bohemia. The duke invited the young man to a coronation in Prague. The boy suspected that their secret was known and that he would never return from the journey. He was right. The Duke of Burgundy had the young man executed in front of Platýz. The cruel deed did not go unpunished. From that moment the duke was constantly able see the eyes of his unfortunate servant and they drove him insane.

In 1586 Jan Platejs and his wife bought the palace. An imperial magistrate of the Old Town, and later a secret councillor of Emperor Rodolph II, he gave the palace its name. Platejs's son, Jan Arnošt, was a zealous Catholic, later becoming a canon and the Bishop of Olomouc. His attitude during the estates rebellion earned him many advantages, and because he did not even have to pay property tax, he could afford to renovate the whole palace. In 1611, though, his life was hanging in the balance. Somebody shot from the Platýz windows at the estates soldiers and killed one of them. The infuriated crowd attacked the house, threw its furniture into the street and stormed into the cellars. There the people found barrels of beer and chose "sampling" over further rioting.

ST. MARTIN IN THE WALL

Practically next-door to Platýz there is the interesting Church of St. Martin in the Wall (kostel sv. Martina ve zdi – *photo below*), probably dating from as early as the first half of the 12th century. When the Old Town fortification was built in the 1230's, the aisle of the church was included. Hence the unusual name "in the Wall" that has been used ever since. In 1414, on the impulse of Hus's pupil Jakoubek of Stříbro, minister Jan of Hradec started to serve the communion "in both kinds"- i.e. both the bread (wafer) and the wine from a chalice. Until that moment the wine had been reserved for priests alone. Thus their superiority was challenged, suddenly every believer shared both the bread and the chalice, the latter thus becaming a symbol of Hussitism. The designation Utraquists is derived from the term "in both kinds" (*sub ultraque* in Latin). During the Hussite Wars the Church of St. Martin in the Wall was spared any damage, as it was a Hussite church. It was modified several times before it was sold to a private owner in an auction in 1784. It was reconstructed as a residential building with shops on the ground floor, including a renowned delicatessen. In 1904 the Prague municipality bought the building and the restoration of the church commenced according to a design by K. Hilbert. Remains of the original Romanesque structure were uncovered during research. The three-nave basilica belongs to the Evangelical Church of Czech Brethren (Českobratrská církev evangelická).

During the era of the next owners, the Sternbergs (Šternberkové), from 1672 to 1797, social events flourished here. Balls were held, there was an excellent school of swordsmanship, and nomadic artists staged performances. Then landowner Jakub Wimmer moved in. He was followed by František Knight Daubek, who, like Wimmer, made his wealth from army commissions. Daubek supported art as well, partly due to the influence of his wife, the daughter of the famous poet Hněvkovský. Daubek reconstructed Platýz into the first tenement house in Prague, Jindřich Hausenknecht designed it. Between 1813–1847 Platýz was given a new appearance in Empire style. On the one hand Platýz offered shelter to the aforementioned carters, on the other it was a famous centre of culture. In 1840 and 1846 Ferenc Liszt performed here in a large hall that occupied two floors. The insurance bank Slavia bought Platýz from the Daubeks, and rebuilt it in 1938–1939. Another significant reconstruction took place in the 1980's. In the cellars the remains of Gothic fortification are still visible. Nowadays Platýz is used for art exhibitions.

Above: *Platýz viewed from National Avenue*
Opposite page below: *a café in the courtyard*

THE NATION
FOR ITSELF

THE NATIONAL THEATRE
(NÁRODNÍ DIVADLO)

THEATRE ON FIRE!

The ceremonial opening of the National Theatre had been planned to take place in September 1881. In fact, although the theatre had not yet been completed, minor adjustments still being made, Smetana's opera *Libuše* was staged here on 11 June 1881. The following afternoon people noticed smoke rising from the roof of the theatre. People started running from all directions and confusion arose; the fire brigade was late, their water tank not full enough, the hydrants in the theatre did not work. A bang was heard from inside; the chandelier, weighing 1500 kg, broke off, then the curtain came down and finally the roof collapsed. The fire, which was allegedly caused by the tinsmiths who had not put out the charcoal under a pot on the roof, could not be stopped. But neither could the Czech people's desire for a national theatre be extinguished. On the same day the first florins were collected for the construction of a new theatre. Ten days after the tragedy half a million florins had been collected, after one month a million. So as early as the 18th November 1883 the theatre was ceremonially opened with the festive fanfares of Smetana's *Libuše*; this time for good.

Above: *external view of the National Theatre*
Opposite page above:
*the auditorium
and Hynais's curtain*
Opposite page below:
a three-horse carriage

The building of the National Theatre (Národní divadlo) is both an excellent example of Neo-Rennaisance architecture and an important national cultural monument. It became a symbol of the existence of the Czech nation and an expression of the people's desire for independence. The Czech spoken word was meant to be a powerful weapon in the struggle for the restoration of the Czech language. The inscription "The Nation For Itself" is a perfect expression of the strength and resilience of this longing; after all, an enormous amount of money was collected during the the initial fund-raising campaign and then again after the tragic fire, so that the theatre could be opened as soon as possible. All the best Czech artists worked on its decoration. People started to call the National Theatre the Golden Chapel (Zlatá kaplička). In some sense it was never really just a theatre, but a very special sacred place, a national temple.

In 1845 a group of Czech patriots asked the estates assembly to establish a permanent Czech stone theatre in Prague. At that time Prague already had such a theatre, the Estates Theatre (Stavovské divadlo) but Czech was hardly ever heard there. In 1850 the preliminary general meeting of the Board for the Establishment of the National Theatre was held, and the first fund-raising campaigns organized. Volunteers carried money boxes in the shape of the intended building with the words "Na zdar" (To success, by which success in building the theatre was meant). This is probably where the Czech informal greeting "Nazdar" originated. First a location had to be chosen. Nine places were considered, among them the Old Town, Wenceslas Square and Charles Square (Staré město, Václavské náměstí, Karlovo náměstí, respectively). In the end a property next to the chain bridge across the Vltava was chosen, an inauspicious location, far below the level of the embankment,

The National Theatre has been a symbol of Czech national identity from its very beginning, so any step towards its foundation was an important event. On 7 March 1868 the celebratory board announced that on 16 May the foundation stone of the National Theatre would be laid. The Czech people were overjoyed, all kinds of clubs and societies entered their names to take part in the parade which would celebrate the event. Foundation stones set out from places of historical importance on festively decorated carriages. The first stone had arrived already by 5th May from Radhošť (a mythical mountain in Beskydy connected with legend about the Slavic missionaries Cyril and Metoděj). Then a six-ton boulder came from Říp (the place where forefather Czech stopped his journey with his people, according to legend). A stone from compatriots in America with the inscription "what is united by blood the ocean cannot divide" only arrived in 1869. The festive day commenced with a massive parade of twenty thousand people, walking across Prague to the construction site of the National Theatre. The foundation deed was signed and was put in a casket, along with several coins, valid currency at that time, a written note about the origin of the theatre and a few stones from Hus's prison in Konstanz. The casket was then set into the foundations. In the evening the first performance of Smetana's opera Dalibor was staged in the New Town Theatre (Novoměstské divadlo), which was in the location of the present-day State Opera (Státní opera). Today the foundation stones are set in the cellars of the National Theatre and can be viewed by visitors to the theatre during the main recess of each performance.

with a rubbish dump and lines of washing hanging around. The future architect would not have been very pleased with the shape of the plot either; it was an irregular trapezoid. Only the patriots were overjoyed, the plot was right between Prague Castle and Vyšehrad. However because there was not enough money, the Provisional Theatre was established in 1862, later being incorporated into the new structure. In 1886 the design of architect Josef Zítek (1832 to 1909) won the competition for the best theatre building. But before its ceremonial opening the theatre burned down and was reconstructed in 1882–1883, after a new fund-raising campaign. Architect Josef Schulz continued the work, basically following the design of his teacher, Zítek, who withdrew from the project with a feeling of injustice, the councillors having criticized him for neglecting safety measures in his design. On 18 November 1883 the theatre was handed over to the ensemble before the opera *Libuše* was symbolically re-staged. Special celebratory coins were issued for the occasion, which were cast from the metal of the partially melted chandelier.

The building, constructed in the Italian Renaissance tradition, contains works by the most prominent Czech artists of the time. Sculptor Myslbek created the portal with the sculptures Opera and Drama Schnirch sculpted the bronze carriage drawn by three horses, the so-called triga, carrying the goddess of victory, on the pillars of the main frontage (the original models burned in the fire, and

so the sculptor had to create new ones, but he died before he could see the final casts). Mikoláš Aleš painted the Homeland cycle of lunette paintings, Ženíšek created the ceiling paintings in the auditorium, the triptych Downfall, Resurrection and the Golden Age of Art. Hynais was responsible for the curtain and the paintings paintings in the presidential loge, Tulka produced the loggia decoration, Mařák paintings of memorable places. Liebscher decorated the foyer antechamber and Brožík created paintings in the gentlemen's parlour.

In 1977–1983 a large reconstruction took place, the vast underground parking area being established at that time, as well as the New Scene, (Nová scéna) which replaced three pulled-down buildings, the so-called Choura Houses. The New Scene was built according to a design by K. Prager. Its façade consists of 4306 glass prisms, and inside there is a circular stage. The reconstructed National Theatre was re-opened on 18 November 1983 again with Smetana's *Libuše*.

TUNES ABOVE
THE RIVER

SLOVANSKÝ OSTROV

A LOCOMOTIVE
ON THE ISLAND

A remarkable attraction was installed here by Mr. Borrosh and Mr. Evans. They laid out 158m of wooden rails, which were used for a steam locomotive with two wagons. The locomotive was the first of its kind to be made in Prague and was called the Czech Lion. Much to people's amazement, Josef Božek's invention could reach a top speed of 15 km/h.

Slavic Island (Slovanský ostrov) was formed by silted dirt downstream from the Šítkovský weir in the 18th century. It is the most famous, the most popular, and from a historical viewpoint probably the most interesting island in Prague. After a great flood in 1784 it was stabilized with a barrier wall and planted with trees and thus it was given a firm shape, identical to its present-day form. The island is approximately 350 meters long and almost 100 metres wide. Sometime before 1817 a small spa and leather dyeworks were established here; the original name of the island actually being Dyer's Island (Barvířský ostrov). In 1830 the plot was purchased by miller Novotný, who renamed the island Žofín as a tribute to Žofie (Sophia), the mother of the emperor-to-be Franz Joseph. He started to create an important social and cultural centre. At first, in 1837, he reconstructed the spa and built a two-storied Classicist edifice with a beautiful dance hall, which was opened with a great festive ball on 30 May 1837. In 1841 the second Czech ball was held here and the other events also had a marked patriotic character. The writer Božena Němcová attended

the third Czech ball two years later. The gentlemen were charmed by her beauty and intelligence, and the ladies were given a small volume of eighteen poems as a keepsake from the great social event. In 1840 the Žofín Academy, a Czech-German musical project, was established here. Josef Leopold Zvonař, composer of the song *Beautiful Bohemia, My Bohemia (Čechy krásné, Čechy mé)* was one of its members. The famous Hlahol choir performed here, and Hector Berlioz, Petr Ilyich Tchaykovski, Ferenc Liszt and Richard Wagner gave concerts. On the eve of the revolutionary riots of 1848 the Slavic Convention had a meeting in Prague, and the name Slavic Island has been used ever since to commemorate the event. Three hundred forty delegates from the Slavic nations of the former monarchy attended the Convention, demanding the formation of states with equal powers under a constitutional government. Ludovít Štúr of Slovakia even demanded that Austria be broken into independent states.

The island became a pleasant destination for walks, with a band playing on Sundays. In summer the local river spa and in winter a skating rink were popular. People watched the construction of the National Theatre (Národní divadlo) from the island, salvaging costumes and various props here during the tragic fire. In 1878 Antonín Dvořák gave his first solo concert here. On 5 November 1888 the work of Bedřich Smetana *My Homeland (Má vlast)* was performed here for the first time. Zdeněk

Fibich was inspired by Žofín, and it was also here that virtuoso-to-be Jan Kubelík was first introduced to the public at the age of ten.

In 1884 Prague City bought the complex. The main building was reconstructed in Neo-Renaissance style from a design by Fialka. In 1928 the spa was pulled down and three years later the island was converted into a park. From 1991–1994 the building was extensively reconstructed. Today Slavic Island (Slovanský ostrov) remains a pleasant place and Žofín *(photo below)* a traditional cultural and social centre.

Entering Slavic Island (Slovanský ostrov) from Masaryk Embankment (Masarykovo nábřeží), we are able to enjoy the most famous panorama of Prague; the view of Prague Castle (Pražský hrad) and Hradčany across the river. In front of us we can see other prominent features, including a constructivist building dating from 1930, Mánes – the House of Visual Artists (Dům výtvarných umělců). Next to it there is the tower of Šitkov Waterworks (Šítkovská vodárna). Originally a waterworks tower for the upper New Town, established at the end of the 15th century, it had to be rebuilt after several fires. It was damaged by the Swedes during the siege of Prague in 1648. Šitkov mills (Šítkovské mlýny), mentioned in records as early as 1178, used to stand next to the tower until 1928. The collection of Art Nouveau houses *(main photo and photo above)* on the embankment also presents a fine sight. Hlahol house from 1905 is also interesting. Three bronze plaques on the façade commemorate three important Hlahol choirmasters: Smetana, Bendl and Knittl. Hilbert House (No 234) has a remarkable Art Nouveau vestibule, and house No 224 is also a rare example of Art Nouveau architecture.

THE TALLEST CHURCH IN PRAGUE

CHURCH OF THE VIRGIN MARY OF SNOW

When one views the vast structure of the Church of the Virgin Mary of Snow (kostel Panny Marie Sněžné – *main photo*), it is hard to believe that it is actually just a torso of an intended cathedral. The church was founded on the edge of New Town (Nové město) by Charles IV himself to commemorate his coronation in 1347. He gave the church to the Order of the White Friars. The church was supposed to be a place for the coronation of Czech kings, which is why it covered an extensive area (its intended length was more than 100 metres) and its magnificence was meant to compete with St. Vitus's Cathedral (Chrám sv. Víta). The construction of the church dragged on until the Hussite Wars, after which there were insufficient funds for its completion. The incomplete walls were pulled down. Only the presbytery was left, and was adapted into a church. As the chancel was neglected, the vaulting and frontage collapsed during the 16th century. In 1603 the Franciscans took over the church with the monastery and had it repaired. The presbytery was vaulted with new Renaissance vaults *(photo opposite page above)*. Despite these setbacks, with its 34m-high cupola, this church remains the tallest in Prague, dwarfing even the St. Vitus's Cathedral. The original, unfinished cupola

A CUBIST LANTERN

By the side gate, originally a cemetery gate, to the grounds of the Church of the Virgin Mary of Snow (kostel Panny Marie Sněžné), we can admire fascination with detail. There a cubist column supports a street light *(photo above)*, this remarkable technical gem being the work of Vlastislav Hofman from 1913.

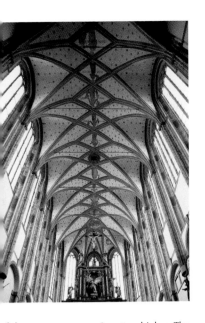

of the nave was even 6 metres higher. The most dominant feature of the church is the main altar, dating from 1650, an example of early Baroque column architecture, it is the tallest in the country. Alongside the walls

there are ten wooden statues of saints. On the side altar there is the painting Annunciation of Virgin Mary by Reiner from 1724. On the southern side of the grounds there is the 17th century Chapel of St. Michael (kaple sv. Michala) and in the courtyard in front of it there is a 17th century chapel dedicated to the Virgin Mary the Helpful (kaple Panny Marie Pomocné). On the northern side of the courtyard is the Chapel of St. Johanes Nepomucensis, which dates from the 18th century. The former monastery is adjacent to the southern side of the church. The original building was erected between 1347–1352, with further construction in 1379, but in the 17th century it went to ruin. The Baroque buildings we see today were built in the 17th century during Franciscan renovation of the whole grounds. Some Gothic elements were preserved, and a Gothic cellar has been transformed into a period Franciscan Winebar (Vinárna U františkánů). A presbytery built in front of the church in the 17th century was renovated in Classicist style in 1778, this creating the courtyard that can be seen today. By the northern side of the church is a doorway with a Gothic tympanum, dating from the mid-14th century, it is decorated with a sculpture of the Tree of Life, which includes scenes from the coronation of Charles IV and his wife Blanche of Valois.

The church has made its mark in history, particularly during of the Hussite revolution. Thousands of poor people came here to listen to the sermons of preacher Jan Želivský.

THE FRANCISCAN GARDENS

A surprising oasis of quiet and greenery occupies the small area (0.6 hectares) found among the residential buildings between Wenceslas Square (Václavské náměstí) and Jungmann Street (Jungmannova ulice), practically in heart of the busy city centre. It is one of the few preserved medieval monastery gardens in Prague, established in the second half of the 16th century by the White Friars from the monastery next to the Church of the Virgin Mary of Snow (kostel Panny Marie Sněžné). Here they grew mostly medicinal herbs and flowers for altar decoration. From 1604 the property belonged to the Franciscans, who modified the garden. As the years went by, space dedicated to the garden was reduced, not least when two water tanks, a fire safety measure, were insensitively installed. From 1985–1992 the garden was modified again and complemented with two sculptures, a Boy with a Shell by Honzík and Dancing Fairies by Klimeš. In the centre of the garden is a Baroque arbour (photo above), dating from the late 17th or early the 18th century. There is a herb garden next to it. The gardens are open to public and are very popular; when the weather is nice it is hard to find an unoccupied seat…

WENCESLAS SQUARE

**I'LL MEET YOU
AT THE HORSE**

When Praguers agree to "meet at the horse", it means at the statue of St. Wenceslas on the horse *(photo above)*, which has been standing in the upper section of Wenceslas Square (Václavské náměstí) since 1913. It is the work of Myslbek, who, in colaboration with the architect Alois Dryák, placed a patron saint of the nation at each corner of the pedestal: St. Ludmilla, St. Prokop, St. Vojtěch and St. Agnes. This monument became a symbol of Czech statehood, similar to Wenceslas Square itself, which has been the scene of events of great importance in recent years.

Photo right: at Můstek
Main photo: the view from the National Museum

The main thoroughfare, the centre of both business and social life, in short the "heart of Prague"... ...that is Wenceslas Square, 750m long and 60m wide. It was established by Charles IV in 1348 as a link between the New and Old Town fortifications. However, the area soon primarily became a large New Town marketplace, and because regular horse auctions were held there, it earned the name Horse Market. As early as 1362 annual markets were held there, wirh fabrics, weapons, and up to 1877 grain being sold here. The lower end was taken up by New Town huts, and after they were pulled down in 1786 a wooden theatre, called the Shack (Bouda), grew in their place. Czech plays were staged here for three years, not a long period, but it was important to the process of national revival. The Shack was pulled down at the same time as the two gates, the Old Town Havel Gate and the New Town Horse Gate. The stone statue of St. Wenceslas by Bendl is no longer here, either, in 1879 it was moved to Vyšehrad. The square was paved as late as the end of the 18th century, but from the beginning Horse Market had a complete-

ly rural character, after all, a typical waysid cross stood in the middle of the square. I 1848 the name was changed to Wencesla Square (Václavské náměstí) at the sugges tion of Karel Havlíček Borovský. Sometim in 1875 it turned green with rows of linden planted, but in 1184 these had to make wa for horse-drawn carriages, taking passenger from Můstek to Nusle. In 1894 the first elec tric lamps were switched on, and the horse drawn carriages were replaced by an elec tric tramcar. Today the tram line only crosse Wenceslas Square (through Vodičkova an Jindřišská Streets), a pedestrian precinct lead

sitive construction of the so-called North-South motorway in 1967. The absurd project is unpararalleled in developed countries. The most prominent feature of the upper end of the square, the National Museum (see separate chapter), built between 1885–1890, was separated by a main thoroughfare, becoming a deserted island between two busy roads. Below the museum, across the motorway, we can see the remarkable statue of St. Wenceslas by Josef Wenceslas Myslbek, dating from 1913.

The square is lined with hotels, restaurants, clubs and shops. Besides the palaces, we will take note mainly of several other important architectural "gems". These include the Hotel Europe (Šroubek), an Art Nouveau structure from 1903 to 1905, which features a façade with gilt nymphs at the top and its original preserved interior, including bars and huge mirrors. The Neo-Renaissance Wiehl House (Wiehlův dům – *photo left*), dating from 1895–1896, has a façade decorated according to sketches by Mikoláš Aleš and Josef Fanta.

rough a part of the middle section of the quare. At both ends of Wenceslas Square here are underground stations (Muzeum at e upper end and Můstek at the lower). The hole area was disrupted with utterly insen-

THE CHARM OF PALACES

The shops and palaces in the busy Wenceslas Square are typical of this part of Prague and offer a variety of architectural styles to the connoisseur. Crown Palace (palác Koruna, No 846 – *photo above*) is found at the lower end of the square. This shopping and administrative centre was built in 1912–1914, according to a design by Pfeifer, and is decorated with sculptures by Štursa and Sucharda. The top of the building has the shape of a crown. In 1931–1932 Crown Palace was adapted by Machoň, and a self-service restaurant was established here. Today there is a shop for luxury goods. Alfa Palace (also called U Stýblů, No 758) is a precious example of constructivist architecture. The work of Kysela and Jarolím, it dates from 1927–1929. You can walk through a passage to the Franciscan Garden (Františkánská zahrada) or to Vodičkova Street. In the past the famous Semafor Theatre used to reside here. Lucerna Palace is the first structure in Prague made of reinforced concrete. It was built by Wenceslas Havel, an ancestor of the first Czech president Wenceslas Havel. In 1907–1910 the wing facing Vodičkova Street was built, in 1913–1921 the wing facing Štěpánská Street. The complex includes vast passages with shops, restaurants and a cinema, as well as a renowned underground hall, in which balls, concerts and other cultural and social events take place.

THE MOST VALUABLE HERITAGE

THE NATIONAL MUSEUM

PANTHEON

The most valuable part of the National Museum is the Pantheon *(photo opposite page below)*, which is dedicated to the memory of great figures of the Czech nation, who are commemorated in statues and busts. The Pantheon is inlaid with five kinds of polished marble, the columns are made of granite, syenite and Carrara marble. The great lunettes above the balconies depict four scenes from Czech history: "Přemysl Being Summoned to Rule" and "St. Metoděj Completing the Translation of the Bible in a Slavic Language" by František Ženíšek; and "Charles IV Establishes Charles University in 1348" and "Jan Ámos Komenský Presents his Work to the Amsterdam City Council" by Wenceslas Brožík. The paintings by Vojtěch Hynais consist of the allegoric figures of Art, Inspiration, Progress and Science.

The Neo-Renaissance exterior of the National Museum *(photo above)* creates a noble and and majestic impression. It envelopes the upper end of Wenceslas Square (Václavské náměstí), although it is absurdly encircled by a motorway. The National Museum is truly a national institution, housing the nation's most valuable heritage, and symbolising Czech culture, science and learning. On the initiative of Count Kašpar Maria Šternberk and Count František Antonín Kolovrat-Libštejnský, it was founded on 15 April 1818, initially as a private scientific institute, and later on it became the Patriotic Museum of Bohemia Society. In 1854 it was renamed the Museum of the Czech Kingdom, serving an important centre of national revival, which many outstanding personalities took turns to head, including Josef Dobrovský and František Palacký. The collections, at first rather small, were placed in the Church of St. Jacob (kostel sv. Jakuba) in the Old Town of Prague, next in Šternberk Palace in

Hradčany, then in Count Jan Nostic Palace Na Příkopě Street. The collections grew and there was never enough space for them. The Museum Society searched for a suitable location for the construction of their own building, in the end accepting František Ladislav Rieger's suggestion to acquire the area behind the former Horse Gate. A competition was announced, and out of 27 designs that by a professor at Czech Technical University, architect Josef Schulz, was chosen. Under the leadership of architect Čeněk Gregor the building we can see today was constructed between 1885 and 1890 and decorated by prominent Czech artists of that time. Upon entering, immediately the two flights of stairs are interesting, with their allegoric sculptures representing Bohemia, Moravia and Silesia, as well as the Vltava and Labe rivers. The square-shaped vestibule looks regal with its caisson ceiling and columns of Swedish granite, between which stand bronze statues of Libuše, Přemysl Oráč (the Ploughman

inces Wenceslas and Přemysl Ottocar II by
unich artist Schwanthaler. The main stair-
ase is framed by three floors of arched ar-
des, *(photo opposite page left)*. On the
nding there are Schwanthaler's statues of
iška Přemyslovna and George of Podě-
ady. Between the arcades of the first floor
ang portraits of Czech kings, on the second
oor there are busts of men who rendered
utstanding service to Czech science and the
ational Museum. From the gallery of the
rst floor and on the staircase to the second
oor we can see paintings of the royal castles
Prague, Karlštejn, Křivoklát and Zvíkov by
ařák, who also created the paintings above
e right-hand side staircase. These works
art represent six important places: Tetín,
bušín, Říp, Budeč, Vyšehrad, Levý Hradec.
bove the left-hand side staircase there are
ore paintings from Czech history.

In the complex we can find mineralogi-
al, anthropological, archaeological, zoo-
gical, osteological and palaeontological
xhibitions.

WHERE THE MUSES RESIDE

Surrounded by the motorway, not far from the National Museum, stands the building of the State Opera (Státní opera – *photo above*), separated from the Museum by the massive building of the former parliament, the latter dating from 1973 and incorporating the building of the money market dating from 1936–1938. Originally, the State Opera had been the site of the wooden New Town Theatre, which, for the time, had an enormous capacity of three thousand seats. A large space like that was practically impossible to heat in winter, so plays were only staged in summer. In winter, balls and circus performances were organized. The theatre was pulled down in 1885, and in 1886–1887 replaced with the Neo-Renaissance structure of the New German Theatre. Of sculpture decoration, Dionysos' Carriage and Thalia above the portal are worth noting, both by Theodor Friedl. In 1945, having been bombed, the theatre was repaired, and renamed the 5th May Theatre. Opera was prevalent in the repertoire, and so the name was changed to the 5th May Great Opera, then again, and after merger with the National Theatre in 1948 to the Smetana Theatre. In 1967–1973 extensive reconstruction took place, and after the theatre became independent again, its name was changed to the State Opera of Prague.

Above centre: *a skeleton of a whale*

CHURCH OF A ROYAL COUPLE

HENRY TOWER
AND THE CHURCH OF ST. HENRY

**AN ART NOUVEAU
GATEWAY TO EUROPE**

The railway is a symbol of far-away places and adventure. Prague's Central Railway Station (which is only a few minutes' walk to the Church of St. Henry) connects it to the whole Europe. The original Neo-Renaissance building was constructed in 1870–1871, according to a design by Barvitius and Ullman. At that time it was necessary to dig a tunnel under the Vinohrady crest. Soon the railway station was too small, so an architectural competition was announced in 1899. The design of architect Josef Fanta (1856–1954) won. And so the original main building was pulled down and between 1901–1909 replaced by a new Art Nouveau structure, rich in shape as well as decoration. The station building was 214m long. The arches spanning the platforms were also imposing, 235m long, 76m wide and 18m high. Between 1972–1977 a vast modern departure hall was added to the existing building. The hall has three floors. On the ground floor there are technical services and some public utilities. The middle floor serves as an entrance area (including the Metro (underground) station on line C), and consists of various utilities, ticket-offices, left-luggage offices. The third floor is level with the underpass beneath the platforms. The branches of the North-South motorway cross the ceiling of the hall, a part of which is taken up by a large parking area.

The present-day Senovážné Square has an interesting history. Charles IV himself decreed that it would become one of the three large New Town markets, and so Hay Market (Senný trh) was established. The pubs of the area used to be pretty lively, and the large open space was used for military drill as there were barracks nearby, but the main focus of attention was a measuring scale for wagons situated in a small wooden building. Wagons loaded with hay, straw or grain would drive onto it. Carters' wagons clattered through here, and prisoners sentenced to death were led through here on their way to the Žižkov scaffold. Hay Square was connected to Wenceslas Square by the present-day Jindřišská Street. On the corner of Jindřišská Street and Hay Square the Goth

ic Church of St. Henry and Kunhuta (kostel sv. Jindřicha a Kunhuty – *photo on opposite page*) was founded, dedicated to a royal couple. Henry II was a capable ruler, who was responsible for the reform of the Church and the establishment of the Bamberk Bishopric. For this he was canonized in 1146, his wife also being proclaimed a saint in 1200.

The church was one of two parochial churches founded in the newly established New Town during the reign of Charles IV. The Church of St. Henry is an interesting example of a Gothic aisled hall with a long chancel and a pentacle chevet, to which a Renaissance antechamber was added in 1562, as well as a Baroque chapel at the sides in the 17th century. In the south-western corner a prismatic tower is built. Each of the three naves originally had its own roof, but during re-gothisation during 1875–1879, following a design by Mocker, a single roof was constructed covering the whole church. The original graveyard was replaced by a park, only a row of headstones has been left *(photo below right)* by the outer wall of the church.

By the church entrance there are Baroque statues of Johanes Nepomucensis, created n Brokof's workshop, and St. Juda Tadeáš, by an unknown author. The paintings are he work of Škréta, Heinsch, and Reiner. The sculptures were made by Bendl and Prach-er. The tin font dating from 1487 and the tatue of Jindřich from around 1500 are very aluable.

Opposite the church, across Henry Street lindřišská ulice), looms Henry Tower (Jindřiš-

ská věž – *photo left*), which originally served as a bell tower for the church. It was built on a former graveyard between 1471–1476. In 1879 it was re-Gothicized by Mocker. The bell tower is connected by a bridge to the former Cukerní Palace. The bell called Maria *(photo above right)* is worth noting. It weighs 500 kilograms and was cast by master bell founder Bartholomew in 1518. The bell clock is just a little younger, having been made in 1577.

AN INTERESTING WEDDING

On the 4 November 1817 the Church of St. Henry witnessed an extraordinary event. The famous composer Carl Maria von Weber, head of the Estates Theatre (Stavovské divadlo) between 1813–1816, married the ensemble soloist Karolína Brandtová here. Another occasion is definitely worth mentioning. In December 1875 Father Ignác Hanka baptized here a certain Reiner Maria Rilke (1875–1926), who was born in 16 Jindřišská Street and later became famous as a poet, in whose work many Prague motifs appear.

IN CELEBRATION
OF BEER

"U FLEKŮ" BREWERY

FOERSTER AT
ST. VOJTĚCH'S

In a little square by Vojtěšská Street, just a few steps from the "U Fleků" Brewery, is the Gothic Church of St. Vojtěch *(photo above)* dating from the 14th century, but later modified in Baroque style before being re-Gothicized in 1875–1877. When the church was renovated in 1930–1932, valuable wall paintings from the first half of the 16th century were uncovered. At that time Josef Bohuslav Foerster (1859–1951), a famous-composer-to-be, worked in the church as an organist. It is interesting that he did not want to pursue a career in music at all, he wanted to study natural sciences. Eventually, he became a student at the Prague organist school and graduated with great success in 1882. In September 1888 he married Berta Lauterer in the Church of St. Vojtěch. She was a member of the National Theatre Opera, and, two months later, sang the first Czech Tatyana in Tchaykovski's opera Eugen Onegin. Tchaykovski himself attended the first night and pro claimed lady Berta as the best Tatyana ever.

ery" *(main photo)*, instead of numerals, is set into a wrought iron frame on the façade.

The vast complex replaced three older houses, one from the Gothic and two from the Renaissance periods, the remains of which have survived below the ground level. The "house with the right to brew" is the heart of the whole complex. It used to be called Na Skřemenci (Na Křemenci), later U Domažlíků, and finally U Fleků, after its owner Jakub Flekovský. The building went through Baroque and Classicist alternations. The interior was refurbished in Romantic style from a design by František Sander. Beer was brewed here as early as the end of the 15th century (1499). In 1986 a large reconstruction took place and, on the occasion of the 500th anniversary of brewing here, a Brewery Museum was opened with a permanent exhibition in the building of the former malt-house. The equipment of the brewery is a monument to the history of brewing, including the machines, tools and vessels. A Renaisance room in which malt used to be dried with hot smoke from burning wood is a much sought-out section of the museum. Here we find the original malt-kiln called "valach" and learn about such unique objects like the historic brewing equipment *(photo below)*, cooling channels and fermentation vats made of oak wood in the old custom.

you want to have a beer, you go first to the "U Fleků" Brewery; this is the unwritten rule or most Prague's visitors. The smallest brew-ry in Prague, with its Old Czech alehouse nd superb-quality Flek 13° stout, is also the ost famous one. The alehouse is somewhat idden in the narrower lanes of New Town, ut on entering Křemencová Street we can-ot miss either the brewery or the alehouse. clock, with letters reading "U Fleků Brew-

FAMOUS GUESTS

Staročeská chmelnice (Old Czech Hop-garden), Václavka, Emauzy, Kufr (Suit-case), Velký sál (Large Hall); these are the names of the individual rooms of the alehouse. However, the most famous one is the Academy (Akademie), where the elite of Prague artistic society used to meet. On 24 June 1908 the painter Láďa Novák was crowned Flek king. With his colleagues, Jindřich and Ota Bubeníček and Vilém Trsek, he decorated the rooms with various little drawings and imbiber's slogans celebrating beer. For his work on the interior of the alehouse he was awarded a lifetime of free beer. Writers such as Jakub Arbes, Jan Neruda and Jaroslav Hašek, playwright Josef Kajetán Tyl, and actors Jindřich Mošna, František Karel Kolár, Rodolph Deyl senior and František Ferdinand Šamberk all used to come here for a pint. It was the latter that introduced the excellent Flek speciality, the Flek toast. One night the society apparently felt like having something spicy, and Šamberk himself prepared some toast. Since that time guests have always wanted the crunchy delicacy. There was also a cabaret at the "U Fleků" Alehouse, where old-Prague songs by Karel Hašler prevailed; Hašler himself was a frequent guest here, for that matter. The society included various peculiar figures. Perhaps the most popular was a man called "Ferda – matches – Europe". He carried his tiny shop, a little box, around his neck, sold matches and boasted that the address mentioned above was enough to reach him.

Above left: a gable in the yard

PRAGUE'S
BASTILLE

THE NEW TOWN HALL

THE PRAGUE ELL

On the eastern wing of the New Town Hall (Novoměstská radnice) we see a chain, which is a reminder of past security measures; such chains were used to close up Prague streets. Another interesting feature is the so-called Prague Ell (photo above), a steel rod exactly 57.27 cm long. In 1760 it was set into the brickwork two metres above the pavement, so that it could not easily be damaged by vandals. At market time, a stoop was placed next to it and a clerk would verify the correct measure of fabric for a small fee. It is said that merchants liked to use one measure for buying and another for selling…

The New Town Hall (Novoměstská radnice – photo below) is a prominent feature of Charles Square (Karlovo náměstí). Today it is a national cultural monument; history and its famous figures walked through this place. It used to serve as a tough prison, the Town Hall being for some time called the "Prague's Bastille" after the infamous Paris prison. The first record of the Town Hall dates from 1377, the eastern wing facing Vodičkova Street comes from that time. During an extensive reconstruction, led by Martin Frička and master Kříž between 1411 and 1416, a southern wing was added, fac-

ing Charles Square. The Gothic two-nav entrance hall is the reminder of this period From the eastern wing, the cellars and a two aisle columned hall (photo on opposite pag below right) have survived. Between 145 and 1456 a 42m high corner tower wa built. On its second floor there is the Nev Town emblem, alongside the Czech, Impe rial and Polish emblems. A further radical re construction followed between 1520–152 and then another, after a fire in 1559; th southern wing being rebuilt in Renaissanc style. A four-wing building, with an arcad courtyard, was formed. Until 1784 the Nev

The New Town Hall lived through a number of important historic events, the most significant one being the first defenestration of Prague on 30 July 1419. On that day, a former Premonstratensian monk, Jan Želivský, preached in the Church of the Virgin Mary of Snow (kostel Panny Marie Sněžné) in New Town. It was a more fiery sermon than usual, and got the gathered crowd of supporters of the chalice stirred up. The people, led by Jan Želivský, seized the Church of St. Stephen (kostel sv. Štěpána) before going on to the nearby New Town Hall, where they demanded the release of the imprisoned supporters of the reformation. The councillors refused, and reportedly somebody threw a stone at a priest carrying a monstrance. The infuriated crowd attacked the Town Hall and threw all councillors present out of the windows. Those not killed by the fall were mecilessly clubbed to death. It was on this day that the Hussite revolution de facto started. When Czech King, Wenceslas IV, who was staying at New Castle in Kunratice, was informed of the events, he suffered a stroke and died shortly afterwards.

al of sixteen participants of the Břevnov Social Democrat Convention was held here. In 1920 participants of a large strike were put in prison. More than half of those arrested were socialites, and the Town Hall became jokingly nicknamed the "People's House in Charles Square" (People's House being the seat of the Social Democrats at that time, as it still is today). In the meantime several other modifications took place. From 1806 to 1811 the Town Hall was reconstructed in Empire style according to a design by Schmidt. In 1905 the complex was given a 16th century appearance (a design by Wiehl and Hilbert). Another reconstruction has taken place in recent years. Today the New Town Hall serves cultural and social purposes.

Above: the interior of the New Town Hall

own municipal administration resided here, and after the alliance of the four towns of Prague, the criminal court and a prison with ts torture chamber were also situated here. Towards the end of the 17th century the Chods together with the leader of the great rebellion, Jan Sladký-Kozina, experienced life in prison, and were all later sentenced to death. The revolutionaries of 1848 served their sentences here, as did the members of the Youth Society (Omladina) in 1893 (e.g. the future Secretary to the Treasury of the first Czechoslovak government, Alois Rašín, and the poet Stanislav Kostka Neumann were among those imprisoned). In 1879 the tri-

CHARLES SQUARE

JESUIT LIFE

The former Jesuit College *(photo above)*, together with its church, dedicated to the founder of the Jesuit order St. Ignatius of Loyola, forms a vast complex that cannot be missed even in the large area of Charles Square (Karlovo náměstí). The college was built between 1658–1667 from a design by Lurago, in place of twenty-three building plots and thirteen gardens. After the order was abolished in 1773, the complex was converted into a hospital. Lurago also designed the church, constructed between 1665–1670 and complemented with a tower designed by Bayer in 1686–1687. At the top of the façade there is a statue of St. Ignatius surrounded by a golden halo. This got the Jesuits into trouble. The Dominicans pointed out that there was a statue of Jesus Christ in the same church with a halo only around his head, which was a striking disbalance. The honour given to St. Ignatius belongs only to God or the Virgin Mary. The dispute had to be solved by the Pope himself, and the Jesuits won. And so St. Ignatius kept his halo from head to toe…

When Charles IV was establishing the New Town of Prague, he also wanted to create a dignified counterpart to Old Town Square. Eventually there were three squares; besides Hay Market (Senovážné náměstí today) and Horse Market (Wenceslas Square), Cattle Market (from 1848 called Charles Square) was the largest public area by far. It was founded in 1348 on an area of 80550 m². It was a high-minded project, one of the "visiting cards" of the "Father of the Nation", a creation that has lasted throughout the ages. At first, though, it looked quite different, as the impression of the marketplace was not

exactly welcoming. However, the importan thing was that almost any kind of goods coul be purchased here, cattle of course, but als pickled herring (Prague had a monopoly i salted herring), timber and all sorts of tools. I the middle of the square there was a wood en tower where the imperial jewels were dis played every year. In 1382 it was replaced b the Chapel of the Body of God (kaple Božíh těla) a variation of the Chapel of Charles th Great in Aachen). In 1437 the Basel Compac was declared here; an agreement betwee Hussite Bohemia and the Basel Counci Leading scholars were buried here, the las

There are several houses in Prague named Faust House, but the most mysterious and famous one is found in Charles Square, next to a garden which used to be the entrance to the Church of St. Johanes Nepomucensis. In the 14th century the palace of the counts of Opava stood here, and at this time the first stories and rumours concerning what was going on inside probably developed. Wenceslas Opavský was a great natural science enthusiast. In 1434 the house was damaged, and around 1543 reconstructed in Renaissance style. It was then purchased by Emperor Rodolph II's renowned alchemist, Edward Kelley. Between 1740 and 1770 Faust House *(photo below)* was the residence of the Mladota of Solopysky family, the pretty late Baroque façade we can see today coming from this period, designed by Kaňka. Ferdinand Antonín Mladota was always doing some experiments, and with flames often seen in the windows, people started to avoid the house. The names of the actual owners or tenants were soon forgotten, but the mysterious house remained, people transposing to it the legend of doctor Faust, who sold his soul to the Devil in return for being able to summon ghosts from their graves and make gold from dirt. When the time came, the Devil took Faust away through the ceiling. Then, the story says, a poor student moved in. In vain he tried to brick up the hole in the ceiling. Eventually he found a book of magic, repeated the formula, and in the arms of the devil followed Faust. That is what the story says, the fact is, though, that for a long time nobody wanted to move into the house. Only after a thorough fumigation and cleaning was the house again fit for human habitation. Between 1833 and 1902 it housed the first Prague Institute of the Deaf and the Mute, and later a large hospital pharmacy.

ne being writer Jan Campanus Vodňanský 1622. In 1791 the chapel was pulled own. Between 1843–1863 a public park as created in its place *(main photo)*, with number of statues of famous figures (poet

Hálek, writer Světlá, botanist Roezl, natural scientist Purkyně, amongst others). Besides the New Town Hall and the Church of St. Ignatius (see separate section), other architectural sights can be found here: Neo-Renaissance-style building of the Czech Technical College (České vysoké učení technické, No 293) *(photo above)* designed by Ullman and dating from 1872–1873. The Black Brewery (Černý pivovar, No 292) built in 1934, Salmovský House (No 671) where Braun died, Stone Table House (U Kamenného stolu – No 550), which in 1910 replaced the original building that had a stone table for laying out money for cattle bought at the market.

WHAT THE BUILDER
NEVER SAW

KARLOV

ŽIŽKA AMONG
THE CATHOLICS

When visiting the Karlov Church, we may notice several interesting features. In the fresco beneath the organ-loft there is a depiction of the Hussite general Jan Žižka. In a Catholic church that is a very strange motif; we know from history that Žižka and the Catholics waged war against each other. The appearance of the Virgin Mary of Karlov is also rather unusual. She is obviously pregnant, which contradicts the Church doctrine of the Immaculate Conception. The Archbishop of Prague, Jan Josef Breuner, demanded that the painting be removed. A copy of the painting, created by Hellich from the original by Heintsch, hangs on one of the side altars.

A stone statue of Charles IV, the work of Josef Max created in 1837 was brought here from Charles Street (Karlova ulice) to commemorate the fact that it was the "Father of the Nation", as he is often called, who in 1350 founded the Church of the Virgin Mary and St. Charles the Great (kostel Panny Marie a sv. Karla Velikého), along with the monastery of Austin Friars (photo above). The burial chapel of Charles the Great in Aachen served as a model for the church, consecrated in 1377. At that time the octagonal church with three cupolas probably only had a provisional ceiling. The gorgeous and boldly conceived Renaissance stellar vaulting, 24m in diameter and 19m in height was constructed as late as 1575 according to a design by Bonifác Wohlmut. It is said that the young builder was so concerned about this unusual creation that he formed an alliance with the Devil to ensure that the work

was completed faultlessly. When the vaulting was finished, no one wanted to dismantle the scaffolding for fear that the ceiling would collapse. So the builder himself set on fire. After a while a ramble was heard and clouds of dust surged out through the windows. The desperate builder, thinking that the vault had collapsed, ran away and took his own life. However, the racket and the dust were caused by the collapsing scaffolding, the vault remaining intact and beautiful. Only the builder never saw it.

Between 1708–1711 the Holy Staircase was constructed on the southern side of the church. It is made of red marble, and has the remains of saints buried in it, their names on the brass crosses by the sides of the staircase. Below there is an imitation of Bethlehem Chapel with an almost life-size sculpture of the Holy Family. It is said that whoever comes to pray will have a lucky thought.

ic elements can still be found in the interior. The monastery was damaged during several further military campaigns (for instance in 1742 the French drank all the wine the monks had been storing for 19 years), as well as by fires, before being abolished in 1785. In 1789 the facility began to be used for the incurably ill. The sanatorium was here until the 1920's. In 1975 a museum was opened in the complex.

THE POLICE MUSEUM

The Museum of the Police of the Czech Republic (photo above) is situated in the complex of the former monastery today. At first, from 1975, there was the Museum of the National Security Corps, which replaced the Museum of the Borderline Guard and Internal Guard. A combat hall of fame with a plaque commemorating 386 members of the police force who died on duty was part of this exhibition. There were also documents which were a product of their time, documenting the building of socialism for example. On 12 April 1991 the exhibition we can see today was opened to the public. It is more oriented towards daily training and education. We find out about the work of the police and see collections documenting the development of the police force from the formation of the country to the present day. The museum has two exhibition halls, and there are about thirty themed exhibitions a year. The all-year-round programme of traffic education for children is really remarkable, from theory to practice, there is a children's traffic playground at their disposal. Moreover, there are lectures and specialized seminars.

The interior of the church (photo below) outstandingly decorated in Baroque style, created in the 1730's. The main altar, dating from 1872, is in Neo-Gothic style.

The Austin Friar monastery, to the west of the church, was damaged and burnt by the Hussites in 1420. The complex was restored as much as possible, but another disaster, the Thirty-Years War, came along. The monastery has retained its original layout even after a Baroque reconstruction. Some Goth-

Above left: the church vaulting
Centre left: Karlov and its Gothic fortification

GEMS OF GOTHIC PAINTING

NA SLOVANECH MONASTERY

A MONUMENT REBORN

Below Emauzy, on the right bank of the Vltava in Palacký Square (Palackého náměstí) there is a monument commemorating František Palacký (*photo above*), a Czech historian, politician and one of the most important figures of the national revival movement of the 19th century. The bronze statue is the work of the sculptor Stanislav Sucharda, dating from 1905–1907, and crated in cooperation with Josef Mařatka. The statue of the seated figure accompanied by various allegorical figures mainly bears the characteristics of Art Nouveau, but also of impressionism and symbolism. This is not surprising, as the authors were inspired by the work of their great idol, French sculptor August Rodin. Mařatka had been his direct pupil. During the occupation the monument was a thorn in the Nazis' side so they ordered it to be destroyed, but the bronze sculptures were re-cast.

A rarity among Czech medieval monasteries is the one that bears the name Na Slovanech, or V Emauzích. Charles IV initiated its establishment in 1347, and insisted that the liturgical language used should not be Latin but Old Slavic. Therefore he invited an order of Slavic Benedictines from the south of Europe, whose members were able to speak the language. In accordance with tradition, the emperor himself and other important guests attended the ceremonial consecration of the monastery and the church on Easter Monday, 1372. Because the Gospel about the meeting between Christ and his disciples on the road to Emmaus was read in churches on that day, the monastery was later called Emauzy or V Emauzích. It soon became renowned as a centre of learning and art. Around 1360 a valued painting of the so-called Crucifixion of Emmaus was created here, approximately at the same time as the exceptionally valuable Gothic wall paintings in the cloister of the paradise garden,

depicting scenes from Old and New Testaments. These are thought to have been painted by the same group of court painters who worked on the decoration of Karlštejn Castle. It is the most extensive cycle of wall paintings in Bohemia, 73 paintings altogether, and one of the most valuable relics of Czech Gothic painting. In 1395 the local monks produced the Glagolitic version of the so-called Reims Gospel, which was in 1546 acquired by French kings, who subsequently swore an oath on it during their coronation in Reims until 1782. In 1419 the monastery was seized by the Hussites, but because most of the Benedictines accepted their teaching, it was spared, unlike the others. In 1455 the first and only Hussite monastery in Bohemia was founded here. In 1636 Benedictine monks from the Spanish Montserrat were introduced here, being replaced in 1880 by monks of the same order, but from Beuron in Germany. In 1941 the Nazis occupied the monastery and used it for their own purposes. During an a

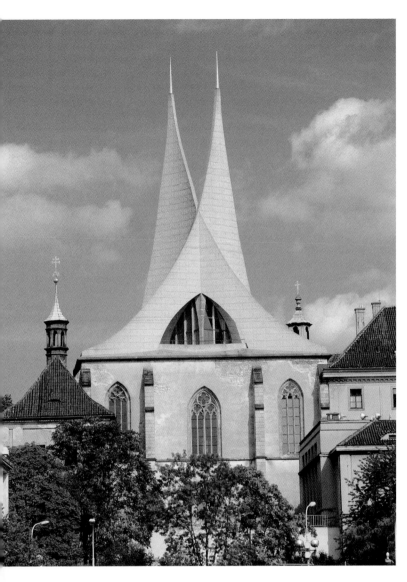

Opposite Na Slovanech Monastery is the Church of St. Johanes Nepomucensis on the Rock (kostel sv. Jana Nepomuckého na Skalce), standing in a dominant position on a raised terrace above Vyšehrad Street. Built between 1730–1739, it represents an excellent piece of architecture by the master of Czech high Baroque, Kilián Ignác Dienzenhofer, a central structure with the nave of an octagonal ground-plan. The dynamics of the richly shaped frontage are heightened by two obliquely positioned prismatic towers, as well as by two flights of steps, built by Antonín Karel Schmidt in 1776. He also created the garden, which is encircled by a stone wall and decorated with statues by Ignác František Dienzenhofer. A wooden statue of St. Johanes Nepomucensis by Jan Brokof, dating from 1682, was used as a model for the famous sculpture of the saint on Charles Bridge. It became an iconographic model, from which later statues of the saint were made in Bohemia as well as in other European countries.

ck by allied bombers on 14 February 1945 e complex burned down, but was rebuilt ter the war was over. The greatest dam- ;e was suffered by the monastery Church ^f the Virgin Mary, St. Hieronymus and the avic saints, which consisted of a Gothic sled hall dating from the 14th century, ba- quized and made up with a pair of spires the 17th century. In 1966–1969 these were placed by a pair of architecturally success- l majestic concrete wings, resembling sails a ship; creating a perfect balance between edieval architecture and its twentieth cen- ry sibling.

The monastery is a four-wing Gothic struc- re surrounding a paradise garden with

a cloister. Another floor, added in 1640, has a Gothic royal chapel, a capitular hall and a stucco-decorated Baroque refectory.

The most interesting sections of the monas- tery are open to the public.

A KINGDOM
OF BLOSSOMS

THE BOTANICAL GARDENS "NA SLUPI"

**THE KARLŠTEJN
OF PRAGUE**

A section called Karlštejn is
a remarkable part of the
Botanical Gardens. This
romantic corner was artificially
created in 1904. We see
a quaint grouping of rockeries
here *(photo below right)*, there
is even a cave.

A beautiful realm of blossoms is found in
the Botanical Gardens "Na Slupi", not
far from Charles Square (Karlovo náměstí).
The gardens are quite young, nevertheless,
several predecessors. The first botanical gar-

dens, dating from as early as the 14th cent
ry, covered the area of the present-day ce
tral post-office as early as the 14th centur
Charles IV himself liked to visit them. Othe
botanical gardens, which occupied the si
of the later Straka Academy in Lesser Tow
were tended by the Jesuits from 1600 unt
the abolition of the Jesuit order in 1773. The
in 1778 botanical gardens were establishe
on the initiative of Marie Therése at Smícho
in the place of the Slavata (Jesuit) Garde
These gardens had a pavilion, designed b
Dienzenhofer, a summerhouse and a fou
tain, and were among the most beautiful i
the country. In fact, the collections of plar
and flowers were among the best in Europ
However, neither the quickly growing indu
try nor the frequent floods suited them. I
1902 the garden ceased to exist, the plot wa
built up, and a section of the area was desi
nated for the Dienzenhofer Orchards.

At that time the gardens we can see to
day were already developing. In 1845 th

Czech Society for the Cultivation of Gardening established the so-called Social Garden on the sloping terrain of the fruit orchards Na Slupi. Greenhouses were constructed in 1882. In 1897 the state bought the gardens and gave them to Ferdinand-Charles University. The university had Czech and German sections, and so did the botanical garden, a lower and slightly larger Czech garden and a German garden above it. Professor Ladislav Čelakovský became the director of the Czech section. Plants from the perishing Smíchov Gardens were brought here. Greenhouses and other buildings of the botanical institute gradually developed. Alpine rockeries, collections of swamp, water and grove plants were established, an arboretum with ponds was formed. During the time of the protectorate on 17 November 1939 Czech universities and colleges were closed by the Nazis. So the Czech botanical gardens lost their purpose and a year later they were attached to the German gardens. During an air-raid on 14 February 1945 some of the greenhouses in the upper part of the garden were damaged. After World War Two ended, the Botanical Department of the Biological Faculty of Charles University (Faculty of Natural Sciences today) took over care of the garden. Between 1946–1949 the damaged greenhouses were replaced by new ones.

MIGHTY VICTORIA

The Botanical Gardens offer a really varied selection to a keen visitor. A large collection of native Czech plants can be viewed, including medicinal herbs. The cacti collection is also renowned. The greenhouses are interconnected, and so we gradually learn about the vegetation of subtropical and tropical areas. The massive Amazonian Victoria is an often-admired rarity. It is a water lily, discovered by the Czech botanist Tadeáš Haenke in 1801. The huge leaves can support a baby. However, it is in bloom for only one day a year. Another item of interest is an enormous bonsai, the only specimen of its kind in the world.

Photos left and opposite page
below left: cacti collections

REMINDERS OF HEROISM
AND BETRAYAL

THE CHURCH
OF ST. CONSTANTINE AND METHODIUS

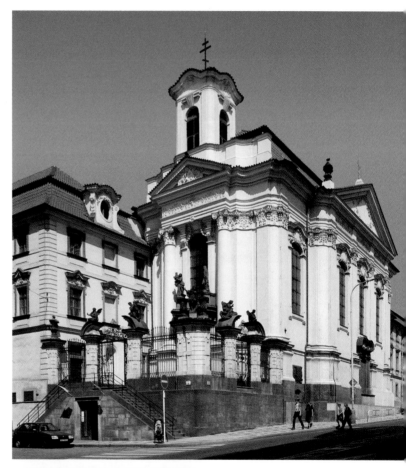

ST. WENCESLAS'S SPA

There used to be a small castle of Wenceslas IV in Dittrich Street near the church, later used by barefoot Austin Friars in the construction of a monastery. The ruler took advantage of the curative spa waters of the spring Pučka (the water was reputed to be especially good for gout). The king had disputes with the high aristocracy, once his entourage was even attacked and Wenceslas IV was put in the council jail. After fifteen weeks in jail he was beginning to lose hope. At one time he went for a bath at the spa near Charles Bridge and when he came out he asked his guards to be allowed a walk. They let him go alone, after all, he was not properly dressed, so where could he run? At that moment a little boat with a girl in it appeared on the river. She introduced herself as Susannah from the spa. The king quickly jumped into the boat and the girl rowed upstream to a place from which they could get to Wenceslas's castle near Kunratice. The king rewarded Susannah, he had the old spa near the bridge pulled down and gave the new one to her. And St. Wenceslas's Spa at Zderaz? It made its mark in history in 1848; people assembled there to signal the beginning of a revolution.

The crypt wall of the Church of St. Constantine and Methodius *(photo above)* in Ressl Street (Resslova ulice), pockmarked with bullet holes *(photo opposite page below)*, is a reminder of the dramatic climax of a story of heroism and betrayal. In 1942 seven paratroopers, sent to the occupied Czechoslovakia from England, were hiding inside the church – including those who had assassinated the Deputy Protector of the German Reich, Reinhard Heydrich. Within a few hours they were supposed to move to another

One of the many villages that merged with the newly established New Town was Zderaz. The name was allegedly derived from Zderad, a favourite of King Vratislav I, who was willfully murdered during the siege of Brno. The village is commemorated by the street name "Na Zderaze" and above all by the Church of St. Wenceslas *(photo above)*. The Romanesque church was constructed between 1170 and 1180 as a parish church of the village of Zderaz. In the first half of the 14th century the church was enlarged in late Gothic style; the remnants of a tower and a nave of the original Romanesque building have been preserved in the western façade; in the front we can clearly see two double Romanesque windows. In 1623 the barefoot Austin Friars acquired the church and built the adjacent monastery. They used the remains of a small Gothic castle, established by sovereign Wenceslas IV in the 14th century. In 1785 the monastery was abolished and converted into a jail named St. Wenceslas Jail. After the jail was moved to Pankrác in 1893, the former monastery was pulled down and replaced with residential tenement houses. Fortunately, the church was spared, and after re-gothization in 1909 re-consecrated. Since 1926 the church has belonged to the Czechoslovak Hussite Church. The beautiful late Gothic vault, dating from 1586–1587, was made by Karel Mělnický. The new altar and the pews are the work of František Bílek from 1930.

hiding place outside Prague, but somedy betrayed them to the Gestapo. On 18 ne Gestapo and SS forces besieged the urch. After a desperate fight lasting severhours the paratroopers themselves chose ath. Since 1947 these heroes have been mmemorated by a memorial plaque, on ich are depicted their names and portraits relief by Bělský. In the crypt, still marked h bullet holes, there is the National Merial to the Victims of the Heydrichiade *oto above)*; the period during which the zis unleashed horrible reprisals for the assination. The events are also commemted by the nearby Gorazd Street which s named after the Orthodox bishop, Matěj lík Gorazd, who was executed for giving lter to the paratroopers.

he Baroque single-nave church was orially dedicated to St. Charles of Boromea. as built in 1730–1739, together with the jacent emeritus house for elderly priests, h designed by Bayer. The frontage, partined by semi-columns and pillasters, with riangular gable and spire rising from the c, is a beautiful example of the high Baque era. In the interior we can view Baque frescoes of the legend of St. Charles Schöpf, surrounded by stucco decoration Palliardi. The elevated terrace on which church was built was formed by terrain

modifications and the lowering of the street in 1885. The little garden by the entrance is framed by an original Baroque lattice. The pillars in which it is set are decorated with sculptures of angels. In 1783 the church was closed, but in 1934–1935 it was restored as a Czech Orthodox Church and dedicated to St. Constantine and Methodius. After 1783 the emeritus house was used as a barracks for almost a hundred years, before being given to the Czech Technical College in 1866.

GINGER
AND FRED

THE DANCING HOUSE

JIRÁSEK SQUARE
(JIRÁSKOVO NÁMĚSTÍ)

From the Dancing House we see a square which bears the name of one of the most productive Czech writers, Alois Jirásek. His most famous novels were inspired by Czech history, and so were his plays. In all his work Jirásek tried to strengthen the nation's self-confidence. In 1903 he settled in house No 1 on the corner of the square and Ressl Street. Today this is commemorated by a memorial plaque. Jirásek's statue *(photo above)*, created by Pokorný and Fragner, was unveiled in 1960. Jirásek Bridge (Jiráskův most) has an interesting history. Built between 1929–1933 according to a design by Vlastislav Hofman and František Mencl, it connected the New Town and Smíchov. A suitable place for its construction was long searched for. Initially it was supposed to be a continuation of Myslík Street (Myslíkova ulice), even the abutments had been installed. Eventually the plan chosen was the one which meant that the corner house would not have to be pulled down (the same house that was damaged during the air-raid and the site of the future Dancing House. Unfortunately, the valuable Dienzenhofer Pavilion on the opposite bank had to be demolished. It is made of reinforced concrete and is 297m long.

The Dancing House on the corner of Jirásek Square and Rašín Embankment (Jiráskovo náměstí and Rašínovo nábřeží) is one of the most frequently discussed pieces of architecture in Prague. Its critics pointed at its excessive complexity, and the fact that it does not fit its surroundings in the least. On the other hand, its admirers were enthusiastic about the originality of the structure, which it even received a prestigious international award. For many years, all that existed there was a vacant space caused by an American air-raid on 14 February 1945. Most of the rubble had been cleared away by 1946, but only in 1955 it was decided that the site should not be built up so that the road could be widened. However the demolition of the remaining brickwork took until 1960. Years of red-tape followed, involving piles of paperwork every time a request was made for a construction permit for a building up this spot. In 1992 events gathered momentum, when the plot was purchased by Nationale Nederlanden, an insurance company. The highly avantgarde design of Slovenian architect Milunič was selected from the designs submitted. The investor recommended that he should cooperate with one of the world famous architects in the project, so the American Frank O. Gehry got involved. In June 1996 the administrative building of Nationale Nederlanden, known as the Dancing House, was opened. The structure is made of reinforced concrete, and there are 99 original facade panels. The building was named after its two towers, called Ginger and Fred after legendary dancers Ginger Rogers and Fred Astaire, the stars of American musicals of the 1920's and 1930's. Fred is the straight concrete tower, while Ginger is elegantly curved. On top of the straight tower is a cupola with a construction of metal pipes coated with stainless wirework, as if veiled by hair, this represents the head of the Medusa.

CUBIST HOUSES

**FLOATING DOWN
THE RIVER...**

The famous settlement called "Under-the-rock" (Podskalí) because of its position below Vyšehrad Rock, used to be on the bank of the Vltava as early as the 12th century. It became part of New Town in 1348. It was a distinctive settlement of people who made their living floating timber on the River Vltava and its tributaries, selling and processing timber, as well as mining sand, fishing and selling ice. The settlement vanished during the construction of the embankment at the turn of the 19th and 20th centuries. Today the only reminder of it is an old customs-house (No 412) in the small park near Rašín Embankment (Rašínovo nábřeží – *photo above*), in which duty used to be paid for floated timber. It is a two-storied building dating from around 1500 with a Gothic core, later modified several times. Above the entrance it is decorated with the New Town emblem from 1671.

Above right: tenement House Hodek
Below right: a house in Rašín Embankment (Rašínovo nábřeží)

The famous Spanish painter Pablo Picasso was the father of the art style called Cubism, which was born as a reaction against impressionism and attempted greater scientific veracity. He was the first to suppress atmosphere, colour and curved lines in his paintings, concentrating instead on the structure of objects and shapes. The basis of cubism is the cube, cubus in Latin, its decomposition, division and re-composition. This style was used mainly in painting; but one of the first Europeans to apply these processes in sculpture was a Czech, Otto Guttfreund. Czech artists took it a step further, as the only ones who managed to apply cubist principles to architecture. Thus an expression arose, special and unique in the European context. Cubist architecture with three-dimensional façades formed by crystal-like shapes and motifs of cubes and pyramids can, outside the Czech Republic, only be found in Austria.

In this respect Prague has a lot to offer. Besides Black Mother of God House (dům U Černé Matky Boží) by Josef Gočár in Celetná Street and blocks of flats by Otto Novotný in Bílek Street (Bílkova ulice), the cubist villas by Josef Chochol below Vyšehrad are among the most beautiful and characteristic. At Rašín Embankment (Rašínovo nábřeží) there are three interconnected hou

A ROMANTIC TUNNEL

Between New Town (Nové město) and Podolí rises Vyšehrad Rock, which at one point falls almost straight down all the way to the River Vltava. For centuries it stood in the way of the construction of a road on the right bank of the river; this stage of the journey had to be made either by a detour around the top or by a boat on the river. Finally between 1902–1905 a tunnel was bored through the rock at the expense of the city. It is 32m long and 9m high. The designers, whose aim was to emphasize the closeness of the ancient seat of the Přemyslide family, decorated the tunnel in Romantic style, with cylindrical towers and battlements, imitating the architecture of medieval castles. To this day we can still see the watchman's house and a building that was used for collecting the toll for passing through the tunnel.

Left: *a Cubist house in Libuše's Street*
Below: *a detail of cubist decoration*

s (Nos 42, 47 and 71), which not only have
cubist façade, but also Cubist interiors and
Cubist fence around the dooryards. The
egmental bay and the staircase leading to it
re also impressive. House No 49 in neigh-
ouring Libuše's Street (Libušina ulice), with
s stylishly conceived garden, was created in
similar style by the same architect. In near-
y Neklan Street (Neklanova ulice) we can
nd probably the most beautiful creation of
hochol's, the tenement Hodek House (No
8) built in 1913–1914. The loggias are set
a sharp corner, which is highly prominent,
s are the attic cornice and the three-dimen-
ional segmentation of space.

A WORLD OF LEGENDS
AND MYTHS

VYŠEHRAD

ŠEMÍK'S LEAP

One of the most famous legends connected with Vyšehrad is about Horymír, a member of the Czech lower nobility, and his loyal horse Šemík. Horymír, who had been sentenced to death, saved his life by jumping from the bulwark on his horse. Horymír survived, the horse did not. The legend is so vivid that Šemík even has a grave in Neumětely near Prague, in the Czech Karst area (Český kras), close to the redoubt of his master.

In Vyšehrad, there was once a Stone Age settlement. By the first half of the 10th century the princely castle of the Přemyslides stood here. However, the notion that the first Přemyslides resided here remains just a romantic idea, in fact Vyšehrad is not as old as Prague Castle. Vyšehrad used to guard the entrance to Prague. Deniers from the Vyšehrad mint, dating between 992–1012, are the oldest proof of its existence. The first written record comes from 1003. In 1067, after disputes with the Bishop of Prague, Prince Vratislav II moved here from Prague Castle for good, converting Vyšehrad into a splendid residence. In 1070 he established a chapter and the Church of St. Peter and

Paul, the main church of Vyšehrad. Its mod el was St. Peter's Cathedral in Rome. Vrati lav II himself helped with the construction carrying twelve baskets of stones and clay t the site on his shoulders. A fragment of a wa with a window is all that has survived fron the triple-nave Romanesque basilica. Some time before 1129 Soběslav I enlarged th church. After a fire in 1249, the church wa reconstructed in early Gothic style. Anoth er reconstruction followed after 1396, whe the church was modified in high Gothic styl with five naves. In 1420 the Hussites plur dered the place, the church was not repaire until 1495. Between 1723–1729 it was ba roquized. In 1885 purist re-gothization be

THE PROPHECY OF LIBUŠE

The oldest Czech legends speak about the forefather Čech (Czech), who arrived here with his people, looked at the landscape around him and, enchanted by its beauty and abundance, made the historic decision to stay. His successor Krok, whose seat was in Budeč, looked for a new place to stay. On a high rock he built a fortress, which he called Vyšehrad (derived from Czech for a 'high castle'). After he died one of his three daughters, Libuše, was elected princess and seated on the stone throne to rule over the people. Ploughman Přemysl of Stadice was summoned, so that men would not feel humiliated at having a woman as their ruler. Libuše had the gift of prophecy. It was at Vyšehrad that she foretold the existence of Prague: "I can see a great city, its fame will reach the stars one day! Well, if it is the will of the gods, let it happen. Therefore I myself will lay the foundation stone of that city, and then let it grow and flourish towards the glory of my race and the future times." The following day she sent out her servants, who came across two men hewing a doorsill ('práh' in Czech). Exactly on that spot Libuše founded the city, which she called Praha.

Above: *the sculpture of Přemysl and Libuše*
Below left: *Leopold's Gate*

gan from a design by Mocker. In 1902–1903 the church was given a Neo-Gothic façade with a pair of spires. Only the torso of the original early Gothic nave has survived in the church. The furnishing is in Art Nouveau and Neo-Gothic styles. A rare panel painting of the Virgin Mary from around 1350 can be found in the interior. To the south of the church in Soběslav Street there are the remains of the walls of the early Romanesque Basilica of St. Lawrence (bazilika sv. Vavřince), dating from the 11th century.

St. Martin's Rotunda (rotunda sv. Martina – *photo above*), dating from the same century, is the only building in Vyšehrad that has kept its original Romanesque form. It is the oldest building of its kind in Prague. During the reign of Josef II it was abolished and until 1848 served as a home for the poor, as well as a storehouse. It got its present-day appearance during a modification in 1878.

After 1140 Soběslav I moved to Prague Castle and Vyšehrad fell to neglect. It was Charles IV who can be credited with its renovation. He decreed that the coronation journey of every Czech king was to begin in Vyšehrad. In 1348–1350 he had the grounds fortified with a new stone wall. The remains of a once spectacular gate, which used to be called Špička, and of a Gothic palace also come from the era of Charles IV. In 1448

George of Poděbrady seized Vyšehrad, and from there he gained control of the whole Prague. After his time the grounds went to ruin. Reminders of the earliest era are provided by the remains of a Romanesque bridge and the ruins of a Gothic guardhouse, called Libuše Spa, on the rock above the river. According to legend Libuše used to bathe here with her lovers before throwing them over the rock.

ETERNAL RESTING PLACE
OF THE FAMOUS

VYŠEHRAD

Many years passed before the old fortress at Vyšehrad was replaced with a new one. The decision was made in 1654, but the work on the new Baroque fort went on until 1678, by which time Vyšehrad had something like its present-day appearance. In 1742 the French seized Vyšehrad without a fight and repaired the fort. Casemate also forms part

THE RESCUE

In 1744 the Prussians seized Vyšehrad and decided to blow it up before they left Prague. Fortunately, one of the Prussian deserters gave the plan away. The locals began to guard the citadel carefully and so they noticed that the Hussar regiment arrived with the chief explosives engineer. Three citizens then quickly descended to the underground, where they found two slow-burning matches, leading to 133 barrels of gunpowder. They managed to avert the explosion, but their troubles were not yet over. The following day the Prussians returned to try again. The people of Vyšehrad resisted them openly and their adversaries began to shoot. But one of the women resorted to a little trick and shouted that Austrian soldiers were nearing Vyšehrad from the east. The Prussians took fright and left, and the fort remained intact.

Above: *the Vyšehrad emblem*

THE SLAVÍN OF VYŠEHRAD

Vyšehrad Cemetery is definitely the most famous one in the Czech Republic. At first it was just a small burial ground, but in the 1860's there was a clamour for a dignified eternal resting place for the great figures of the Czech nation. Primarily the newly-established association of Czech writers, called Svatobor, promoted the idea. Many spots in the area around Prague were considered (Budeč, Levý Hradec, Liběchov), before Vyšehrad was agreed upon. Even before the Slavín of Vyšehrad was established, Wenceslas Hanka, a Slavist and the author of Manuscripts (the famous literary forgery), was buried here in 1861. In 1869 the burial grounds were enlarged according to the design by Viktor Barvitius, later followed by further enlargement and modification including the arcades and Slavín, the work of Antonín Wiehl. The most dominant feature of the area is Slavín, situated in the eastern part, the joint headstone of the most deserving men and women of the nation. On the sarcophagus with its winged genius there is an inscription saying: "Although they died, they still speak."

of the complex, the passageways and rooms serving as a storage place for weapons and an assembly area for the garrison.

Vyšehrad is usually entered from the direction of Pankrác by Na Pankráci Street. Walking through the Baroque Tábor Gate (Táborská brána), which dates from around 1655, we pass Špička on the way to Leopold Gate (Leopoldova brána), through which we enter the fort itself. After passing St. Martin's Rotunda (rotunda sv. Martina) we arrive at Brick (New or Chotek) Gate (Cihelná, Nová or Chotkova brána), one of the most beautiful examples of Empire style architecture in Prague. It was built in 1841.

At the Rotunda we turn to the centre of Vyšehrad. On the right-hand side we can see the former farmstead of Vyšehrad chapter, on the left-hand side the building which houses the Vyšehrad canons. The Neo-Gothic New Deanery (Nové děkanství) dates from 1877. On the edge of the park there is the so-called Devil's Column (Čertův sloup – *photo left*), broken into three pieces. Although some romantics claim that it is a timekeeping column used by the old Slavs or the milestone of a Roman road, it probably is the remains of a public pillory. Legend has it that the devil broke it into pieces in anger after he lost a bet with a priest, the priest completing his service before the devil managed to bring the column from Rome.

The most dominant feature of the complex is the Church of St. Peter and Paul (kostel sv. Petra a Pavla). The Vyšehrad Cemetery with its Slavín memorial *(main photo)* is the burial ground of many famous Czech people, and a popular destination for visitors. In the Vyšehrad Gardens we can see the sculpture of Přemysl and Libuše by Josef Wenceslas Myslbek, as well as other sculptures from the 19th century. We should also visit to the permanent exhibitions; the casemate and Gorlice Hall (sál Gorlice), in which six statues from Charles Bridge are found, are both open to the public. The Information Centre is found in the torso of Špička Gate, and above Libuše's Spa is the Vyšehrad Gallery.

Above: *the graves of Smetana and Dvořák*

LIKE NOAH'S
ARK

THE CHURCH OF THE SACRED
HEART OF LORD

Not far from Žižkov Tower (Žižkovská věž) in the park George of Poděbrady Square (náměstí Jiřího z Poděbrad) is the amazing and unique Church of the Sacred Heart of Lord (kostel Nejsvětějšího Srdce Páně). Deservedly considered to be the finest modern religious building in the area of the capital, it was designed by a professor of the Academy of Applied Arts, Slovenian-born architect Josip Plečnik, who is best-known for the most recent modifications of Prague Castle. The church was built between 1928–1932. Its designer was inspired by the architecture of antiquity, and like the ancient temples, this Vinohrady church was supposed to be surrounded by pillars.

steel tubes were erected (two with a diameter of 4.8 m, the third with a diameter of 6.5 m). The two smaller tubes reached the height of 134m, the longer one, with its aerial extension, reached 216 meters. The Žižkov Tower weighs approximately 11 800 tons, it is about seventy times heavier than the Petřín Look-out Tower. At first the modern construction had many opponents, citizens of the capital finding it hard to get used to a new dominanting feature. Today the tower is an accepted part of Prague and the number of its visitors increases every day. They are also interested in the small artefacts by artist David Černý – his figures "climb" the steel construction...

BY LIFT TO A LOOK-OUT

The television tower in Žižkov is open to the public. Next to the entrance there are two high-speed lifts, connecting the ground floor with three cabins situated one above the other. In the lowest one, 66 meters above the ground, there is a café and restaurant, from which Prague can be viewed through glass walls. An even more breath-taking view opens up from the glassed-in observation terraces 93 meters above the foot of the tower. When the weather is fine we can see not only the famous monuments of Prague, but also an area extending about 100 kilometres.

Plečnik was inspired by Noah's Ark, and the church does resemble a ship with high rising sides and an unusually broad spire, taking up the whole width of the church, and symbolizing a mast with blowing sails. The interior is a single space with a caisson ceiling, creating the impression of a lower deck.

Another prominent feature, located within the sight of the church in Mahler Gardens is the Žižkov Television Tower, the work of Wenceslas Aulický, Jiří Kozák and Alex Bém. The design was completed in 1984, and the construction itself took place between 1985 and 1992. The massive structure had to be anchored. At first a 4m thick and 30m wide concrete panel was inserted to a depth of 15 meters. Above it three

THE MEMORIAL PLACE
OF HISTORY

THE NATIONAL MONUMENT IN ŽIŽKOV

Many years ago there used to be deep impenetrable forests here. After the forests were cut down, Charles IV had vineyards established on the hillsides. These remained until the end of the Thirty-Years War. The names of the former vineyards (Ohrada, Pražačka, Smetanka, Perníkářka etc.) have been kept as local place-names to this day. Vineyards also covered the hill that rises distinctly from the landscape. This hill is called Vítkov, after Vítek

THE ARMY MUSEUM

Just below the National Monument at the foot of Vítkov Hill, there is a building that houses the Historical Institute of the Army of the Czech Republic and the Army Museum *(photo above)* with permanent exhibitions dedicated to the history of the Czech Army and to the history of the resistance movement from the beginning of World War One to the end of World War Two.

f Hora, the owner of one of the vineyards. It was here that the Hussites, led by Jan Žižka, fought a victorious battle against the superior crusader army on 14 July 1420. And so the place entered Czech history. People began to call it Chalice (Kalich), then Tábor, eventually the name Žižkov took hold. In 1868 a large meeting took place here, the 15 000 participants manifesting their support for the patriotic movement. In the same year one of the foundation stones of the National Theatre was quarried out here. And so, when a place was being sought for the construction of the National Monument, Žižkov was unequivocally chosen. Two architectural competitions were held and Jan Kotěra's pupil, Jan Zázvorka, was awarded the first prize. One of the requirements was that the National Monument (main photo) should be a dignified counterpart to Prague Castle and Vyšehrad. Its contruction took place between 1929 and 1933, but the ceremonial opening was postponed, as more time was needed to construct sufficient roads, promenades and complete the decoration of the interior. The interior is the work of Max Švabinský, Jan Štursa, Jaroslav Horejc and Karel Obrovský, amongst others. The National Monument, a massive building 142m long, 31.5m high and almost 28m wide was opened to the public on the 20th anniversary of the founding of the republic, on 28 October 1938. The fast-approaching Nazi occupation was a pointer to the cheqered history the Monument would experience. The establishment of the Protectorate saw the Monument closed, some of the in-

terior decorations stolen, and its metal melted for military purposes. Army materials were stored in the monument. Thanks to the courage of anonymous Czech patriots many valuable relics were saved. The events of February 1948, with the Communists gaining power, also meant changes for the National Monument. It was as if the section dedicated to pre-War Czechoslovakia had never existed; many exhibits were removed and gradually replaced by communist artefacts. Urns containing the ashes of important Communist functionaries were placed in the Monument. The embalmed body of the first Communist president, Klement Gottwald, became the central exhibit. His embalming was of such poor quality that the stench soon emanating from the "mausoleum" became unbearable. Even strong ventilation did not help. An unbelievable circus commenced; during the day "the leader of the working-class" was displayed to the public, during the night a team of specialists intensively worked on the body. Eventually this absurd charade came to an end, the body was cremated and the urn containing the ashes was exhibited in the Monument. In 1990 the urn was taken over by Communist functionaries; the same happened to the other figures of the past regime.

This remarkable monument slowly ceases to be connected with the Communist regime in people's minds. After all, it was originally intended to be "for the whole nation". In the year 2009 the National Museum opened here a permanent exhibition called The Crossroads of Czech and Czechoslovak Statehood.

On the anniversary of the Battle of Vítkov on 14 July 1950 a colossal bronze equestrian statue was unveiled in front of the National Monument, a memorial to Jan Žižka of Trocnov. The sculptor Bohumil Kafka (1878–1942), a professor of the Academy of Fine Art in Prague, created the largest equestrian statue in the world. The height of the statue is 22m including the pedestal, and it weighs 16.5 tons. In fact even the details make one wonder; the hand of the rider weighs 195 kg, the sword 110 kg and the mace 52 kg!

Above left: the look-out arbour in Žižkov
Facing page below left: *the detail of the door of the monument*

PRAGUE
1:432

LANGWEIL'S MODEL OF PRAGUE

THE CITY MUSEUM

The idea of establishing a City Museum emerged for the first time at a municipal council meeting as early as 1877. Within three years a committee, led by historian Wácslav Wladiwoj Tomek, had been established. In 1883 the museum's board, led by Dr. Miroslav Tyrš, the famous co-founder of Sokol (a sports organization), organized the first small collections. They were exhibited in the former café in Poříčí Park. Naturally, the café pavilion, built in 1878, was not big enough, and so between 1896–1898 a New Renaissance building, designed by Antonín Wiehle and Antonín Balšánek, was constructed. The museum collections were not strictly defined. Unique objects covering all branches of human activity were being collected, continuously purchased or donated. Nowadays there are about half a million different exhibits, spanning the time from the prehistoric town settlement to the present-day. The museum is open to the public, and short-term exhibitions and lectures are held there.

Langweil's model of Prague *(main photo)*, currently displayed at the Museum of the City of Prague *(photo opposite page above)*, near the Florenc bus station, holds a privileged position among the vast number of other museum exhibits. A three-dimensional model of Paris was displayed in Prague in 1826 and Antonín Langweil, then a servant in the university library, was enthralled. This was the crucial moment in his career. He thought of nothing but the construc-

tion of a model of Prague and devoted a his free time to it. He followed a city pla drawn between 1811–1815 by Josef Jü tner published by the National Museum i 1820. Langweil built 600 models of the Ol Town houses within three years, and the displayed his work for the first time. Ther was a positive response so he carried o working, even more eagerly. The Old Tow churches, Jewish Town, Lesser Town an Hradčany were added. In 1834 he showe

ANTONÍN LANGWEIL

Antonín Langweil (1791–1837) did not live a long life, but he has become immortal through his work. The son of a peasant from the town of Žatec, he briefly stayed in Český Krumlov after finishing his studies. He was interested in drawing, so he left south Bohemia to study at the Academy of Fine Art in Vienna. In 1819 he settled in Prague to found a lithographic workshop. Lack of money, however, forced him to sell his equipment to the printer Schönfeld and to close down his business. He was employed at Schönfeld's for some time, but in 1822 he left to work as a servant in the university library. It meant having a roof over his head, but minimal wages. However, he could indulge his hobbies, painting miniature portraits and vistas, which were more important to him. Inspired by the three-dimensional model of Paris, he started constructing the work of his life, a model of Prague. Only the problem of sustaining a wife and five daughters remained unsolved. He even put his work aside for a while and asked the Emperor himself for help. After waiting for three years he received 150 guldens. By that time he was already seriously ill. He tried to sell the model, offering it to Count Chotek in order to cover at least the costs, which included the materials (carton and inks) and labour (plumbing, carpentry, lithography, and turnery). Chotek negotiated with the President of the Museum, Kašpar Šternberk, but he thought the price of 800 guldens was too high. So Langweil died poor.

his model to the public again. And again it met with general approval. However, Langweil's health was deteriorating and he desperately lacked money. He was forced to stop work on the model, unable to finish it before he died quite young of tuberculosis and oedema. He left an extraordinary model covering an area of 20 square metres. The buildings were made with total precision on an unusual scale of 1:432. Langweil's model of Prague has become a much sought-after tourist attraction, and, moreover, an irreplaceable study material and teaching aid for all generations of art historians. Only this model enables us to know what the houses, indeed what whole parts of Prague originally looked like, especially as most of the buildings have either been rebuilt or pulled down.

Below: the detail of the model

IN PRAISE
OF FUNCTIONALISM

THE EXHIBITION PALACE

LIKE A BURNING TORCH

Late in the evening on 14 August 1974, the press agencies issued a strict embargo on the news that the Exhibition Palace had caught fire. Nobody could imagine what a frightful sight it would be. The palace resembled a huge burning torch. It was indeed one of the most extensive fires in modern history of Prague. It was reported at 21:33, seven minutes later the fire fighters arrived. Initially, only the fourth and fifth floors were on fire but due to the hardboard and wooden partitions, as well as the large amount of files in the offices, the fire spread fast. Even water from the Vltava had to be used, as more and more fire brigades even from outside Prague were summoned to help. The floors collapsed and heavy safes fell through. Only at daybreak did the fire brigades manage to put out the huge fire, apparently caused by an electric cooker someone had forgotten to switch off. Only a gigantic burnt skeleton remained of the whole palace.

Practicality and functionality, these were the chief requirements for the Exhibition Palace (Veletržní palác) which was meant to become a kind of a world trade centre. This goal was never accomplished, but nevertheless, the most distinguished example of Czech functionalism was erected at Holešovice near the Exhibition Grounds (Výstaviště). It is one of the most important buildings of modern European architecture. The renowned French architect Le Corbusier, fascinated by the size of the Palace, called it "a magnificent work". Its history dates back to 1924, when a competition was announced, concerning the construction of an exhibition complex. A plot of 33 000 square metres near the railway station at Holešovice and the river wharf was eventually chosen. Two designs, one by architect Oldřich Tyl (1883 to 1939) and the other by Josef Fuchs (1894 to 1979), were declared the winners. Thus both men worked together on the execution of the project, which began in 1925. However, only about a quarter of the origi-

nal plan was carried out. For example, a other identical palace was supposed to ha been built where the Parkhotel is situated day. Administrative buildings, a post-offic a telephone exchange building, resident homes and a hotel were also supposed have been part of the project. Even a goo station was included in the constructi plans. The palace was officially opene on 25 September 1928 and a collection paintings, entitled the Slavic Epic (Slova ská epopej), by Alfons Mucha was unveil on this occasion. The large canvases we placed in the grand hall, so the people Prague could see the complete work. T huge Exhibition Palace was seven store high, with further two underground floo and covered an area of 140m x 60m. Tv halls surrounded by galleries dominated t building. The large one, with its 15m hi roof, served exhibition purposes. Admin tration was the purpose of the small one. 1948 the government decided that big indu try and trade exhibitions would only be he

Above: H. Rousseau – Self-portrait
Below: P. Cézanne – A House in Aix
Opposite page below left:
A. Rodin – St. John the Baptist (all photos © 2010 Národní galerie v Praze)

Brno, and the Exhibition Palace ceased to rve its original purpose. The splendid inte- r now spoiled by partition walls was con- rted into a multitude of offices, occupied iefly by companies dealing with foreign de. After the huge fire in 1974 all the in- tutions moved to different locations and e palace (or rather its skeleton) was aban- ned for quite a while. In 1978 it was de- ded that this important building would be apted to suit the needs of the National allery. However, there was still a long way m the decision to the actual execution; body wanted to work on such a complex oject. Finally between 1986–1995 the Ex- bition Palace was expensively reconstruct- according to a design by architect Miro- v Masák. Only then were the Collections Modern and Contemporary Art of the Na- nal Gallery placed here as had long-since en agreed.

FOR ENTERTAINMENT
AND BUSINESS

THE EXHIBITION GROUNDS (VÝSTAVIŠTĚ)

The Jubilee Provincial Exhibition which took place in Prague in 1891 was a very special event. It was a tribute to the 100th anniversary of the Industry Exhibition held by the Czech Estates on the occasion of the coronation of Leopold II. The latter exhibition celebrated the development of industry, arts, science and culture. From 15th May to 18th October it was attended by two and a half million visi-

tors. An appropriate site was required for such an event. Part of the Royal Game Reserve was earmarked and the Exhibition Grounds, designed by Wiehle, were built there on an area of 40 ha. The Industry Palace (Průmyslový palác) became the dominant feature of the site. Münzberg was its chief designer but he cooperated with Prášil (who also designed the lookout tower on Petřín hill). The intricate ste-

UNDER THE STARS

The humble building of the Planetarium *(photo above)* is found in the Exhibition Grounds complex, just on the edge of Stromovka Park. Its ground plan is circular and was designed by Jaroslav Fragner between 1960–1962. Inside we can experience the perfect illusion that we are sitting under the stars on a clear night. The screen on which the night sky and the movements of the celestial bodies are projected is installed in the cupola. The Planetarium offers an extensive range, from popular science programs, lectures and exhibitions about astronomy to literary and music events.

mework was spoken of in awe; the contemprary press even considering it as significant the National Theatre (Národní divadlo) d the National Museum (Národní muzm). Figural windows, designed by Mikoláš eš, were fitted into the two long side wings. ne million different panes of various colours ere used to assemble the array of patterns. ne square steel tower, with a clock above e main frontage, is considered to be its typal and most prominentnt feature. The exbition was extremely successful and even nperor Franz Josef I himself visited it seval times. In 1895 the Ethnographic Exhibin took place here. After 1918 the Prague mple Fairs were held here. The First Chef d Waiter Exhibition in October 1922 was nother event to remember. The International hibition of Cars took place a year later. On February 1948 representatives of the works

LET THERE BE LIGHT!

During the Jubilee Provincial Exhibition in 1891 visitors experienced a number of surprises, mostly arranged by the famous Czech engineer and inventor František Křižík (1847–1941). He was a real star of his time. He built and ran a trial tram line from the upper cable-car station in Letná to Stromovka. However, his main achievements were the installation of electric lights covering the entire site of the exhibition and the construction of a beautiful illuminated fountain (photo left). Nowadays the newly reconstructed Křižík Fountain is a spectacular attraction and provides an impressive backdrop to the theatre stage. The Křižík Pavilion is named after him. Křižík, born in Plánice near Klatovy, was a very interesting person. He graduated at Prague Technical College and first attracted attention for his invention for improving railway signals. Then in 1880 he designed a brand new type of arc lamp for a paper mill in Plzeň. These started to be used throughout the world, only becoming obsolete with Edison's invention of the light bulb. By in 1888 he had erected a power station at Žižkov, the first one in Bohemia. While watching the amazing light effects of the Křižík Fountain one should not forget its famous creator. Not long ago there was a large fire in the Industrial Palace (Průmyslový palác), during which the whole western wing burned down. After a reconstruction the building should have its original appearance, which can be seen in the photograph from the time before the fire.

councils met here at a congress. They ratified a resolution demanding the expropriation of all factories and enterprises with more than 50 employees. It was a turbulent year, which decided the future of Czechoslovakia for the next 40 years. Industry Palace was renamed Congress Palace. In 1952 and 1953 the Exhibition Grounds (Výstaviště) was renamed the Julius Fučík Park of Culture and Relaxation (Julius Fučík was a communist journalist executed by the Nazis) and reconstruction of the site followed shortly afterwards. Nowadays the site is again known as the Exhibition Grounds. Apart from Industry Palace and the four wings of Křižík Exhibition Pavilion, a number of other buildings are found there, including a pavilion containing Luděk Marold's painting, GoJa Music Hall, T-Mobile Arena, a hotel and so on. Sea World, a permanent exhibition, was opened only recently. About three hundred species of sea animals, including sharks, inhabit ten gigantic aquariums. There is also a unique underwater coral cave. Upon entering we notice twelve fountains with ceramic groups of animals as well as the Pavilion of the City of Prague which nowadays hosts the Lapidarium of the National Museum. The Exhibition Grounds boast a variety of shows throughout the year. There is a succession of exhibitions; the extensive cultural programme also includes musical and theatrical performances; favourite musicals being staged in the permanent theatre. There are lots of sports and entertainment centres and, of course, the traditional spring Matthew Fair (Matějská pouť) takes place here.

LAPIS
MEANS STONE

LAPIDARIUM (MUSEUM OF SCULPTURES)

SAND EXHIBITS

During World War Two the Lapidarium was closed. As Prague was in serious danger of being bombed, the collections were moved away; part of them to Zbraslav and Troja Castles, some to the National Museum. The larger exhibits were dismantled and deposited in the basement of the Lapidarium, some of them being covered with sand. After the war it took several years of hard work to restore the collections. The original idea of the lapidarium was eventually realised. Only Langweil's Model of Prague was submitted to the Museum of Prague City.

Below: sculpture decoration next to the entrance

Lapis means stone in Latin, hence the name lapidarium for a collection of stone sculptures and architectural objects, or a building containing such a collection. The Lapidarium of the National Museum, situated in the Exhibition Grounds, is exceptional indeed. In 1995 it was singled out as one of the ten best in Europe. Its purpose was to hold big exhibitions taking place at the turn of the 19th century. The Neo-Renaissance building, designed by Wiehle, was constructed in 1891 as one of the many pavilions to be used for the Jubilee Exhibition. In 1895 it was reconstructed in Baroque-Art Nou-

veau style, according to a design by Hruby, so that it could be used for another special event, the Exhibition of Architecture and Engineering. A display of ancient architecture was part of that exhibition, and this particular display became the core of the future lapidarium. In 1905 the collections were opened to the public for a short time before World War One. Exhibition Grounds were taken over by the army, the building housing the lapidarium served as a storehouse. Even when the war was over the outlook for the Lapidarium did not improve, as it was part of the National Museum and "taking up

EQUESTRIAN STATUES

In sculpture, equestrian statues are among the most favoured and admired. The portrait of St. George is one of the most beautiful and valuable works of Gothic sculpture *(photo above)*. The statue is dynamic, St. George is stabbing his lance into the dragon, which is writhing beneath the horse's hooves. The creator of the model probably worked in Parler's workshop. The statue was only cast in bronze in 1373 by Jan and Martin of Kluž. St. George is the first statue that was not meant to be part of a building, but to adorn an open space. Its original location remains a mystery. Later on it was moved to the courtyard of Prague Castle. Nowadays a copy stands at Prague Castle, the original forming part of the Lapidarium collections.

and in 1987 a reconstruction of its building even commenced. In April 1993 it was reopened again. Nowadays its visitors can admire a splendid exhibition of Czech stone sculpture ranging from the 11th to the 19th centuries. Only about four hundred showpieces out of a two-thousand-piece collection are on display, including fragments of Romanesque cloister in Ostrov by Davle, a 13th century base of a pulpit with two resting lions from a fort in Kouřim, tombstones from ancient times and works from Peter Parler's smeltery. There are also examples of Renaissance and Baroque styles.

pace" in the Exhibition Grounds. But busy xhibition life required space, and there was o place to which the collection could be noved. Eventually the Lapidarium was reoened to the public, partially in 1931 and s a whole a year later. During World War wo the collection "survived" in various loations, before its problems started again. he National Museum was under constant ressure to vacate the lapidarium building. he exhibition had to be closed in 1967, ecause the building had become unfit for se. In 1973 the National Museum was givn a written notice, backed by the decision f the municipal committee of the Commuist party. The keys from the empty premises ere to be handed over within one month. he decision made no sense – there was o other location the collections could be noved to, moreover, the deadline was ridiclously tight. And as the underground was eing built in Prague at the time, architecturl fragments of great value had been piling p. The Lapidarium was eventually saved,

Above left: a view of one of the halls
Central left: busts of Charles IV and Jan of Luxemburg from the triforium of St. Vitus's Cathedral
Below left: late Gothic pulpit from the Church of St. Bartholomew in Rakovník, by Matěj Rejsek

THE LARGEST
OF PAINTINGS

THE MAROLD PANORAMA

wanted to see something extraordinar*
a display of the panorama of the Battle *
Lipany. The painting depicts the famous ba*
tle in which Prague citizens fighting in th*
Nobility Union army (Panská jednota) con*
tributed to the defeat of the Taborites an*
the so-called Orphan army on the hillock *
Lipany on 30 May 1434. This event basica*
ly put an end to the revolutionary phase *
the Hussite movement. The work, a remar*
able size at 95 m wide by 11 m high, is sure*
ly one of the biggest paintings in the Czec*
Republic. It was painted by Luděk Marol*
(1865–1898), together with his assistant*
On his return from Paris in 1897 the pain*
er approached the members of the exhib*
tion board and offered to arrange somethir*

A COLLECTIVE WORK

Luděk Marold is usually
portrayed as the only painter of
the Marold Panorama, so it is
necessary to point out that it
was a collective work that he
organized. His participation
was obviously major, but
a number of other artists left
their mark as well. From his
time in Paris Marold knew Karel
Rašek very well. He also
employed Wenceslas Jansa,
a distinguished landscape
painter, Theodor Hilšer,
a talented colourist, and Ludvík
Vašátko, who was good at
painting horses, Karel Štapfer
was in charge of the installation
works and the actual terrain in
front of the painting.

At the turn of the 19th century several significant events were organized on the
site of the Exhibition Grounds in Holešovice.
The Exhibition of Architecture and Engineering was one of them. Between 15 June and
17 October 1898 it was attended by half
a million visitors. Eighty two thousand people headed into a wooden pavilion next to
the right wing of the central palace. They

unique. His suggestion was met with a pos*
tive response, although the theme arouse*
discussion; the Battle of Lipany being con*
sidered a sad episde in Czech history. Ther*
was very little time, but eventually the*
managed to finish the work shortly befor*
the exhibition was due to open. The sam*

Above: the Marold Panorama
(the building on the left)
Other pictures: battle scenes

ear the wooden pavilion was replaced ith a new wooden construction and, after ng discussions, the colossal painting was nally attributed a permanent place, beoming a widely admired attraction. On 25 bruary 1929 a disaster occured. The roof the pavilion collapsed under wet snow. he painting was left in shreds beneath the eams and walls. Fortunately the renowned storer Bohumír Číla was able to save it. here were insufficient funds for a new, ore solid ferro-concrete building, which ould cost more than a million crowns. owever, the money was raised through ublic collections and in 1932 final approv- to commence construction was passed.

The restored painting was then pasted onto a cylindrical shaped plaster wall. There was only one slight problem; the wall was about a meter longer than the painting. So a suitable part of the painting was chosen, a piece of canvas inserted there and the missing section of landscape painted. The restored work was presented anew to the public on the anniversary of the battle, on 30 May 1934. The magnificent painting was endangered again in the 1980's when the canvas was exposed to rain. With the Jubilee Exhibition in 1991 was approaching the painting was again put into the care of the restorers. Nowadays the Marold Panorama is once more a first-class attraction.

WHERE TO PUT IT

The exhibition was over, the enthusiasm gradually died down and the usual question arose – where should it be put? The colossal work had enchanted the visitors but now the problem of its future use needed to be solved. The Association of Architects and Engineers in the Kingdom of Bohemia offered the painting for free, on the condition that it would be put on public display. The Prague Municipality did not accept the offer, neither did the Royal Vinohrady nor the Modern Gallery. Moreover, the pavilion had to be removed from its location. It seemed that the painting would be cut into pieces and the building demolished. However, the aforementioned Association of Architects decided to preserve the work. The Prague Municipal Council granted them a loan and councillor Ludvík Čížek designed a new building, as well as intricate machinery to fold and stretch the painting. The architect Jan Koula devised an external cover for the new building. And so a new dodecagonally shaped pavilion was successfully built. The artists who had created the vast painting then worked on its restoration. Only Luděk Marold was missing. He had died on 1 December 1898.

THE OLDEST
GREEN JEWEL

THE ROYAL GAME PRESERVE
(PARK STROMOVKA)

THE RODOLPH GALLERY

The so-called Rodolph Gallery, situated in the Royal Game Preserve, is a technical achievement of great historic value. Rodolph II comissioned this extraordinary work between 1584–1593. The gallery was driven through under the Letná massif so that water from the Vltava could flow from New Mill weir (Novomlýnský jez) to the big pond in the Royal Game Preserve. The gallery is more than one thousand metres long. It was made by digging five pits on the Letná surface and at the same time tunnelling both its ends simultaneously. Real experts, miners from Kutná Hora, worked on it. The gallery still serves its purpose today and is occasionally open to the public.

The Royal Game Preserve, since the 19th century called Stromovka (Tree Garden – the name is probably an incorrect translation from the German word Baumgarten), is a green jewel of the busy city. It takes up an area of 95 ha between Bubeneč and Holešovice, near the arm of the Vltava known as the Little Brook. Its history stretches back to 1268 when King Přemysl Ottocar II fenced a plot, which was at that time the property of the nuns of Chotěboř convent, as a hunting ground. It is possible that he even built a hunting lodge there. In 13? the game preserve, the oldest in Prague, b came the property of the Crown. During t' Hussite Wars the game preserve was cor pletely ruined. In the 16th century it w newly planted and divided by a wall, w' the eastern side containing a summer p ace and the western side with a pheasant. The reign of Rodolph II was a golden a for the game preserve; he built a gallery, e larged the pond and extended the preser as far as Imperial Mill (Císařský mlýn), h

Above: the gate to the Rodolph Gallery
Main photo: romantic spots in the preserve

xotic woody plants and game brought in. After his reign the imperial court moved o Vienna and the importance of the Roy- l Game Preserve somewhat decreased. Al- hough the damage caused during the Thir- y-Years War was repaired, real catastrophe ame with the wars that occured during he reign of Marie Therése. The Saxon and russian armies used it as their encamp- nent and chopped down practically all the rees. The enormous damage inflicted near- y resulted in the preserve's closure. How- ver, the Czech nobility, led by Count Kin- ký, was given permission to restore the ame preserve, and so in 1792 the corona- on ceremony of Franz I could take place here. Game, though, never again returned. his helped Burgrave Jan Rodolph Chotek, vhose aim was to open the game preserve o the public. He succeeded in 1804 when he entire property was excluded from he use of the Senior Provincial Master of Hounds. Stromovka was gradually turning

into a landscape park. However, the plans of landscape gardeners Bedřich Wünscher and Jiří Braul were too ambitious, requiring about two hundred thousand guilders to im- plement, and so their ideas were never com- pletely carried out. In 1845 part of the park was used for building a railway track, and then it was further altered to meet the needs of the Buštěhrad railway, which opened in 1867. Other significant changes took place after 1880, for example several fully grown trees were moved here from the castle gar- dens in Vlašim and Sychrov. In 1891 the first Jubilee Exhibition was held in the eastern section of the park – this very section was separated and developing independently af- terwards. The last major man-made altera- tion happened in 1920, but Stromovka has also been "checked" several times by nature itself. The extensive floods of August 2002 were disastrous, and as a result the majority of trees had to be cut down.

THE GOVERNOR'S SUMMER PALACE

The most beautiful view of Stromovka opens up from the picturesque Governor's Summer Palace (photo above). The building has always been associated with the game preserve. It was in fact originally constructed as a royal hunting lodge of Vladislav Jagello between 1495–1503. In 1594, under Rodolph II, it was converted into an observation building with loggias. Between 1805 and 1811 it was rebuilt in romantic Gothic style, at the same time the flower gardens were created. Water was supplied with the help of a water pump created by a Czech inventor Josef Božek. Ever since members of the Czech Estates offered the building to Burgrave Jan Rodolph Chotek, the building has been called The Governor's Summer Palace. Its sculptures are worth noticing, they are the work of Ignatius Michael Platzer and Josef Kranner, the painting of the rooms was created by Josef Navrátil. The sculptured sundial is also remarkable.

TROJA CASTLE (TROJSKÝ ZÁMEK)

Above: wall paintings in the main hall

The majestic double-flight staircase leading from the main hall to the French garden is considered to be the most remarkable feature of Troja Castle (Trojský zámek), which is situated on a low terrace above the Vltava in the neighbourhood of Prague Zoo. The staircase is richly decorated with Baroque sculptures depicting a battle between the gods of Olympus and the Titans, the work of Dresden sculptors John George Hermann and his nephew Paul. However, people confused it with scenes from the Trojan War, so both the castle and the village in the vicinity started to be called Troja. The

castle itself is also extremely valuable. Cour Wenceslas Vojtěch Baltazar of Šternberk ha it built between 1679 and 1705. It was sup posed to become his family's seat, therefor the designer of the project, Burgundian Jea Baptist Mathey, looked for inspiration Ital ian Baroque-style country villas. The palac is one of the most remarkable buildings c its type north of the Alps. It is a three-win two-storey building which has a three-sto rey section in the middle with adjacent sid wings that have turret-like belvederes. Th castle courtyard contains the out-buildings The main frontage, including the aforemen tioned staircase, faces the French garden, which has strict geometrical layout, complemented by a fountain *(photo right)* and hedges arranged in various patterns. In the direction of the Vltava the converging hedges form an arc gateway. The clipped hornbeam shrubberies are planted in the shape of a circular maze, situated in the centre of a geometrically designed intersection. The axis of the garden is an extension of the central axis of the castle and is oriented in the direction the Royal Game Preserve and Prague Castle. Reputedly the builder deliberately designed it this way, assuming that the monarch would drop in more often when hunting, as the castle provided more comfort than the lodge in the Royal Game Preserve. He was absolutely right, Emperor Leopold I paid Troja several visits and liked the castle very much. In 1699 the count of Šternberk was even awarded the high-

st Austrian order, the Order of the Golden Fleece. In 1763 Empress Marie Therése bought the castle and moved some of its furnishing to Vienna. Prince Alfred Windisgrätz, the infamous military commander of Prague, who brutally suppressed the Prague revolution in 1848, was also one of its owners. After 1918 the last owner offered the run-down castle to the state. The castle then served cultural purposes. After an expensive reconstruction between 1977 and 1989 it was given to the Gallery of the

City of Prague, which opened it to the public, placing there painting collections and an exhibition of ancient prints and maps from the Far East. Visitors can also admire the amazing wall paintings by Abraham and Isaac Godin and Francesco Marchetti in the interiors. The paintings represent the peak of Czech Baroque art.

GRAPES FROM ST. CLARA

The Troja Castle complex used to include a vineyard, which was founded in the 17th century on the slope above the castle and restored by prince Windisgrätz in the first half of the 19th century. Nowadays it is separated by Troja Street (Trojská ulice). It is one of the few vineyards in Prague still preserved to this day and covers an area of 3.5 ha. The early Baroque Chapel of St. Clara (kaple sv. Kláry), which dates from about 1685, is situated there *(photo left)*, and a little further down the slope there is a Classicist vineyard house.

Centre left: *front garden with a staircase*

THE MOST BEAUTIFUL
IN EUROPE

THE ZOOLOGICAL
AND BOTANIC GARDENS

TROJA HOMESTEADS

The southern slopes of Troja made perfect vineyards. Only some have been preserved, for example the vineyard at St. Clara's managed by the Prague Botanic Gardens. Several vineyard homesteads remain. They are typical of this rather remote part of Prague, and give Troja a somewhat rural atmosphere, although it is not far from busy roads. The Kázanka homestead (photo above) is perhaps the most beautiful. This exquisitely reconstructed two-storey building has a Baroque layout and façade, and is covered with a mansard roof. The 17th century central building is adjoined to single-storey outbuildings. Pazderka, another well-known homestead, consists of several buildings surrounding a small yard. Its construction began in the 18th century and continued into the first third of the 19th century. It is located high on the slope overlooking the suburb of Bohnice. The vineyard homestead Sklenářka is quite secluded as well. Its corners are strengthened by abutments and the building is covered with a hipped roof.

We have a plot envied by the experts: that was the appraisal given in 1924 about the site by the founder and first director of Prague Zoo, professor Jiří Janda, a traveller, renowned zoologist and popularizer of the natural sciences. On 28 September 1931, when it was officially opened, visi-

tors could see for themselves – at that time the zoo included three hundred animals and covered an area of eight hectares. Since then it was enlarged to more than sixty hectares (two thirds of which are open to the public) but the relief of its terrain has not changed at all. From the often flooded meadows on the banks of the Vltava (in fact, in 2002 widespread flooding caused enormous damage) it rises through steep rocks and warm hillside all the way to the original dry steppes.

Anywhere else rocks would have be artificially and expensively installed, but here it was just a question how to integrate and use them within the zoo. Additionally the site also benefitted from the existing vegetation and a hospitable climate. As in other big cities, the idea of having a zoo in Prague has already been considered in the 19th century. A small zoo existed in Vrchlický Garden (Vrchlického sady) for a short period of time. After the independent state came into exist

reared here. In 1942 the first polar bear in the world born in captivity made the zoo famous, followed by a Siberian tiger, a clouded leopard, a cheetah and so on. The Przewalski horse is one of the most valued species of the zoo, Prague Zoo being prominent in helping save it from extinction.

The zoo provides further services such as restaurants and children's corners; the feeding of some animals is a sought-after attraction. A number of rare plants grow here as well. If you are really keen on botany you can visit another place of interest at Troja, Prague's Botanic Gardens. The entrance is in nearby Nádvorní Street. The idea to establish a large national botanic garden emerged shortly after the "Na Slupi" Botanic Gardens were founded. Eventually the property in Troja was chosen from many other options, the official "blessing" being finally attained in 1968. The Prague Botanic Gardens have only been open to the public since 1992. The opening exhibition occupied a three hectare area, but in 1997 the display was complemented by an interesting Japanese Garden, below which a section introducing the flora of Turkey and the Mediterranean can be found. An interesting exhibition can be seen in a tropical greenhouse named Fata Morgana *(photo below)* opened in 2004. Every spring many exotic butterflies can be seen flying freely in the greenhouse. Of interest is also the large pool with an underground tunnel and a waterfall.

...nce in 1918 the intention to build a large zoological garden became more realistic. The committee offered a selection of 14 plac...s, and today's site was surely a good choice. The zoo lies in a quiet part of the city at Troja, ...early on the outskirts of Prague. It is quite re...note, so the journey itself makes it an inter...esting day trip. There is also a cableway and ...a new wooden lookout tower for the visitors.

The zoo at Troja is considered by many ex...perts to be the most beautiful in Europe. It ...also boasts excellent achievements in breed...ng. In 1937 a condor *(Vultur gryphus)* was

PAVED PATH (DLÁŽDĚNKA)

The narrow lane called Na Dlážděnce very much resembles a country road. It ascends through a grove, then along gardens to a hillock above the right bank of the Vltava. The paved road is not only significant evidence of the craftsmanship of our ancestors, but also its history is interesting and worth mentioning. According to legend, one of the owners of Troja Castle was guilty of wrongdoing and as penitence he had to pave a path from the river as far as the road to Stará Boleslav. The work went on for several years until it was interrupted by the lord's death. The unfinished path then started to be called Dlážděnka, Paved Path *(photo above)*. The reality is a little different, though. From the end of the 16th century Emperor Rodolph II and his company had been using the path to go hunting in the woods of Stará Boleslav. It was a very pleasant journey as far as Holešovice. Then the gentry got on boats and crossed the river to Troja. From there the track ascended steeply, was often muddy and the horses could not pull the carriages and hunting wagons. The Senior Controller of the Kingdom of Bohemia, Adam of Wallenstein, had material brought and the track, the length of which exceeded 1 000 m, paved between 1628–1629.

AN IDEAL PLACE
TO LIVE

BABA

AT ST. MATTHIAS'S

In the Baba neighbourhood there is a lovely spot, the main feature of which is the Chapel of St. Matthias (kaple sv. Matěje). It is in a picturesque location above Silent Šárka (Tichá Šárka) Valley. It used to be the natural centre of Dejvice and a place where the first spring fairs (on 24 February) called Matthias Fairs (Matějská pouť), were held. Originally, a Gothic shrine mentioned as early as 1404 stood there, later replaced by a late Baroque chapel. According to legend it was Prince Boleslav II who founded the shrine in 971 at the place where Ctirad's squad, known from Czech mythology (the story of the War of the Czech Amazons), was buried. Boleslav, called the Pious, was attacked by a bear when hunting and nearly breathed his last. Suddenly St. Matthias appeared and scared the bear away. Then he explained to Boleslav that it was not an ordinary animal, but an infernal beast that usually visited the places where the corpses of people who had not been christened were resting, such as fighters massacred by Šárka and her women co-warriors. He asked Boleslav to build a house of God on that spot. In 1890 several bronze objects were excavated by a local undertaker. Archaeologists later confirmed that a prehistoric Knovíz settlement (Knovízská kultura) had once existed here.

Main photo: *a villa in Na Paťance Street*

One of the most attractive residential areas is found in a quiet part of Prague 6, on the edge of Dejvice. It is situated on a promontory from which on one side rocks descend as far as the Vltava, and on the other forested hillsides slope into the Silent Šárka valley. The history of this quiet and in many cases exclusive residential area dates to 1932–1940. At that time the Association of Czechoslovak Work built an estate that was supposed

to demonstrate ideal housing. They constructed a variety of houses, arranged horizontally in several rows, one above the other, on ascending terrain. They were positioned alternately so that they would not block one another's view. The town-plan was prepared by Pavel Janák and the individual houses were designed by both renowned and unknown architects. The latter were actually given their first opportunity to demonstrate their faculties

solving a task representative of European trends of that time. Among the architects who participated in the project were Adolf Beneš, Antonín Černý, Josef Fuchs, Josef Gočár, Josef Grus, František Kavalír, Ladislav Machoň and Oldřich Starý. The area is attractive from other points of view as well. The edge of the promontory is dominated by the ruins of a folly which commands an amazing view of Prague, presenting a beautiful vista – from Petřín Hill to Prague Castle, the Vltava valley as far as the suburb of Bohnice. And nature fanciers can discover something worth their attention, as Baba is a protected area in which thermophilic rock vegetation can be found.

A FOLLY OR A WINE PRESS?

High above the left bank of the Vltava at the edge of the Baba housing estate, there is an interesting ruin. Sometimes it is referred to as a wine press but it is actually a former folly. Originally in 1622 there was a vineyard. In 1650 one of its owners, Servatius Engel, built a "lusthaus' (folly) there. He chose the place with the most beautiful view, and we can see for ourselves that he was right. However, the folly gradually went to ruin, because people in the nearby vicinity used it for building material for their houses. The destruction of the folly was eventually completed by Bavarian and French soldiers in the early 18th century. The folly was burned down and the garden with a number of rare trees was destroyed. In the 19th century workers building a railway track in the river valley strengthened the remains of the walls, made a hole in one of them and fitted in a Gothic arc. That is how the former folly became today's romantic ruin.

Above: the ruins of Baba
Centre left: villa, No 9
Matthias Street (Matějská)
Below left: Janák's Villa

A BREATHTAKING SPOT

GOAT RIDGES – BARE HILL
(KOZÍ HŘBETY – HOLÝ VRCH)

The Prague area definitely does not want for romantic spots so each of us will surely find a place worth visiting over and over again. Goat Ridges (Kozí hřbety), on the northern edge of Prague near Suchdol, is such a breathtaking location. A marked hiking trail crosses the road from Suchdol, leading us through a lovely grove before disappearing among rugged rocks. The upper parts offer unexpected views, not only of Prague but also of faraway northern Bohemia. There are beautiful views of Říp Hill, the distant hills of the Czech Low Mountains (České středohoří) and Ještěd mountain. From Goat Ridges the path descends into Silent Valley (Tiché údolí), which is part of a nature reserve named Si-lent Valley – Roztoky Grove (Roztocký háj) Sedlec Rocks (Sedlecké skály). It encompasses an area of 185 hectares.

The Chapel of St. Wenceslas *(photo opposite page above)*, which was founded at the plague cemetery, can be found near Goat Ridges. The city district of Suchdol, known apart from other things as the seat of the Agricultural College, is very interesting. A manor house called the Brandejs Estate is situated in the upper part of the town. Originally, there used to be a fortress of which only its Renaissance layout was preserved. In the mid-18th century the fortress was rebuilt as a Baroque manor house and later on it was used as a farm. The courtyard is surrounded by four

ÚNĚTICE CIVILIZATION

Goat Ridges (Kozí hřbety) offer a lovely view of the rocky Bare Hill (Holý vrch) *(photo above)* situated on the other side of Silent Valley (Tiché údolí). Bare Hill is a well-known prehistoric site. In 1928 passionate amateur archaeologist discovered 70 graves here dating from the earliest Bronze Age in Central Europe. He had uncovered a real treasure, a settlement of the so-called Únětice Civilization (únětická kultura). Bronze daggers adorned with amber, gold and engraved ornaments were excavated here. The culture is named after the village of Úňetice. The valley is a popular tourist destination; its rugged rocks, made of slate and Lydian stone, being often admired. A lot of disused quarries can also be found in this area.

Main photo: *view from Goat Ridges*

SILENT VALLEY

A comfortable path leads from Únětice to Roztoky through Silent Valley (below), a green oasis surrounded by slate and Lydian stone rocks. Several mills can be found in the valley, some reconstructed, others neglected, yielding to time. The beautifully reconstructed Trojan Mill (Trojanův mlýn) (photo above) is a place painter Mikoláš Aleš liked visiting. In the early Middle Ages a road from Prague to Levý Hradec, called the Přemyslide Road (Přemyslovská), used to lead through a side gorge, which forks away from Silent Valley here. Downstream we discover Burnt Mill (called Spáleník), which got its name from a long-ago fire.

ings of a single-storey building. The famous ainter Mikoláš Aleš often visited one of the nants on the estate, Alexander Brandejs, etween 1877–1879. Aleš would meet his friends there to discuss Czech history, and there he also created some of his works (e.g. The Meeting of George of Poděbrady and Matthias Corvinus). Only a simple memorial made of boulders commemorates Aleš's stay, with the inscription of his motto: "…I long to serve my country through art." We can take a bus to Suchdol and get off at the Výhledy terminus. The interesting building No 15 is a former carters inn called Na Chumperku, which served as a postal station for changing horses on the so-called Serbian Road as early as the 16th century.

THE MOST BEAUTIFUL
VALLEY

WILD ŠÁRKA

THE GIRL'S LEAP

The most famous of several awesome look-out spots created by the rugged rocks of Wild Šárka Valley is Girl's Leap (Dívčí skok), its name refering to an incident which supposedly occured during the Wars of the Czech Amazons. According to legend a war took place here, in which women, led by militant Vlasta, fought against men. One of the warriors from Vlasta's squad, beautiful Šárka, betrayed brave Ctirad, who was captured and killed. The conscience-stricken girl then jumped from the rock into the chasm. The story became a popular source of inspiration for a number of artists, for example in 1896 the opera *Šárka* by Zdeněk Fibich was staged. Wild Šárka also serves as a setting for Eduard Štorch's novels, *The Raven Settlement* and *The Mammoth Hunters*, the tribe of hunters having to leave the valley because "the most terrible beast of all time, the giant cave bear" raged there.

Perhaps the most beautiful valley in Prague runs parallel to the upper end of European Street (Evropská ulice), stretching out towards the airport in Ruzyně. Šárka Brook (Šárecký potok) had to make its way through th Lydian stone rocks, creating the magnifice scenery that makes the area so popular fe outings. Wild Šárka (Divoká Šárka) is one o

JENERÁLKA

At a place called Jenerálka the road from Red Hill (Červený Vrch) to Horoměřice crosses the valley and divides it into Wild and Silent Šárka (Divoká and Tichá Šárka, respectively). An important trade route led there in the Middle Ages. In the second half of the 18th century part of the Austrian general staff resided there. Since that time the place has been called Jenerálka (general's seat). A farmstead there was bought by Prague baker Ignatius Komm in 1926, who converted it into a gorgeous manor house. Komm was a good friend of Karel Hynek Mácha, a romantic poet who dedicated his lyrical poem called May (Máj) to him. Praguers used Jenerálka for their summer vacations; the landscape painter August Friedrich Piepenhagen liked working there. The manor house (photo above) later served various purposes. From 1926 it was the Legionary Invalids Home. In 1942 a Children's Home was established here by Germans for orphans whose parents died in concentration camps. After 1990 the building was expensively and carefully reconstructed by the Baptist Church. Nowadays we admire a spectacular estate with a park. A lovely period restaurant is situated nearby. The quieter part of the area, the Silent Šárka, is also worth visiting, but unlike Wild Šárka, there is a road leading through this valley. A number of homesteads are typical of this part (Vízerka, Kaplanka, Žežulka, Heřman's Estate).

he oldest protected areas in Prague (1964). Nowadays it is hard to believe that motocross aces used to be held here. A place called Džbán (photo above), which has a water reservoir used for swimming, is found at the entrance of the valley. There is also a swimming pool (photo right) in a romantic place between rocks a bit further downstream on árka Brook. Džbán Pass (soutěska Džbán – he main photo), between Šesták and Kozák Rocks, is the gate to the most beautiful part of ne valley. On Šesták Rock there was a possibly fortified prehistoric settlement during the Neolithic and Eneolithic periods. On the opposite Kozák Rock (photo below) once stood he acropolis of the largest ancient settlement n the Prague area, which had replaced an neolithic altitudinal settlement of the so-alled Řivnáče Civilization (řivnáčská kultura). Hardly any traces remain; overgrown dges indicate the former mounds, but just s the settlement on Šesták Rock, its fortification was later damaged by a quarry. The lavs built their hill-fort here as early as the th century. However, from the 9th century its mportance began to decrease due to the establishment of Prague.

The area is also famous for several interesting finds. In 1964 some playing children ound a Frankish coin of Charles the Bald 43–877) made in Melle mint. Thermophilc flora of rock steppes is worth mentioning, o (Pulsatilla pratensis ssp. bohemica, Au-

rinia saxatilis, Stipa joannis). Rare species of moss and fern grow profusely on shady spots, and the remains of alder growth can be found along the brook.

BEAUTY AS THE ULTIMATE PERFECTION

MŰLLER'S VILLA

Below: Ořechovka

$\mathbf{B}$eauty as the ultimate perfection; that was the artistic motto of the great architect Adolf Loos (1870–1933), whose most famous work, the Müller Villa, can be found in Nad Hradním vodojemem Street at Střešovice. The building, constructed between 1928 and 1930, was commissioned by Dr. František Müller, the co-owner of a big building company Kapsa-Müller. Apart from designing the actual building, Loos also chose the furnishings and the art objects. The perfectly reconstructed villa is national cultural heritage nowadays. It is mentioned in every book on modern architecture.

It is hard to believe that the building wa once in jeopardy. After World War Two th house ceased to be used as a domestic re idence, and became the seat of the Sta Pedagogical Publishing House, even hou ing its printers. Later, until 1990, it was a re idence of the Institute of Marxism-Leninisn During those times admirers of unique arch tecture could only have a look at the buil ing from the outside. In 1993 the busines man Viktor Kožený expressed his interest i the villa, but both experts and the public pr tested. The voice of the people was even li tened to by politicians. The Prague Muni

ADOLF LOOS

On 21 October 1870 a son Adolf was born into the family of sculptor Loos from Brno. After finishing elementary school and passing the final exams at School of Crafts in Liberec Adolf Loos went to Dresden to study architecture at Technical College. Between 1893 – 1896 he travelled in North America. Later he lived in Paris and London. He eventually settled down in Vienna but he frequently travelled to Prague and Brno. On his sixtieth birthday he received a personal financial present from President Tomáš Garrigue Masaryk and was also awarded a honorary pension. Loos did not have much time to enjoy his pension, though, he died on 23 August 1933 after a long illness in a sanatorium near Vienna. Müller Villa, which he designed together with Prague architect Karel Lhota, remains his supreme work. Their other works include Winternitz Villa at Smíchov.

ality intervened, and after purchasing the building, initiated an extensive reconstruction in 1997. The villa, including the interiors, was restored the way it looked in the 1930's. It was then officially handed over to the Museum of the City of Prague. Nowadays is open to the public who can admire both the exterior and the interiors with a permanent exhibition dedicated to architect Adolf Loos. The interior layout of Müller Villa is remarkable. Loos used his own invention, the so-called interior Raumplan, in which rooms were conceived to be at different levels. So the building is not divided vertically into floors, as it would be in a usual house. Rather the rooms have different heights, the designer winding them in a spiral around an imaginary axis. The magnificent spatial layout closes up with a summer dining room on the top floor of the house. From the dining-room there is an entrance to a large upper terrace, which offers a splendid view of the Prague Castle, Hanspaulka and Baba. The interior is in direct contrast to the exterior,

which is conceived as a pure cube with bare, plain white walls.

While viewing the villa, we may also take a stroll in the neighbouring quarter, Ořechovka, which is a model of pleasant housing surrounded by greenery.

Above: exterior view
Opposite page above: the living room with the dining room above it
Below: the study

THE FIRST
IN BOHEMIA

BŘEVNOV MONASTERY

BŘEVNOV AND VOJTĚŠKA

The area around the brook Brusnice used to be quite unwelcoming, covered with dense forests, in which there were a few hidden farmsteads. When building began to flourish in Prague, felling trees became a welcome source of sustenance. According to legend brothers Janek and Matěj set out along the brook to a place their father had told them about. They came to a small spring with a huge smoothly hewn beam lying next to it. The brothers decided to build a cottage on that pleasant spot. They felled trees and hewed them, and the place to which they carried the beams they called Břevnov ('břevno' means 'beam'). A monastery was then founded near the spring. The monks named the spring Vojtěška. It never ran dry, even when there was severe drought, but on 16 August 1419 the surface of the spring turned bloody, which people took as a bad sign. Shortly afterwards King Wenceslas IV died at his fort, then the Hussite rebellion broke out and the monastery was plundered and burnt. Nowadays the Baroque pavilion Vojtěška *(photo above)*, built by Kilián Ignác Dienzenhofer, towers above the spring and a vast garden extends from it.

T he extraordinary complex of the Břevnov Benedictine Monastery is situated on the outskirts of Prague. Founded in 933 by Boleslav II and Bishop Vojtěch as the second cloister in Bohemia (the first was the Benedictine nuns' convent at Prague Castle), it was also the first monastery. During the reign of Prince Břetislav I, around 1040, the monastery had to be rebuilt after an extensive fire, and an early Gothic reconstruction followed around 1300. During the Hussite Wars the monastery was burnt down and went to ruin. The present-day Baroque complex was built only between 1708–1745 according to a design by Pavel Ignác Bayer, and Kryštof and Kilián Ignác Dienzenhofer. The 1740 entrance gate alone, the work of Kilián Ignác Dienzenhofer, is splendid. The individual buildings surround a large courtyard. The monastery Church of St. Margaret has a crypt *(photo opposite page below)*, which, built as part of the earlier construction, is considered to be the most important monument. The tombstone of a Benedic

tine hermit Vintíř, dating back to the beginning of the 14th century, can be found on the southern side. The sculptures on the moulding of the church nave are the work of Matěj Wenceslas Jäckel from 1712. In 1725 he also decorated the organ with his sculptures and together with the joiner Josef Dobner he created the pulpit in 1719. Dobner also made the main altar (1718), probably designed by Kryštof Dienzenhofer and decorated with Jäckel's sculptures. The nave vault *(photo to above)*, created between 1719–1721, adorned by paintings by Jan Jakub Steife and is truly remarkable. The paintings celebrate St. Benedict, St. Vojtěch, St. Margaret Czech saints and the saints of the order. Paintings by Peter Brandl adorn the side altars.

Between 1709–1720 a convent with two courtyards and cloisters, a capitular hall, winter refectory and sacristy was built near the eastern side of the church, according to a design by Kryštof Dienzenhofer. The prelacy was completed after 1720 by Kilián I.

c Dienzenhofer, its famous Theresian Hall commemorating a visit by Marie Therése d Franz Lotharingian in 1753. There is al- a superbly preserved Baroque fresco, dat- 1727, the work of Kosmas Damian Asam. e reception salon, the Chinese Salon and the Classicist room are decorated with paintings by Antonín Tuvora.

The wing of the summer refectory, with a library and a billiards salon, extends out to the garden. A beautiful large garden with an 18th century layout stretches behind the monastery.

ST. VOJTĚCH

St. Vojtěch, the co-founder of the Břevnov monastery, came from the Slavník family and at his confirmation was named Adalbert (Vojtěch in Czech) after his teacher, the Bishop of Magdeburg. In 982, at the age of 26, he was entrusted with the Prague bishopric, but, because of conflicts with the ruling prince, he soon left for Rome, where he entered a Benedictine monastery. In 983 he returned to Bohemia, bringing with him a group of his fellow friars from the Roman monastery. However, even after the foundation of the Břevnov Monastery he did not stay in Bohemia for long. In 995 he went as a missionary to the pagan Prussians, and was murdered in 997. Later on he was canonized.

Opposite page below: the entrance gate
Above: overall view of the complex

IN THE SHAPE
OF A STAR

STAR SUMMER PALACE
AND GAME PRESERVE (HVĚZDA)

THE FATAL BATTLE

The inconspicuous grassy hillock called Bílá hora (White Hill), rising to 381m on the right-hand side of the road to Karlovy Vary, gave this district of Prague its name. Until 1974 it was the highest point in the capital. In 1920 a stone mound *(photo above)* was piled up as a reminder of the battle that took place there on 8 November 1620, a battle considered fatal for the Czech Kingdom. The Protestant Estates Army fought against the Catholic League Army and the imperial army of Ferdinand II. It seemed that the Estates Army was winning, but then, suddenly, for no apparent reason soldiers from Jindřich Matyáš Thurn's Czech infantry regiment threw their muskets away and beat a retreat. In vain Thurn tried to stop his running soldiers, but more and more joined them. The Estates Army was heading towards the well-fortified city of Prague, which had enough food supplies to cope with a siege, and moreover a strong allied Hungarian army was approaching. Most commanders did not want to continue to fight and opted for surrender. The White Hill defeat resulted in the 300-year-long subjection of the Czech Kingdom to the Habsburgs.

A pleasant destination for walks, a beautiful green area (86.5 ha) on the edge of the [ci]ty, enlivened by training runners and cross-[co]untry skiers in winter; that is the Star Game [pr]eserve. However, the game preserve has [n]ot always been open to the public. Found[e]d by King Ferdinand I in a wood in Malejov [in] 1534 as the second royal game preserve [a]fter the one at Bubeneč), it was called the [N]ew Game Preserve (Nová obora). Between [1]555–1556 Archduke Ferdinand of Tyrol had [a] summer palace built there. As its ground [pl]an uses the shape of a six-point star (central [ph]oto), the game preserve began to be called [St]ar (,Hvězda' in Czech). Sir Ferdinand was [s]o concerned about the construction that he [d]esigned the magnificent Renaissance build[in]g and dug the hole for the foundation stone [h]imself. According to romantic legend Fer[d]inand built the summer palace as a resi[d]ence for his secret wife Filipina Welser. As

palace. The palace was also 'checked out' by soldiers from time to time, for example the Swedes took away the entire gilded copper roof in 1648. Between 1785–1874 it served as a gunpowder storehouse. The restoration work in the first half of the 20th century was carried out by the famous architect Pavel Janák. In 1951 a permanent exhibition dedicated to the writer Alois Jirásek and later also to the painter Mikoláš Aleš was opened in the palace. Another extensive reconstruction took place during the 1980's and 1990's (apart from other features the valuable tessellated floor in the banqueting hall, dating from 1562, was restored). Nowadays the building is again open to the public, its permanent exhibition focusing on the construction, development and function of the palace from the 16th to the 20th centuries. The Star game preserve has an interesting history too. In the second half of the 16th cen-

A REMINDER OF VICTORY

The Battle of White Hill brought victory to the Catholics, and the Chapel of the Virgin Mary was built between 1622 and 1624 to commemorate this victory. In 1628 a Servite monastery was established by the chapel, but it never served its purpose. The incomplete Baroque building was converted into an inn called the Great Inn (Velká hospoda), and also occasionally served as hospital. Nowadays there is a popular restaurant here. The chapel went to ruin, but between 1704–1712 the painter Kristián Luna instigated its replacement with the Church of Virgin Mary the Victorious (photo above). Between 1710–1714 it was enclosed within a wall which had corner chapels, and between 1721–1729 cloisters were added. In 1714 its prominent feature was erected, the high dome with a lantern which is the work of the great Baroque master John Santini (as is the surrounding wall), possibly in collaboration with Kilián Ignác Dienzenhofer.

[G]overnor of Bohemia and second son of Em[p]eror Ferdinand I he simply could not afford [t]o officially marry a merchant's daughter. So [t]he clever Ferdinand set up an irresistible [tr]ap for the Emperor. The Emperor got thirsty [w]hen hunting and suddenly, a charming girl [e]merged from the bushes carrying a jug of [w]ater. The Emperor was enchanted and pro[c]laimed the marriage legitimate…
Prominent Italian artists Giovanni Campi[o]ne de Bossi and Andrea Avostalis decora[t]ed the palace. The stucco decoration is one [o]f the most beautiful in Central Europe. In [1]610 the sovereign, Frederick Palatine (Frid[ri]ch Falcký), was officially received at the

tury plenty of feasts and shooting competitions were held there. Not only game was kept in the game preserve, it is said that in 1592 twelve lions lived there under the supervision of a trained tamer. However, the military campains of 17th and 18th centuries proved disastrous. The armies were encamped in the Star (Hvězda) and, as a consequence, many trees were cut down for firewood. The game was therefore moved to the Deer Moat (Jelení příkop). At the turn of the 18th century the area was converted into an English-style park, three wide avenues leading from the main gates to the palace creating its axis.

Main photo: a pleasant path through the game preserve to the summer palace

THE GREATEST
TRANSFORMATION

THE GOLDEN ANGEL AT SMÍCHOV

THE 'INTERMIGLED' PLOTS

There are several explanations for the origin of the name Smíchov, the most likely one being associated with the distribution of plots to new settlers, which resulted in an intermingling ('smísit' in Czech) of the citizens. Jan Smíchovský, who bought several plots there during the Hussite Wars, is also mentioned. The man really existed but by his time Smíchov was already known as Smíchov. If we prefer a mythical explanation we can accept a story about the militant fighter Vlasta, who laughed ('smích' means 'laughter') at the men defeated in the War of the Czech Amazons. The old Smíchov gradually became just a distant memory. However, quite a few historical buildings remain there, including the Baroque summer palace, Portheimka, built in 1725 by the excellent Baroque architect Dienzenhofer for his family, the Neo-Gothic cloister and Church of the Heart of Jesus, constructed in 1882–1884, the Neo-Renaissance Church of St. Wenceslas by Barvitio, which dates from 1881–1885, and the Neo-Renaissance town hall *(photo above)*.

Since its establishment the Prague quarter Smíchov has undergone some interesting changes. According to the Zbraslav Chronicle (Zbraslavská kronika) the coronation banquet for King Wenceslas II was held in this area as early in 1297. In 1409 Smíchov itself was mentioned in written records for the first time, at that time still being a pleasant area with gardens, vineyards and a few isolated homesteads, just as in the time of Wenceslas II. The district kept this character until the 19th century and the fierce arrival of industry. In 1815 the Przibram calico factory commenced production, in 1816 it was the Porges factory, followed a little bit later by the Portheim china factory and the the Ringhoffer factory. Smíchov has officially been part of Prague since 1922, but it underwent its greatest transformation at the end of the 20th century, when the oft-neglected suburb became a modern city district. A multifunctional complex called the Golden Angel (Zlatý Anděl – *photo below left*), consisting of four separate buildings designed by world renowned French architect Jean Nou-

vel (1945), replaced the original historic in Golden Angel in November 2000. The buil ings have a joint ground floor, which is divide into bigger and smaller shopping units. In th buildings there are offices and shops; a guar ian-angel watches from the corner outside. O the façade there are excerpts from the works Franz Kafka, Gustav Meyring, Jiří Orten, Rai er Maria Rilke and other famous Prague wri ers. A restaurant and a freely accessible terrad

with twelve grown trees can also be found in the complex. Nouvel has established himself as a representative of Rational Constructivism and designs mainly technical buildings. One of his valued projects is for example Institut du Monde Arabe in Paris, assessed the best French construction of 1987.

Like the Dancing House, the Golden Angel at Smíchov roused contradictory responses. The Angel, however, is not the only construction that has contributed to the transformation of Smíchov, the shopping and cultural centre accross Pilsen Street (Plzeňská ulice) called New Smíchov (Nový Smíchov) *(photo left and the main photo)*, the Möwenpick Hotel (with a cable car going to the upper part of the complex) are remarkable features too. The character of the neighbourhood has also been changed by two tunnels; Strahov and Mrázovka. Old Smíchov really does remain just a distant memory.

ETERNAL REST

One of the most beautiful historic cemeteries in Prague extends along Pilsner Street near the Golden Angel. Although situated in Smíchov district, it belongs to the Lesser Town. It was founded in 1679 as a plague cemetery far from built-up areas, in a small settlement out of which industrial Smíchov gradually developed. Years later it was enclosed within a wall, together with the Chapel of St. Roch and the cemetery church of the Holy Trinity. The cemetery became surrounded by swiftly expanding housing developments and in 1910 it was due to be demolished. However, the protests of both the public and experts were so strong that the cemetery was preserved. The surrounding wall, though, was pulled down during the First Republic and the cemetery was converted into a public garden, which led to the destruction and close-down of the chapel. Nowadays the cemetery is walled again and a lapidarium (museum of sculptures) covers an area of 2.2 ha. It contains valuable examples of funeral sculptures from the classicism period. The Platzer family, Wenceslas Prachner, Josef and Emanuel Max, Jan Ludvík Kranner and others were among the sculptors. Important figures of Czech culture rest in the cemetery, including the singer Josefína Dušková, the painters Josef Vojtěch Hellich, Adolf Kosárek and Antonín Mánes, the sculptors Ignác František, Ignác and Robert Platzer, and the engraver Vincenc Morstadt.

AMADEUS'S HIDE-AWAY

BERTRAMKA

MOZART'S DEATH

When Wolfgang Amadeus Mozart died in Vienna on 5 December 1791 at the age of just 35, all Prague mourned. On 14 December 3 000 people attended his requiem mass in St. Nicholas's Cathedral in the Lesser Town. Rössler's Requiem was part of the programme, with the solo sung by Josefína Dušková. A catafalque formed part of the funeral arrangement, during which Lesser Town grammar school students kept a guard of honour holding burning torches.

A remarkable place, the picturesque estate Bertramka will forever be associated with the name of the musical genius Wolfgang Amadeus Mozart. Bertramka was built in the 17th century, and named after one of its many owners, Františka Bertramská (Vetrabská) of Zornfest and her husband František of Bertrab. In 1784 Bertramka was bought by the famous diva Josefína Dušková and her husband František Xaver Dušek. At that time the thirty-year-old singer had been married to her music teacher, twenty-three years her senior, for eight years. The former vineyard and agricultural estate was soon altered into a sanctuary for music, an oasis of peace outside the city. On their honeymoon in 1777 the Dušeks met the family of archiepiscop musician Leopold Mozart. From that tim they maintained correspondence and th Dušeks invited young Wolfgang Amadeus Prague. Mozart first visited Prague in 178 staying with his wife at Count Thun's in Les er Town. At this time Josefína was performi in Dresden. Prague received Mozart enth siastically, and so the young genius return within the same year to finish his opera Dc Giovanni and to dedicate it to the citize of Prague. He stayed at Three Golden Lio (U Tří zlatých lvů) in Coal Market (Uhel trh), but soon moved into the Dušek's hous In 1789 Mozart visited Prague for the thi time. He was on his way to Dresden ar

Above: Mozart's bust

ipzig and on the way back he called in
ξain. For the fifth and the last time he ar-
ved in Prague on 28 August 1791, staying
  Bertramka again. He left, already ill, for
enna, but in Vienna he only had time to
njoy the first night of his opera The Magic
ute before he died.

In 1799 Dušek died and Josefína sold Ber-
amka. The new owners did not respect its
mous musical history, but fortunately in
338 the Popelka family acquired the estate.
neir son, a wholesaler Adolf Popelka, was
great admirer of Mozart's and assigned the
eation of Mozart's bust to sculptor Tomáš
eidan. After its unveiling he also estab-
hed a memorial book. He looked after Be-
amka faultlessly, even managing to defend
against the Smíchov municipality, which
anted to have the estate demolished so that
new road could be built to the Malvazinky
emetery. In 1925 the estate was bequeathed
the International Mozarteum Foundation
 Salzburg and in 1929 it became the prop-
ty of the Mozart Association in Czechoslo-
kia. However, Betramka was going to ru-
 and it proved difficult to find money for
 reconstruction. Paradoxically, Betramka

found help during the Nazi occupation. The
Mozart Association was taken over by Germans who raised enough funds for its restoration. An extensive reconstruction took place
between 1955–1956 and again 1986–1987.
The estate's main building is a single-storey
residential house. Its most prominent feature is a double-flight self-supporting staircase with a loggia. The southern front opens
through a sala terrena into a garden. Adjacent to the house, the lower part of a wine
press is a reminder of the bygone history of
this estate. Bertramka – the Wolfgang Amadeus Mozart and the Dušeks memorial – was
closed to the public in November 2009.

A GIFT FOR THE HOSTESS

Mozart promised Praguers that
the first night of his opera Don
Giovanni would take place in
Prague as an expression of his
gratitude for their warm
welcome. However, its
completion did not prove so
simple. As the premiere drew
near, the opera had still not
been finished. Young Amadeus
admired the beautiful Josefína
and had promised her the aria
Bella mia fiamma addio. So on
3 November 1787, Josefína
Dušková enticed Mozart into
a pavilion, in which a pen and
sheets of paper were prepared.
She locked him in, saying she
would not open the door until
the promised aria had been
completed. The artist had no
choice but to fulfil his promise.
However, he only agreed under
the condition that Josefína
would sing the entire part
immediately, without making
a single mistake, otherwise he
would destroy the notation.
Josefína Dušková did not
hesitate and the famous aria
was performed on the first
night.

Above: the staircase
In the middle: interiors with
the permanent exhibition
Main photo: overall view

IN SEARCH
OF ROMANTICISM

PROKOP VALLEY (PROKOPSKÉ ÚDOLÍ)

ST. PROKOP
AND THE DEVILS

The Prokop quarry is the most famous of the many quarries in the Prokop Valley. Works commenced here in 1875, with the limestone quarried to be used as building material or to burn lime. Despite numerous protests, between 1883–1887 the quarry even swallowed up all 120m of St. Prokop's cave. The prehistoric man had used the cave as a shelter, remains of mammoth, bear, lion, reindeer, ibex, bison and horse being found here. According to legend even St. Prokop himself used to dwell in the cave. Away from people he was translating the Bible. However, devils kept interrupting him. The saint exorcized them with a cross and the fiends ran away, but, as the entrance was blocked, they smashed the ceiling of the cave with their heads. The place became called Devil Hall (Čertova síň) and the famous Prokop pilgrimages often headed there. The cave has disappeared without a trace, now only a wall of the former quarry remains. However, walking through Prokop Valley we cannot miss a cave tunnel, and, passing through it, we can briefly experience the illusion of what it was like to live underground in Prokop's cave.

Steep limestone rocks are reflected on the surface of a little lake, caves yawn in the rocky slopes; such is the romantic spot found only a few steps from busy roads. It is no wonder that Prokop Valley (Prokopské údolí – *photos above and below*) is a popular location for trips and walks. Experts on fauna and flora come here frequently, and the area is also a palaeontologist's paradise. The valley is usually approached from Hlubočepy, but there is also a romantic path from Nové Butovice. The longest track leads from Řeporyje.

Prokop Valley is a protected area and the most northerly part of the Czech Karst, which extends as far as the south-west edge of Prague. It survived even the huge impact of industry in the 19th century, when factories were being built and quarries opened. Railway track was laid and an asphalt road (on which nowadays you are not allowed to drive!) extended into the valley. Nature has not given in, though, about 400 species of plants (including 26 protected ones) grow

The splendid view of the railway track pressed against the white rocks, climbing up Prokop Valley across daring viaducts, evokes the Alps. The illusion is perfect, this section of the track being commonly known as the Prague Semmering *(photo below).* It was constructed in 1872 as part of the former Buštěhrad railway track. Two viaducts, both more than 20 metres high, were part of it. Two tracks lead through the valley (Prague – Smíchov – Slaný and Prague – Smíchov – Rudná – Beroun). Their double crossing is truly impressive. Travelling by train through this most romantic Prague area is really an amazing experience.

n the valley. A number of invertebrates live here as well, mainly insect and molluscs. Various species of the calciphilic plants can be found; some are relics of cooler climate *(Sesleria albican)*, others of dry continental teppes *(Stipa pulcherrima)* and some are examples of the Mediterranean flora *(Dictamus albus).* The Prokop Valley nature reserve, with its unique geological profile, spanning upper Ordovician to middle Devonian eras, s the subject of continual research.

A nature trail leads through the valley, and can take us to the Lake (Jezírko – *photo above),* which was formed in 1905 by the seepage of underground water into the quarry. Nowadays it occupies an area of 25 are, and is 26m wide and 10m deep. Klukovice Caves (the so-called Coral Caves), which had been settled by the prehistoric man, tower above the former swimming pool in Klukovice. The caves (the longest is about 20m) on the steep side of the rock are inaccessible. The fossil sites (Kovářovic's slope, Boar quarry) are very inteteresting. And the Hemr Rocks (Hemrovy skály), formed by a volcano that erupted in the sea bed four hundred and thirty million years ago, are remarkable. All this can be seen while following the nature trail.

TOUCHES
OF ASIA

ZBRASLAV MONASTERY

**'ROLL OUT
THE BARRELS...'**

Another important monument is situated on Havlín Hill above Zbraslav, the Romanesque Church of St. Galus, which dates from the 12th century and was later rebuilt in Baroque style. A Czech composer, Jan Vejvoda, is buried in the churchyard. He is the author of the world famous polka, 'Škoda lásky' ('Roll out the barrels'). Below Havlín Hill is the villa that used to belong to another significant person, writer Vladislav Vančura. Vančura lived and worked in this very house until he was arrested during the so-called 'Heydrichiade' in 1942 (the period of severe Nazi reprisals which followed the assassination of the Vice-Protector of the German Reich Reinhard Heydrich). Here in Zbraslav Vančura found inspiration for his book Rozmarné léto (A Breezy Summer), one of the most genial works of Czech literature (later made into a superb film by Oscar-winning director Jiří Menzel). Vančura is commemorated by a monument (photo above).

A permanent exhibition of non-European art including works from all over Asia is a singular attraction, and it takes us to Zbraslav Castle and Monastery (Zbraslavský zámek a klášter – the main photo) situated on the southern edge of Prague. In 1952 the National Gallery's Set of Asian Art became the heart of the Collection of Oriental Art (photo opposite page above). It has since been enlarged through purchases and donations. In the Japanese tearoom on the ground floor we can breathe in the atmosphere, while admiring works of Japanese art. A remarkable haptic exhibition, called Japanese Sculpture through Touch, can be found on the first floor. On the second floor works of art from China, Tibet, India and South-East Asia ar presented, together with Islamic art. Topica exhibitions are held here as well.

The village of Zbraslav was originally th property of the monastery in Kladruby. I the 13th century the Archbishop of Pragu obtained it through exchange before givin it up in favour of King Přemysl Ottocar II i 1268. The monarch replaced the original es tate, or provostry, with a hunting lodge, bu his son Wenceslas II founded the Aula Regi monastery (Royal Hall) there in 1292, des ignating it to the Cistercian order. The firs half of the 14th century was the golden age c the monastery, at that time local abbots Ot and Petr Žitavský wrote the Zbraslav Chron

The tetra-nave Church of the Virgin Mary used to be part of the monastery complex. It was considered to be the most splendid building of the Cistercian early Gothic style in Bohemia. Its founder King Wenceslas II chose it as the burial ground of the Royal family, but the Taborites burnt the church down in 1420 and what remained was destroyed during the Thirty-Years War. Nowadays the Church of St. Jacob stands in front of the monastery *(photo below)*. The church has an extremely valuable interior. The main altar is decorated with sculptures by Platzer, the altar painting Assumption of the Blessed Virgin Mary is the work of the Italian painter Piazzetti, dating around 1743–1744. On the side altar facing south there is a copy of the rare panel painting of the Zbraslav Madonna (Zbraslavská Madona), the original dating from around 1350. A stone monument of Přemysl the Ploughman (Přemysl Oráč) contains caskets with the skulls of the founder of the monastery Wenceslas II, as well as Wenceslas III and Eliška Přemyslovna. An interesting legend is connected with the church. It is about a bell-ringer called Jacob whose son Martin was sentenced for an alleged murder of his lover. He was to be executed exactly when the clock on the church tower struck twelve, unless a pardon was delivered before this hour. Jacob was watching for a bearer carrying the good news, but he only appeared in the distance as the clock began to strike noon. The desperate Jacob knew that the rider would not make it. But something unexpected happened; the clock, of its own, began to strike twelve over again. Martin was reprieved, and later even his innocence was proven. Since then the double striking of each hour on the clock on the tower of the Church of St. Jacob has been a common practice…

e (Zbraslavská kronika), thereby providing an invaluable record of Czech history during that period. In August 1420 the monastery was destroyed by the Hussites. Its reconstruction began in the mid-15th century, but the complex was again completely destroyed during the Thirty-Years War. Around 700 things changed for the better when Abbots Wolfgang II Loechner and Thomas Bucius constructed impressive new buildings according to a design by John Blasius Santini. František Maxmilian Kaňka took over from Santini between 1723–1739. In 1785 the monastery was closed down, in 1787 the richly decorated royal hall was even converted into a sugar refinery and the refectory became a hayloft. In 1825 the Bavarian Prince Friedrich of Oettingen bought the prelacy and converted it into a castle. In 1875 his offspring acquired the monastery and restored it. The next owner reconstructed the entire complex between 1912–1926 using a design by architect Dušan Jurkovič. In 1940 he lent the monastery to the state. A collection of paintings was placed there, and after the war the National Gallery started to use the building.

We can admire delicate stuccoes by Tomasso Soldatti in the interiors and frescoes by Wenceslas Vavřinec Reiner in the royal hall. Reiner's frescoes can also be found in the prelacy.

TRACES LEFT
BY THE CELTS

OPPIDUM HILL-FORT ABOVE ZÁVIST

Traces of an extraordinary prehistoric fort, significant even on the European level, can be found high above the right bank of the Vltava above the Prague – Zbraslav railway station. The area abounds with marked hiking trails, offering breath-taking views not only of the river valley, but of the entire area. This place was fortified as early as the beginning of the 1st millennium BC, and in the 1st century BC there was a Celtic settlement. It was one of the largest settlements in Europe until it disappeared after the invasion of the Germanic tribes. Archaeologists have found the remains of stone constructions of secular character, as well as an oblong stone shrine that is recognized as the most advanced structure of the later La Tene period on Czech territory. Nowadays the preserved foundations of this construction can be seen. The area has been researched since 1963.

The prehistoric site called Šance is found on the other side of the Břežany Valley (Břežanské údolí). Throughout the 1st century Šance was connected to the Hill-fort above Závist (Hradiště nad Závistí) by huge mounds. The earthworks and mounds, several metres high, can be seen even today. The oppidum (oppidum is the predecessor of settlements of an urban character) used to oc-

cupy an area of 170 ha and the mounds we 16.5 km long. The area is one of the most s nificant places in Czech history and it is a r tional cultural heritage site.

Břežany Valley itself is a very interesting a ea as well. A road leads through it. A mem rial *(photo below left)* to poet Vítězslav Hál (1835–1874) is hidden in the shade und the trees near the path. It is a sandstone o

NEAR ZÁVIST

The road from Zbraslav forks right after the bridge on the right bank of the Vltava; if we carry straight on it ascends through Břežany Valley (Břežanské údolí), if we turn left the main road leads us to Komořany. A remarkable steep flank of rock can be seen from the crossroads. When the railway track and the road from Zbraslav to Komořany and Modřany were being built, this 400m-long cutting was made *(photo above)*, revealing one of the most beautiful geological profiles of the Letná massif in the Prague area. Notice the superb alternation of dark mica slates with sandstones or quartzites.

Main photo: *the overall view of Závist*

...sk with a portrait plaque, made in 1876
» Myslbek. The popular poet used to like
...lking in the valley. In fact he was doing
...actly that on Sunday 20 September 1874.
...e had just returned from the Giant Moun-
...ns (Krkonoše) and was feeling a little tired.
...e hoped to invigorate himself with the help
... a walk round his favourite places, but his
...ange tiredness proved to be a symptom of
a beginning illness. On 8 October the poet, who was extremely popular with young
people, died unexpectedly. Students had the
aforementioned memorial built.

THE SEAT OF METEOROLOGISTS

The road leading from the crossroads below Závist and the Břežany quarry takes us to Komořany, a Prague district mentioned in the foundation deed of the Vyšehrad Chapter (Vyšehradská kapitula) as early as 1088. In 1304 part of Komořany belonged to the Zbraslav Monastery. The Vice-Judge of the Kingdom of Bohemia bought Komořany in 1589, a fort being mentioned for the first time in the contract of purchase. In 1622 the estate was turned over to Zbraslav Monastery again. Around 1742 the local fort was converted into a Baroque castle (photo above), which served as the summer residence of the Zbraslav abbots. On 2 July 1742 negotiations concerning the possible free departure of the French armies took place there. The two-wing single-storey building, laid out in the same way as the original fort, has Renaissance graffito on the façade of its tower. Inside the castle there is a chapel with a copy of the Zbraslav Madonna on the altar. During the last quarter of the 19th century the castle was modified in Neo-Gothic style. Nowadays this beautifully renovated complex is a seat of the Czech Hydro-Meteorological Institute.

INDEX

We would like to thank the following institutions, whose helpful
approach enabled this book to come into existence:
The National Gallery in Prague
The Prague Castle Administration
The Arts and Crafts Museum in Prague
The Promotional Department of the National Museum
The Jewish Museum in Prague
The Museum of the City of Prague
The Gallery of the City of Prague
The Knightly Order of the Cross with a Red Star
The Capuchin Province in Prague
The Administration of the Church of the Virgin Mary the
Victorious in Prague
and others

Petr David
Vladimír Soukup

WONDERS OF PRAGUE

Picture credits Zdeněk Thoma, the National Gallery of Prague (7)
and the Prague Castle Administration (3)
From the original edition Skvosty Prahy, first published
by Euromedia Group, k. s., in 2004, translated by Zuzana Amchová
Language editor Craig Riddell
Graphic design and setting Martin David
Published by Euromedia Group, k. s. – Knižní klub in Prague
in 2010 as 5499. publication
Editor in charge Jitka Zykánová
Technical adviser Martina Adlová
Number of pages 200
Printed by Tlačiarne BB, spol. s r. o., Banská Bystrica
Second revised edition